Essentials of Applied Portfolio Management

Massimo Guidolin
Manuela Pedio

BUP

EGEA S.p.A.
Via Salasco, 5 - 20136 Milano
Tel. 02/5836.5751 – Fax 02/5836.5753
egea.edizioni@unibocconi.it – www.egeaeditore.it

First Edition: September 2016
Corrected Reprint Edition: March 2017

ISBN International Edition 978-88-85486-08-9
ISBN Domestic Edition 978-88-99902-05-6
ISBN Pdf Edition 978-88-85486-07-2

Print: Digital Print Service, Segrate (Milan)

Contents

Foreword

This book is a mark left in the woods. It is a sign left by two travelers who have chosen every day to share a portion of their fun trip. The woods are the tall trees of the concepts, the methods, and not least, the practice of financial markets. Their journey has been long but fast-paced. At one point, they felt a need to share and leave a mark, to tell others that they had been in these woods and they have tried to find their way through in a manner that they have enjoyed so much, they wanted to invite others along the same path. Of course, the two travelers are us, the Authors, and this corner of the woods is about portfolio management. We hope that the sense of speed through a journey and the fun we had while writing together, continuously swapping ideas and encouraging each other, will spring to life from the pages of our book.

We are both aware that there is a chance that you, the Reader, may be using this textbook to follow one taught course, presumably at the MSc. level. This is the experience from which our joint effort stems as well. The authors crossed paths in such an environment from different sides of the desk, but their paths soon aligned to one, shared direction. We hope that you will feel what our goal has been—to explain the important from the unimportant, the useful from the curious, the feasible from the convoluted (albeit elegant).

The least youthful (we like to see the glass half-full) of the two authors carries a big debt for what he has learned from the more youthful about the real, everyday value of knowledge, its usefulness in practical situations, and a fresh taste for the simple and immediately applicable. On her turn, the most youthful of the two, has derived true inspiration from the enthusiasm, the passion, and the genuine curiosity that the least youngest still places after so many years in sharing his knowledge with students without forgetting that learning is a never ending process.

The book strives to avoid becoming just one more textbook piece in financial mathematics. Although one of the Authors stood at that gate holding an ax to prevent excesses, we cannot rule out that we may have been occasionally carried away. For the Readers who perceive being short of an adequate background, the references are classical, Simon and Blume (1994) and Wainwright and Chiang (2013) in mathematics, Mood, Graybill, Boes (1974) in statistics.[*]

Manuela and Massimo

Additional resources are available online via MyBook:
http://mybook.egeaonline.it

---

[*] Mood, Graybill, and Boes (1974), *Introduction to the Theory of Statistics*, McGraw Hill; Simon and Blume (1994), *Mathematics for Economists*, Norton & Co.; Wainwright and Chiang (2013), *Fundamental Methods of Mathematical Economics*, McGraw Hill.

List of Symbols and Acronyms
(in order of first appearance in the book)

HPR	Holding period return
$R_{i,t}$	Return on an asset or index i
CAGR	Compounded annual growth rate
MV	Mean-variance
$Prob(A)$	Probability of event A
$E[\cdot]$	Expectation (in population)
μ_i	Expectation of asset i (in population)
$Var[\cdot]$	Variance (in population)
σ_i^2	Variance of asset i
$Cov[\cdot,]$	Covariance (in population)
$\sigma_{i,j}$	Covariance between assets i and j
$\rho_{i,j}$	Correlation coefficient of assets i, j
ω_i	Weight of asset i
N	Number of assets in the asset menu
R^i	Return or payoff on asset/security i
S	Number of states in the discrete case
EUT	Expected utility theorem
VNM	Von-Neumann Morgenstern (felicity function)
W	Wealth
CE	Certainty equivalent
DMU	Decreasing marginal utility
p_i	Price of a good or service
MU	Marginal utility
x_i	Quantity demanded of a good or service
H	Zero-mean bet, gamble
RRA	Relative risk aversion
ARA	Absolute risk aversion function
T	Risk tolerance function
CRA	Relative risk aversion function
Π	Risk premium
CER	Certainty equivalent rate of return
LRT	Linear risk tolerance
HARA	Hyperbolic absolute risk aversion

CARA	Constant absolute risk aversion
CRRA	Constant relative risk aversion
LHS	Left hand side
RHS	Right hand side
GMV(P)	Global minimum variance (portfolio)
FOC	First-order condition
R^f	Return on the risk free asset
CML	Capital market line
DARA	Decreasing absolute risk aversion
IARA	Increasing absolute risk aversion
FOSD	First-order stochastic dominance
$F_Y(\cdot)$	Cumulative distribution function of asset/gamble Y
CDF	Cumulative distribution function
SOSD	Second-order stochastic dominance
GARCH	Generalized autoregressive conditional heteroskedastic
PCA	Principal component analysis
CAPM	Capital asset pricing model
$R_{m,t+1}$	Rate of return on the market portfolio
SSR	Sum of squared residuals
OLS	Ordinary least squares
SD[·]	Standard Deviation
ARMA	Autoregressive Moving Average (model)
IP	Industrial production
APT	Arbitrage pricing theory
SMB	Small minus big
HML	High minus low (book to market)
WML	Winners minus losers
IRRA	Increasing Relative Risk Aversion
IID	Independent and identically distributed
TWR	Time-weighted return
NAV	Net asset value
FMV	Fund/Manager/Vehicle
SML	Security Market Line
TR	Treynor ratio
TAA	Tactical asset allocation

1   Introduction to Portfolio Analysis: Key Notions

"Uncertainty cannot be dismissed so easily in the analysis of optimizing investor behavior. An investor who knew future returns with certainty would invest in only one security, namely the one with the highest future return" *(H.M. Markowitz, "Foundations of Portfolio Theory", 1991)*

Summary: – 1. Financial Securities. – 2. Choice Under Risky Situations. – 3. Statistical Summaries of Portfolio Returns.

1 - Financial Securities

1.1 Definition of financial securities

Most people own a "portfolio" (i.e., a collection) of assets, such as money, houses, cars, bags, shoes, and any other durable goods that are able to retain value over time and that can be used to transfer (real) wealth and hence consumption opportunities over time. In this book, we will focus primarily on a certain type of assets, i.e., financial securities. As is generally known, financial securities (or financial assets) can be thought of as a legal contract that represents the right to receive future payoffs—usually but not exclusively in the form of monetary cash flows—under certain conditions. For instance, when you buy the stocks of a company, you are acquiring rights on a part of the future profits of that company (generally distributed in the form of *dividends*, either in cash or shares of stock). Of course, when an asset just pays out money, such monetary payoffs can be used to purchase goods and services subject to a standard budget constraint that forces a decision maker to spend only the available resources (currently or in present value terms). Our seemingly vague reference to what we have cited as "certain conditions" is due to the fact that financial securities are generally *risky*, i.e., they pay out money, goods, or services in different, uncertain *states of the world*, as we shall see extensively throughout the rest of the book.[1]

Financial assets generally serve two main purposes:

I. To redistribute available wealth across different states of the world, to finance consumption and saving;

II. To allocate available wealth intertemporally, i.e., to allow an investor to save current income/wealth to finance future consumption or, on the opposite, to make it possible for her to borrow against her future incomes/wealth to finance current consumption.

For instance, consider an investor who uses a part of her income from wages earned in one productive sector (e.g., banking) to buy stocks issued in another sector (e.g., industrial companies such as in the automotive industry). This individual is thus making sure that her welfare is at least partially disconnected from the fortunes or mis-fortunes of the banking sector to participate in the outlook of the automotive industry. At the same time, this very investor who reduces her consumption stream to save by purchasing automotive stocks is financing her own future consumption, although the exact amount available will depend on the future, realized profitability of the sector. Nowadays there are a large number of different financial securities available, such as stocks (equity), bonds, commodities, derivatives, investment (mutual, pension, hedge) funds, etc. A broad discussion of the specific characteristics of each type of financial securities is beyond the scope of our book and can be found instead in many intermediate finance textbooks (see, e.g., Fabozzi and Markowitz, 2011). However, just to level the playing field in view of the rest of our work, in this section we offer a short review of how returns of financial assets should be computed. In the rest of the chapter we review other basic concepts that are necessary to understand the framework of portfolio analysis. First, we clarify in what sense financial securities are risky and we explain how investors can deal with choice among alternative securities in such uncertain situations. Second, we discuss how returns

---

[1] Throughout the rest of the book, unless stated otherwise, we shall not distinguish between the concepts of risk and uncertainty. Risk characterizes unknown events for which objective probabilities can be assigned; uncertainty applies to events for which such probabilities cannot be attributed, or for which it would not make sense to assign them because they cannot be replicated in any controlled way, thus rendering the calculation of relative frequencies difficult. One simplistic way to think about this issue is to envision all the uncertainty that we shall deal with as risk.

and risk are generally measured and how these measures can be aggregated when securities are collected to form a portfolio.

1.2 Computing the return of financial securities

Consider first an asset that does not pay any dividends or coupon interest. The simple single-period return R_t of this asset between time $t-1$ and t is defined as

$$R_t = \frac{P_t}{P_{t-1}} - 1, \tag{1.1}$$

where P_t is the price of the asset at time t and P_{t-1} is the price of the asset at time $t-1$. Therefore, an investor that has invested a monetary unit (e.g., one euro) at $t-1$ in this security will end up at time t with $1 + R_t$. The return plus one is often referred to as *gross return* or, alternatively, the *holding period return* (*HPR*). If after the first period the investor reinvests her money from time t to $t+1$, at the end of her holding period she will get $(1 + R_t)(1 + R_{t+1})$, where R_{t+1} is the return between time t and $t+1$. This way of aggregating simple gross returns over time generalizes to any possible time interval: the gross return between time $t-h$ and t is simply given by the geometric-style (in the sense that products are considered) product:

$$(1 + R_{t:h}) = (1 + R_t)(1 + R_{t-1}) \dots (1 + R_{t-h+1}) = \prod_{i=0}^{h-1}(1 + R_{t-i}). \tag{1.2}$$

Consequently, the net return over h periods, also known as *compounded* return, is simply equal to $\prod_{i=1}^{h-1}(1 + R_{t-i}) - 1$. However, it generally makes little sense to discuss about returns without defining their investment horizon. Conventionally, practitioners tend to express their returns on an *annualized* basis, as this enhances comparability. For instance, consider the case in which you have invested your money for three years and you have earned a rate of return R over this period. Based on formula (1.2), the annualized return R_a (sometimes called *compounded annual growth rate* or CAGR) of your investment is simply equal to

$$R_a(3) \equiv \left[\prod_{i=1}^{3} (1 + R_i) \right]^{1/3} - 1. \qquad (1.3)$$

More generally, $R_a(n) \equiv [\prod_{i=1}^{n}(1 + R_i)]^{1/n} - 1$. Clearly, it easier to compute arithmetic means than geometric ones. For this reason, it is also quite common to use *continuously compounded* returns, which are obtained from simple return aggregation in (1.2), when the frequency of compounding is increased towards infinity, i.e., as if we could disinvest and reinvest our accrued wealth at every moment. The continuously compounded return (also known as *log-return*) of an asset is simply defined as $R_t^c \equiv \ln(P_t/P_{t-1})$. The advantage of using continuously compounded returns is that the multi-period return is very easy to compute as it consists of the sum of the log-returns of each period:

$$R_{t:h}^c \equiv R_{t-1}^c + R_{t-2}^c + \cdots + R_{t-h+1}^c = \sum_{i=1}^{h-1} R_{t-i}^c. \qquad (1.4)$$

The use of log-returns is widespread not only because they can be easily summed up to obtain multi-period returns, but also because their use simplifies the modelling of statistical properties of return time-series. Unfortunately, continuous compounding has a key drawback: while the return of a portfolio is equal to the weighted average of the simple asset returns, this statement does not hold true for log-returns, as the sum of logs is not equal to the log of the sum. However, when returns are measured on a short horizon (e.g., daily) the difference between the portfolio continuously compounded return and the weighted average of the log-returns of each asset is very small. In the rest of the book, we shall use simple returns when we are not interested in their time-series properties and log-returns in all other cases.

Finally, for assets (generally stocks) that make periodic payments (e.g., dividend) the formula in (1.1) should be slightly modified:

$$R_t \equiv \frac{P_t + D_t}{P_{t-1}} - 1, \qquad (1.5)$$

where D_t is the dividend paid at time t and P_t is the *ex-dividend* price of the stock (i.e., the price of the stock immediately after the payment of the divi- dend). Equivalently, the continuously compounded return of a stock that pays dividends is $R_t^c \equiv \ln[(P_t + D_t)/P_{t-1}]$.

2 - Choices under Risky Situations

2.1 Choices under uncertainty: a general framework

In section 1.2, we have discussed how we can compute the realized returns of financial assets. However, we have noted that most financial securities have a fundamental characteristic: they are *risky*, meaning that their payoff depends on which of the K alternative states of the world will turn out to occur at a future point in time. The states are uncertain because they are not known in advance, when investors make their investment decisions (i.e., whether to buy, not to buy, and—when feasible—sell the securities that be- long to the *asset menu* they face). However, at least under some conditions, we shall assume that investors are able to quantify such uncertainty on fu- ture states using standard *probability distributions* and the entire apparatus that classical probability theory provides them with (a brief discussion of the properties of the distribution of returns is provided in the next section). We also assume that exactly one state will occur, though investors do not know, at the outset, which one, because the states are mutually exclusive. The description of each state is complete and exhaustive, in the sense that all the relevant information is provided to an investor to tackle the decision problem being studied.

In spite of this rather rich structure imposed on the choice problem, the task that awaits us (or our investor) is a complex one and the optimal choice will result from three distinct sets of (interacting) factors:

I.   how an investor's attitude toward or tolerance for risk is to be con- ceptualized and therefore measured;
II. how risks should be defined and measured;
III. how investors' risk attitudes interact with the subjective uncertain- ties associated with the available assets to determine an investor's desired portfolio holdings (demands).

First, we shall consider how the investors' beliefs about future states may be expressed. In the following example, we show how standard probability theory can be used to capture the uncertainty on the payoffs of securities through the notion that different *states* may carry different probabilities. By attaching a probability to each state, we shall be able to distinguish between a decision maker's beliefs (expressed by probabilities) about which state will occur and preferences about how she ranks the consequences of different actions.

Example 1.1. The asset menu is composed of the following three securities, A, B, and C:

State	Security A		Security B		Security C	
	Payoff	Prob.	Payoff	Prob.	Payoff	Prob.
i	20	3/15	18	3/15	18	3/15
ii	18	5/15	18	5/15	16	5/15
iii	14	4/15	10	4/15	12	4/15
iv	10	2/15	5	2/15	12	2/15
v	6	1/15	5	1/15	8	1/15

Security B pays 18 monetary units (say, euros) in both states *i* and *ii*. Therefore, the difference between these two states is not payoff-relevant to security B. However, it is payoff-relevant in the case of security A, in the sense that this asset pays out 20 euros in state *i* and 18 euros in state *ii*. Note that in this example, we characterize securities through their payoffs, but in future examples we shall equally use their period rate of return, computed as discussed in section 1.2.

The table above also shows the (subjectively determined) probabilities of each of the states. Because the states of the economy should be uniquely defined across the entire asset menu, the associated probabilities are simply repeated across different securities.

Of course, the table above reports redundant information because for securities B and C, one can re-define the states to consist of payoff-relevant states only. For instance, for security B there are only three payoff-relevant states, which we can call "*i+ii*", *iii*, and "*iv+v*"; in the case of security C, the payoff-relevant states are *i*, *ii*, "*iii+iv*", and *v*.

State	Security A		Security B		Security C	
	Payoff	Prob.	Payoff	Prob.	Payoff	Prob.
i	20	3/15	18	8/15	18	3/15
ii	18	5/15			16	5/15
iii	14	4/15	10	4/15	12	6/15
iv	10	2/15	5	3/15		
v	6	1/15			8	1/15

Example 1.1 illustrates the interplay among the three ingredients that we have listed above. First, the need to define and measure risk. For instance, if one takes notice of the potential returns, security A may be considered riskier than C because the span, the range of variation of the payoffs of security A (from a minimum of 6 to a maximum of 20), exceeds that of security C (from a minimum of 8 to a maximum of 18). Second, the usefulness of pinning down the concept of risk aversion. For instance, it is not immediately evident why a rational investor should prefer security C over security A (if any): on the one hand, security A threatens to pay out only 6 euros in state v; on the other hand, the same security achieves a very large payment of 20 in state i.[2] It is natural to ask what kind of investor would pay more for security C than for security A. Presumably such willingness would be motivated by a desire to avoid the very low payoff of 6 that the latter security may yield. Third and finally, it is unclear how such inclinations against risk—however measured—may be balanced off in the light of the probability distribution that characterizes different states.

In fact, this state-preference framework is fruitfully employed as an abstract tool for understanding the fundamentals of decision-making under uncertainty, but it is more special than it may first appear. For example, the set of states, S, is given exogenously and cannot be affected by the choices of the investors. In reality, many investment choices change the physical world and create chances for new outcomes and states of the world. For instance, a successful venture capital investment in cold fusion energy production will profoundly affect all other sectors and investment outlooks. Consequently, the state-preference model is not as widely applicable as it

---

[2] By construction, example 1.1 is perfectly symmetric: security C has a minimum payment of 8 that exceeds by 2 euros the minimum payment of security A; however, security A has a maximum payment of 20 that exceeds by 2 euros the maximum payment of security C. Hence the question in the main text stands.

might at first seem, and this should be kept in mind.

2.2 Complete and incomplete criteria of choice under uncertainty

The primary role played by the state-preference framework is to dictate how a rational investor ought to select among the different securities in her asset menu. One important distinction of criteria of choice under uncertainty, is their completeness: a *complete criterion* is always able to rank all securities or investment opportunities from top to bottom on the basis of their objective features. As such, complete criteria form a good basis for portfolio choice. For instance, an investor may (simplistically) decide to rank all available assets and to invest in some pre-determined fraction starting from the top of the resulting ranking.[3] The expected utility decision criterion to be defined in chapter 2 will satisfy this completeness property. By contrast, an *incomplete criterion* suffers from the existence of potential (usually, empirically relevant) traded combinations of the primitive assets that cannot be ranked in a precise way. As we are about to show, the celebrated mean-variance criterion is unfortunately incomplete. Paradoxically, such an incompleteness represents the reason for its success.

Although many other incomplete criteria can be defined (see Meucci, 2009, for a general framework), a first often referred to criterion is (strong) *dominance*:

Dominance: A security (strongly) dominates another security (on a state-by-state basis), if the former pays as much as the latter in all states of nature, and strictly more in at least one state.

In the absence any further indications on their behavior, we will assume that all rational individuals would prefer the dominant security to the security that it dominates. Equivalently, dominated securities will never be demanded by any rational investor. Here rational means that the investor is *non-satiated*, that is, she always prefers strictly more consumption (hence, monetary outcomes that may be used to finance such consumption) to less consumption.

However, the following example shows that the dominance criterion, although strong, is highly incomplete.

---

[3] Many "funds-of-funds" investment selection strategies are well known to be formally spelled out in this fashion, where the asset menu is composed by the (hedge or mutual) funds that can be selected.

Example 1.2. Consider the same asset menu, payoffs, and probabilities as in example 1.1:

State	Security A		D	Security B		D	Security C	
	Payoff	Prob.		Payoff	Prob.		Payoff	Prob.
i	20	3/15	>	18	3/15	=	18	3/15
ii	18	5/15	=	18	5/15	>	16	5/15
iii	14	4/15	>	10	4/15	<	12	4/15
iv	10	2/15	>	5	2/15	<	12	2/15
v	6	1/15	>	5	1/15	<	8	1/15

Clearly, as indicated by the signs in the "D" column (for dominance), the payoffs of security A dominate those of security B on a state-by-state basis. In this case, the exact probabilities that characterize the different states are not relevant. Even if one changes the probability distribution reported in the table, the result will stick. However, this criterion is visibly incomplete: for instance, security B does not dominate security C and, more importantly, security A does not dominate security C (and vice versa). Hence, neither security A nor C is dominated by any other security, while security B is dominated (by security A). A rational investor may then decide to select between assets A and C, ignoring B. However, she cannot find an equivalently strong and impartial rule to decide between security A and C, hence the criterion is incomplete.

The strength of dominance is that it escapes a definition of risk. Indeed, to be able to resort to such a concept may be very useful. However, in general, a security yields payoffs that in some states are larger and in some other states are smaller than under any other state. When this is the case, the best known (and yet still incomplete, as we shall see) approach at this point consists of summarizing the distributions of asset returns through their mean and variance:

$$E[R_i] = \sum_{s=1}^{S} Prob(state = s)R_i(s) \qquad (1.6)$$

$$Var[R_i] = \sum_{s=1}^{S} Prob(state = s)[R_i(s) - E[R_i]]^2, \qquad (1.7)$$

where i indicates a specific security of N and S is the number of states (e.g., 5 in examples 1.1 and 1.2). The following example shows in intuitive terms how mean and variance could be used to rank different securities, on the grounds that variance can be used to measure risk.

Example 1.3. Consider the same inputs as in examples 1.1 and 1.2:

State	Security A		Security B		Security C	
	Payoff	Prob.	Payoff	Prob.	Payoff	Prob.
i	20	3/15	18	3/15	18	3/15
ii	18	5/15	18	5/15	16	5/15
iii	14	4/15	10	4/15	12	4/15
iv	10	2/15	5	2/15	12	2/15
v	6	1/15	5	1/15	8	1/15
Mean	15.47		13.27		14.27	
Variance	16.78		28.46		8.46	

It is indeed the case that security C is less risky than security B.

If we decided to summarize these return distributions by their means and variances only, both securities A and C would clearly appear more attractive than asset B as they have a higher mean return and a lower variance. We therefore say that both securities A and C dominate asset B in terms of a *mean-variance dominance criterion*.

Mean-variance dominance: A security dominates another security in a mean variance (MV for short) sense, if the former is characterized by a higher expected payoff and a by a lower variance of payoffs.

However, security A fails to dominate security C (and vice versa) in a mean-variance sense. This occurs because security A has a higher mean than security C has (15.47 > 14.27), but the former also yields a higher variance (16.78 > 8.46). This shows that, as with to dominance, also the mean-variance is an incomplete criterion, that is, pairs of securities exist that cannot be simply ranked by this criterion.

Clearly, because of its incompleteness, the mean-variance criterion can at best only isolate a subset of securities that are not dominated by any other security. For instance, in example 1.3, security B, being dominated by both securities A and C, can be ruled out from the portfolio selection. However, neither security A nor C can be ruled out because they belong to the set of non-dominated assets.

Implicitly, the MV dominance criterion commits to a definition that requires an investor to dislike risk and that *identifies risk with variance*. Because the criterion implies this need to define and measure both risk aversion and risk, the mean-variance dominance is neither as strong, nor as a general concept as state-by-state dominance. In fact, we know from example 1.2 that while security A dominates state-by-state security B (and we now know that A also MV dominates B), security C does not dominate B on a state-by-state basis, while C MV dominates B.[4] Moreover, this criterion may at most identify some subset of securities (as we shall see, portfolios) that are not dominated and as such are "MV *efficient*". We shall return to these concepts in chapter 3.

3 - Statistical Summaries of Portfolio Returns

In section 2, we have introduced the idea that the returns of most financial assets (and thus of portfolios of such assets) are random variables. A random variable y is a quantity that can take a number of possible values, y_1, y_2, ..., y_n (and the case in which n diverges to infinity cannot be ruled out). The value that the random variable will assume is not known in advance, but a probability π_i is assigned to each of the possible outcomes y_i. The probability π_i can be (does not have to be) thought of as the frequency with which one would observe y_i if the experiment of observing the outcome of y could be repeated an infinite number of times.

We have already seen that the distribution of asset returns is often (and yet incompletely) characterized through their means and variances. In (1.6) and (1.7), we have shown how to compute the expected (or mean) return of an asset and its variance, respectively.[5] However, because we are also (mainly)

---

[4] Although our example does not show this feature, it is possible to build cases in which one asset dominates another on a state-by-state basis, but not in MV terms. This means that just as MV dominance does not imply state-by-state dominance, also state-by-state dominance fails to imply MV dominance. The two are merely different criteria.

[5] In the rest of the book, unless otherwise specified, we shall use the terms mean and expected return interchangeably to indicate the average value obtained by considering the probabilities as equivalent to frequencies.

interested in the risk-return profile of portfolios of assets, we now discuss how to aggregate the statistics of the individual assets to compute a portfolio mean and variance. Indeed, a portfolio is simply a linear combination of individual assets and, as a result, its return, R_P, is a random variable whose probability distribution depends on the distribution law(s) of the returns of the assets that compose the portfolio. Consequently, we can deduce some of the properties of the distribution of portfolio returns by using standard results regarding linear combinations of random variables. In particular, in what follows we focus on two-parameter distributions (sometimes called *elliptical*), of which the normal Gaussian distribution family represents the most important case, both theoretically and practically.

For instance, assume that we know that the returns R_A and R_B of two securities, A and B, are jointly normally distributed and that their means and variances are:

$$\mu_A \equiv E[R_A], \quad \sigma_A^2 \equiv Var[R_A]$$
$$\mu_B \equiv E[R_B], \quad \sigma_B^2 \equiv Var[R_B]. \tag{1.8}$$

Clearly, given these inputs, we can easily compute σ_A and σ_B, the square roots of the variances of the two assets, which are called *standard deviations* or, alternatively, *volatilities*. Yet, this information is not sufficient to compute all the required statistics characterizing the distribution of portfolio returns, and in particular portfolio variance, because asset returns are in general correlated, that is, they tend to show some form of linear dependence which goes to increase/decrease portfolio volatility above/below the variability justified by individual assets. For this reason, we need to introduce the concepts of *covariance* and of *correlation coefficient.*

The covariance σ_{AB} between two securities, A and B, is a scaled measure of the *linear association* between the two assets and it is computed as follows:

$$\sigma_{AB} \equiv Cov[R_A, R_B] = E[(R_{A,t} - E[R_A])(R_{B,t} - E[R_B])]. \tag{1.9}$$

The sign of the covariance reveals the kind of (linear) relationship that characterizes two assets. If $\sigma_{AB} > 0$, the returns of the two securities tend to move in the same direction; if $\sigma_{AB} < 0$, they tend to move in opposite directions; finally, if $\sigma_{AB} = 0$ the returns of the two securities are linearly independent (we also say they are uncorrelated). Intuitively, the covariance has to satisfy the following inequality:

$$|\sigma_{AB}| \leq \sigma_A \sigma_B. \tag{1.10}$$

Indeed, one can demonstrate that the covariance of an asset with itself is simply equal to its variance, $E\big[(R_{A,t} - E[R_A])^2\big]$; consequently, when two assets are perfectly correlated and therefore not distinguishable in a linear sense, then $\sigma_{AB} = \sigma_A \sigma_B$.

Looking at formula (1.9), it is evident that covariance is affected by the overall variability of the two assets, what statisticians call the *scales* of the two phenomena under consideration, in particular their standard deviations. As a result, if we were to rank pairs of securities based on the strength of their relationships, we would find it difficult to compare their covariances. For this reason, we usually standardize the covariance dividing it by the product of the standard deviations of the two assets:

$$\varrho_{AB} = \frac{\sigma_{AB}}{\sigma_A \sigma_B}. \tag{1.11}$$

The coefficient ϱ_{AB} is called correlation coefficient and it ranges from -1 to $+1$, as a result of the covariance bound stated in (1.9). A value of $+1$ indicates a perfect *positive* linear relationship between two assets, while -1 implies a perfect *negative* relationship between them. If two assets are completely linearly independent, they will display a correlation coefficient equal to 0. In this latter case, knowledge of the value of one variable does not give any information about the value of the other variable, at least within a linear framework.[6]

Now we have defined all the elements that allow us to compute the necessary mean-variance portfolio statistics. For the time being, we will take the values of the means, variances, and covariances of asset returns as given and show how these map in the mean and variance of portfolio returns. Later in

---

[6] Our emphasis on the fact that correlation just captures the strength of linear association may be best understood considering the following example: $R_{A,t} = R_{B,t}^2 + \eta_t$. Clearly, securities A and B are strongly associated according to a quadratic function. Yet it is easy to verify that $Cov[R_A, R_B] = 0$, i.e., the linear association between the two return series is zero.

the book (chapter 5) we will address how these can be empirically estimated.[7]

3.1 Portfolio mean

The computation of the mean of portfolio returns is relatively easy: the return of a portfolio simply consists of the sum of the returns of the components weighted by the fraction of wealth that is invested in each asset. Fortunately, the expected value operator enjoys a property called linearity
which states that the expected (or mean) value of a sum of random variables
is equal to the sum of the expected values of the random variables themselves; in addition, the expected value of a scalar multiple of a random variable is equal to the scalar coefficient applied to the expected value. Consequently, if $R_1, R_2, ..., R_N$ are random variables representing the returns of N
securities that compose a portfolio, $\mu_1 \equiv E[R_{1,t}], \mu_2 \equiv E[R_{2,t}], ..., \mu_N \equiv E[R_{N,t}]$ are their expectations, and $\omega_1, \omega_2, ..., \omega_N$ are the weights of each security in the portfolio (expressed as a proportion of total wealth), then the
portfolio mean is equal to:

$$\mu_P = E[R_P] = \sum_{i=1}^{N} \omega_i \mu_i. \tag{1.12}$$

To be more precise, consider the case of a portfolio consisting of the two
securities A and B defined in (1.8), with weights ω_A and ω_B, respectively.
The mean value of the portfolio can be easily computed as follows:

$$E[R_P] = E[\omega_A R_A + \omega_B R_B] = \omega_A E[R_A] + \omega_B E[R_B] = \omega_A \mu_A + \omega_B \mu_B. \tag{1.13}$$

The following example makes these simple concepts more concrete.

---

[7] It is important to recognize that the estimates that are obtained from actual data for
means, variances, and covariances are the observable counterparts of *unobservable* theoretical concepts. Estimates of the mean and of the covariance matrix can be obtained
through a variety of methods (estimation based on past data is just one common example). The way these estimates are constructed is addressed in chapter 5.

Example 1.4. Consider the two stocks A and B described below:

Market Condition	Stock A		Stock B	
	Return	Prob.	Return	Prob.
Bull	12.00%	25%	6.00%	25%
Normal	8.00%	50%	1.50%	50%
Bear	-7.00%	25%	-1.00%	25%
Mean	5.25%		2.00%	

For instance, the expected return of a portfolio composed by 30% of security A and 70% of security B is computed as follows:

$$\mu_P = \omega_A \mu_A + \omega_B \mu_B = 30\% \times 5.25\% + 70\% \times 2.00\% = 2.98\%$$

As a portfolio can be composed of a large number of assets, it may often be convenient to use a more compact matrix notation. If we indicate with $\boldsymbol{\omega}$ the $N \times 1$ vector containing the weights of the N securities that compose the portfolio and with $\boldsymbol{\mu}$ the $N \times 1$ vector of mean returns of the assets, then equation (1.12) can be rewritten as follows:

$$\mu_P = \boldsymbol{\omega}' \boldsymbol{\mu}. \tag{1.14}$$

3.2 Portfolio variance and standard deviation

As already pointed out, the computation of portfolio variance is a bit more complex than the calculation of its mean as it requires knowledge of the co-variances between each pair of asset returns. Following the standard definition of variance:

$$\sigma_P^2 = E[(R_P - \mu_P)^2] = E\left[\left(\sum_{i=1}^{N} \omega_i R_i - \sum_{i=1}^{N} \omega_i \mu_i\right)^2\right]$$

$$= E\left[\left(\sum_{i=1}^{N} \omega_i (R_i - \mu_i)\right)\left(\sum_{j=1}^{N} \omega_j (R_j - \mu_j)\right)\right]$$

$$= E\left[\left(\sum_{i,j=1}^{N} \omega_i \omega_j (R_i - \mu_i)(R_j - \mu_j)\right)\right] = \sum_{i,j=1}^{N} \omega_i \omega_j \sigma_{i,j}, \tag{1.15}$$

where $\sigma_{i,j}$ is the covariance between asset i and asset j; as already discussed, the covariance of an asset with itself is simply equal to its variance. Note that also the variance formula can be rewritten using matrix notation:

$$\sigma_P^2 = \omega' \Sigma \omega, \tag{1.16}$$

where ω is again the $N \times 1$ of the weights and Σ is the so-called *variance-covariance matrix*, which is an $N \times N$ matrix whose main diagonal elements are the asset variances while the off-diagonal elements are the respective asset covariances. To clarify, Σ is a *symmetric, positive definite* matrix structured as follows:

$$\begin{bmatrix} \sigma_1^2 & \sigma_{1,2} & \cdots & \sigma_{1,N} \\ \sigma_{2,1} & \sigma_2^2 & \cdots & \vdots \\ \vdots & \vdots & \vdots & \vdots \\ \sigma_{N,1} & \cdots & \cdots & \sigma_N^2 \end{bmatrix} = \begin{bmatrix} \sigma_1^2 & \sigma_{1,2} & \cdots & \sigma_{1,N} \\ \sigma_{1,2} & \sigma_2^2 & \cdots & \vdots \\ \vdots & \vdots & \vdots & \vdots \\ \sigma_{1,N} & \cdots & \cdots & \sigma_N^2 \end{bmatrix}. \tag{1.17}$$

The second matrix clearly reflects the symmetric property of covariances and variances. Positive definiteness implies that for all N-component real vectors x, $x' \Sigma x > 0$. Clearly, because the vector of weights ω is a just a special case of such a ω, it will be that $\sigma_P^2 = \omega' \Sigma \omega > 0$.

To make the notion of portfolio variance more concrete, we come back to investigate in depth, a portfolio composed of only two stocks, A and B. In this application, the formula to compute portfolio variance simplifies to

$$\sigma_P^2 = \omega_A^2 \sigma_A^2 + \omega_B^2 \sigma_B^2 + 2\omega_A \omega_B \sigma_{AB}, \tag{1.18}$$

which can also be rewritten as

$$\sigma_P^2 = \omega_A^2 \sigma_A^2 + \omega_B^2 \sigma_B^2 + 2\rho_{AB} \omega_A \omega_B \sigma_A \sigma_B, \tag{1.19}$$

where $\sigma_{AB} = \rho_{AB} \sigma_A \sigma_B$.

Example 1.5. Consider again the two stocks mentioned in Example 1.4:

Market Condition	Stock A		Stock B	
	Return	Prob.	Return	Prob.
Bull	12.00%	25%	6.00%	25%
Normal	8.00%	50%	1.50%	50%
Bear	-7.00%	25%	-1.00%	25%
Mean	5.25%		2.00%	
Variance	0.0053		0.0006	
Standard Deviation	7.26%		2.52%	
Covariance		0.0015		
Correlation coefficient		0.83		

For instance, the variance of a portfolio composed of 30% of security A and 70% of security B is computed as follows

$$\sigma_P^2 = \omega_A^2 \sigma_A^2 + \omega_B^2 \sigma_B^2 + 2\omega_A \omega_B \sigma_{AB}$$
$$= 0.30^2 \times 0.0053 + 0.70^2 \times 0.0006 + 2 \times 0.30 \times 0.70 \times 0.0015$$
$$= 0.0014.$$

Clearly, the same result holds if we use matrix notation:

$$\sigma_P^2 = [0.30 \quad 0.70] \times \begin{bmatrix} 0.0053 & 0.0015 \\ 0.0015 & 0.0006 \end{bmatrix} \times \begin{bmatrix} 0.30 \\ 0.70 \end{bmatrix} = 0.0014.$$

Given such variance, it is also easy to compute also the standard deviation (or volatility) of the portfolio, which is simply equal to its square root:

$$\sigma_P = \sqrt{0.0014} = 0.0378 = 3.78\%.$$

Now consider a new asset, let's call it stock C, with the characteristics detailed below:

Market Condition	Stock C	
	Return	Prob.
Bull	-2.00%	25%
Normal	3.50%	50%
Bear	3.00%	25%
Mean	2.00%	
Variance	0.0005	
Standard Deviation	2.32%	

This stock has a negative covariance (hence, correlation) with both stock A and stock B. In particular, stock B and stock C have a covariance equal to -0.0005. Consequently, an equally weighted portfolio of stock B and C will have mean, variance, and standard deviation as computed below:

$$\mu_P = 0.50 \times 2.00\% + 0.50 \times 2.00\% = 2.00\%$$
$$\sigma_P^2 = 0.50^2 \times 0.0006 + 0.50^2 \times 0.0005 + 2 \times 0.50 \times 0.50$$
$$\times (-0.0005) = 0.00004$$
$$\sigma_P = \sqrt{0.00004} = 0.61\%.$$

Noticeably, this portfolio has a similar mean but a considerably lower risk (as expressed by the standard deviation) than both its component stocks. This is a consequence of the high *negative correlation* between the two assets:

$$\rho_{BC} = \frac{\sigma_{B,C}}{\sigma_B \sigma_C} = \frac{-0.0005}{0.0252 \times 0.0232} = -0.88.$$

The result is even more intuitive if we look at what happens when the market enters a bear regime. An investor holding the equally weighted portfolio defined above loses 1% of the wealth invested in stock B, but gains 3% on stock C. Overall, she gains 1% on her total wealth. Conversely, in a bull regime, she gains 6% on stock B, but loses 2% on stock C, with a total return of 2%. It is obvious that this investor would never lose money, while an investor holding only stock B or C would experience a negative return in some regimes. In practice, stock C provides a hedge to stock B in a bear regime and vice versa in a bull regime. As a result, the portfolio has a similar mean but a considerably lower risk than each of the two stocks, a point that we are about to explore in depth.

An analysis of the formula of portfolio variance leads us to a natural discovery of the concept of diversification. To illustrate this in the simplest and starkest set up, consider an equally weighted portfolio of N stocks (consequently, the weight assigned to each stock in the portfolio equals 1/N). In this case, formula (1.15) can be re-written as follows,

$$\sigma_P^2 = \sum_{i,j=1}^{N} \omega_i \omega_j \sigma_{i,j} = \sum_{i=1}^{N} \left(\frac{1}{N}\right)^2 \sigma_i^2 + \sum_{i,j=1}^{N} \left(\frac{1}{N}\right)\left(\frac{1}{N}\right) \sigma_{i,j}$$
$$= \frac{1}{N} \sum_{i=1}^{N} \frac{\sigma_i^2}{N} + \frac{N-1}{N} \sum_{i,j=1}^{N} \frac{\sigma_{i,j}}{N(N-1)}$$

$$= \frac{1}{N}\bar{\sigma}^2 + \frac{N-1}{N}\bar{\sigma}_{i,j}, \tag{1.20}$$

where $\bar{\sigma}^2$ and $\bar{\sigma}_{i,j}$ are the average portfolio variance and covariance, respectively. As N grows to infinity, the term $(1/N)\bar{\sigma}^2$ of equation (1.20) approaches zero. In other words, as N gets large the contribution of the variance of the individual stocks to the variance of the portfolio goes to zero. Therefore, the variance of a large portfolio does not depend on the individual risk of the securities, but only on their average covariance. Figures 1.1 and 1.2, illustrate this result for the US and the Italian equity markets, respectively. In the plots, the vertical axes indicate the risk of the portfolio as a percentage of the risk of an individual security. The horizontal axis represents the number of stocks included in the portfolio.[8]

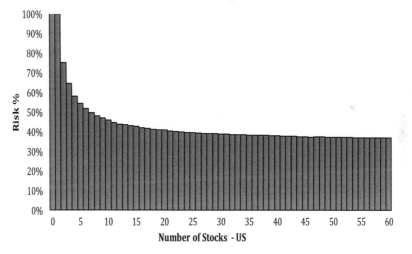

Figure 1.1

<hr />

[8] The two figures were obtained as follows. For the US market, we collect monthly returns for 2,237 stocks from CRSP (Center for Research on Security Prices) over a sample spanning the period December 1994 - December 2015 and compute their variance. Then, we randomly select N stocks (with N increasing from 1 to 60) and calculate the resulting portfolio standard deviation. We repeat the exercise 1,000 times and compute the average standard deviation of all portfolios composed by N stocks. The latter is then expressed as a percentage of the average standard deviation of a single stock, randomly picked. In the case of the Italian stock market, we perform the same exercise, but with a lower number of stocks to start from (60) and a higher number of simulations (10,000) to guarantee sufficient stability in variance estimates. In this case, monthly returns are collected with for the period January 2000 - April 2016.

It is evident that in both cases the standard deviation of the portfolio sharply declines as we add the first 10 stocks, then it slowly converges towards the average covariance of the pool of stocks considered. Interestingly, the average covariance reduction is much larger for Italian stocks than for US stocks. Indeed, the total risk of a large portfolio of Italian stocks is equal to only 14% of the average risk of a single individual Italian stock, while the total risk of a US portfolio cannot be reduced below 35% of the average risk of an individual security. Clearly, the more the stocks are uncorrelated, the lower the variance of a well-diversified portfolio will be. Indeed, the second term of equation (1.20), the average covariance, depends on the average correlation coefficient among stocks. If all the stocks were uncorrelated (the average correlation coefficient would be equal to zero), a well-diversified portfolio would show zero risk, as the second term of (1.20) would be zero as well.

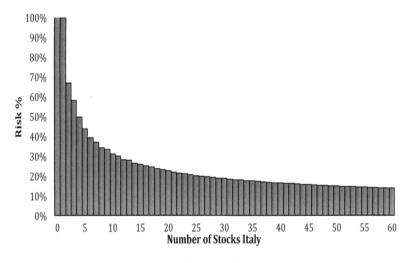

Figure 1.2

Rearranging equation (1.20) helps us understand when a portfolio has reached the minimum possible variance:

$$\sigma_P^2 = \frac{1}{N}\left(\bar{\sigma}^2 - \bar{\sigma}_{i,j}\right) + \bar{\sigma}_{i,j}$$

(1.21)

When the difference between the average variance and the average covariance of all stocks is equal to zero adding a new stock would not help to further decrease the portfolio variance. Since it can be eliminated by holding a large number of stocks, the risk arising from individual securities is often called *diversifiable* risk and an investor should not be rewarded for taking it. We shall examine this concept again in chapter 5.

References and Further Readings

Bailey, R., E. *The Economics of Financial Markets*. Cambridge: Cambridge University Press, 2005.

Campbell, J. Y., Lo, A. W. C., and MacKinlay, A. C. *The Econometrics of Financial Markets*. Princeton, NJ: Princeton University Press, 1997.

Cuthbertson, K., and Nitzsche, D. *Quantitative Financial Economics: Stocks, Bonds and Foreign Exchange*. John Wiley & Sons, 2005.

Danthine, J. P., and Donaldson, J. B. *Intermediate Financial Theory*. Academic Press, 2014.

Fabozzi, F., and Markowitz, H. *The Theory and Practice of Investment Management*, Second Edition, John Wiley & Sons, 2011.

Huang, C.-f., and Litzenberger, R., H., *Foundations for Financial Economics*. Amsterdam: North-Holland, 1988.

Luenberger, D. G., *Investment Science*. Oxford: Oxford University Press, 1997.

Meucci, A., *Risk and Asset Allocation*. Springer Science & Business Media, 2009.

Modigliani, F., and Pogue, G. A. An introduction to risk and return: concepts and evidence, part two. *Financial Analysts Journal*, 30, 69-86, 1974.

2 Choice under Uncertainty and State-Preference Approach to Portfolio Decisions

> *"(...) the determination of the value of an item must not be based on its price, but rather on the utility it yields. The price of the item is dependent only on the thing itself and is equal for everyone; the utility, however, is dependent on the particular circumstances of the person making the estimate." (D. Bernoulli, "Exposition of a New Theory on the Measurement of Risk," 1938)*

Summary: – 1. Representing Preferences and Risk Aversion Attitudes with Utility Functions – 2. Measuring Risk Aversion and Its Economic Implications – 3. A Review of Commonly Used Utility of Wealth Functions.

1 - Representing Preferences and Risk Aversion Attitudes with Utility Functions

In chapter 1, we have introduced the concepts of dominance and of mean-variance dominance, that are useful tools to rule inefficient securities and portfolios from the analysis. However, we have also seen that both these criteria are highly incomplete, as there are many portfolios that are not (mean-variance) dominated by any other. How does an investor choose among such securities? In order to answer this question, in this chapter we shall introduce *expected utility theory*.

1.1 Choice under certainty: preference relations

The first step in developing a theory of rational portfolio selection based on utility maximization focuses on the case of choice under certainty. As a

Reader may recall from her standard courses in intermediate microeconomics, economic theory describes individual behavior as the result of a process of optimization under constraints, the objective being determined by individual preferences, and the constraints depending on an investor's income or wealth level and on market prices (in our cases, for the securities in the asset menu).

To develop such a rational theory of choice under certainty, we begin by describing the objectives of the investors in the most basic way: we postulate the existence of a *preference relation*, represented by the symbol $\gtrsim$, describing the investors' ability to compare alternative *bundles* (collections, lists) of goods, services, and money. For two bundles a and b, we can express preferences as defined below.

Preference relation: when $a \gtrsim b$, for the investor in question, bundle a is strictly preferred to bundle b, or she is indifferent between them; pure indifference is denoted by $a \sim b$, strict preference by $a \succ b$.

What does it mean to be rational in such a framework of choice based on the existence of the preference relation $\gtrsim$? In essence, it turns out that rationality means that you can always express a precise preference between any pair of bundles, that you should not contradict yourself when asked to express preferences over three or more bundles in successive pairs, and some additional technical conditions that prevent the possibility that by considering long sequences of converging bundles you may express equivocal choices. To be more specific, the notion of economic rationality can be traced back to the following assumptions holding true. These are often called *axioms of choice*:

Completeness: Every investor possesses a complete preference relation, meaning that she is always able to decide whether she prefers a to b, b to a, or both, in which case she is indifferent with respect to the two bundles. That is, for any two bundles a and b, either $a \succ b$ or $b \succ a$ or both; if both conditions hold, we say that the investor is indifferent with respect to the bundles and write $a \sim b$.

In practice, the axiom of completeness rules out situations in which an investor may be indecisive when asked to choose between two bundles of goods or services. To turn it into a joke, there is no chance that you would ignore a text asking if you would like sushi or pizza tonight (note that you may reply that you are indifferent, but not that you cannot decide which one you would prefer).

Transitivity: For any bundles a, b, and c, if $a \succsim b$ and $b \succsim c$, then $a \succsim c$.

This axiom in practice rules out contradictory answers; if you like sushi over pizza and pizza over cereals for dinner, you cannot then claim that you prefer cereals to sushi! Note that the framework within which the choice occurs should not matter. For instance, even if we add that each of the three meals listed above will be accompanied by hot, sweet milk, this should not perturb the transitivity relationship that we have just established. If you consider (as we do) sushi or pizza accompanied by hot milk unappetizing (while hot milk with cereals may be acceptable), then the solution is to re-define the objects of your choice to be bundles involving hot milk and—for instance—state that $\{\text{hot milk}, \text{cereals}\} \succsim \{\text{hot milk}, \text{pizza}\}$ and $\{\text{hot milk}, \text{pizza}\} \succsim \{\text{hot milk}, \text{sushi}\}$ implies $\{\text{hot milk}, \text{cereals}\} \succsim \{\text{hot milk}, \text{sushi}\}$.

A further requirement is also necessary for technical reasons:

Continuity: Let $\{x_n\}$ and $\{y_n\}$ be two sequences of consumption bundles such that $x_n \to x$ and $y_n \to y$ as $n \to \infty$. The preference relation $\succsim$ is continuous if and only if $x_n \succsim y_n$ for all n, then the same relationship is preserved in the limit, $x \succsim y$.

To keep using tasty food metaphors (and apologies for those who are reading this book just before dinner time), as a pizza cooks and becomes a golden crusted cradle of ham and cheese, you will keep preferring it to a portion of broccoli while it becomes steamed in your pressure cooker into a healthy mash. Using these conditions, it is possible to prove the following result (the proof is somewhat technical and can be found in most microeconomics textbooks, for instance, Mas-Colell et. al., 1995):

Result 2.1: Completeness, transitivity, and continuity are sufficient to guarantee the existence of a continuous, time-invariant, real-valued *ordinal utility function* $u(\cdot)$, such that for any two objects of choice (consumption bundles of goods and services, amounts of money, etc.) a and b,[1]

$$a \succsim b \text{ if and only if } u(a) \geq u(b).$$

---

[1] The ordinal feature of $u(\cdot)$ means that any nonlinear monotone increasing transformation of $u(\cdot)$ will always represent an identical preference ordering as $u(\cdot)$. Technically, the bundles a and b ought to belong to a convex set for the result to hold, i.e., linear combinations of bundles with positive weights assigned to all of them (say, mixing different shopping carts at the supermarket) will give new, eligible bundles.

Therefore rationality buys us one important result: the ranking of bundles of goods and services that you may determine on a qualitative basis using your preferences as summarized by the relation $\succsim$ corresponds to the ranking derived from the utility function $u(\cdot)$ that maps bundles into real numbers. Of course, real numbers are then easy to compare. Equivalently, a decision-maker, instead of optimizing by searching and choosing the best possible bundle of goods and services, may simply maximize the utility function $u(\cdot)$ (possibly, subject to constraints). Note that the resulting $u(\cdot)$ is a continuous function by construction. Intuitively, this derives from the continuity axiom. Because $u(\cdot)$ is an ordinal function, no special meaning may be attached to its values, i.e., while the fact that $u(a) \geq u(b)$ is meaningful, the exact size of the difference $u(a) - u(b) \geq 0$ is not.

Of course, different investors will be characterized by heterogeneous preferences and as such will express different utility functions, as identified by heterogeneous shapes and features of their $u(\cdot)$ functions. However, because $a \succsim b$ if and only if $u(a) \geq u(b)$, any monotone increasing transformation $v(\cdot)$ will be such that $v(u(a)) \geq v(u(b))$, or, assuming $v(\cdot)$ monotone increasing cannot change the ranking of bundles. Therefore *any increasing transformation of $u(\cdot)$ will represent the same preference relation* because such a transformation by definition will preserve the *ordering* induced by $u(\cdot)$. For instance, if $u(a) \geq u(b)$, then $(u(a))^3 \geq (u(b))^3$ (note that $d((u)^3)/du = 3(u)^2 > 0$) and the function $(u(\cdot))^3$ represents the preference relation $\succsim$ as much as $u(\cdot)$. We summarize this result as follows:

Result 2.2: Given a utility function $u(\cdot)$ and a generic monotone increasing transformation $v(\cdot)$, the function $v(u(\cdot))$ represents the same preferences as the original utility function $u(\cdot)$.

For instance, if John is characterized by $u(\cdot)$ and Mary's preferences are simply derived from John's by transforming his preferences into $v(u(\cdot))$, then John and Mary will display identical rankings over bundles of goods and services. When both $u(\cdot)$ and $v(\cdot)$ are everywhere differentiable, the proof is actually a direct consequence of the chain rule of standard differential calculus. If we define $w(\cdot) \equiv v(u(\cdot))$, then $w'(\cdot) \equiv v'(u(\cdot))u'(\cdot) > 0$. Of course, this result derives from the fact that $u(\cdot)$ just pins down the ordering across bundles, it does not provide cardinal, signed information on their subjective values. For instance, it is not correct to state that because $w(a) = 2u(a)$, the investor with utility function $w(\cdot)$ values the bundle a twice as much the investor characterized by $u(\cdot)$.

1.2 The expected utility theorem

Can result 2.1 above be generalized to the case in which the objects of choice consist of payoffs paid out under varying probabilities that depend on some uncertain state of the world? Under certainty, the choice is among consumption baskets with known characteristics. Under uncertainty, the objects of choice are typically no longer consumption bundles but vectors of state-contingent monetary payoffs. This means that investors generally have no intrinsic like or dislike for securities, but they appreciate their monetary payoffs in different states of the world. Moreover, ranking bundles of goods (or vectors of monetary payoffs) involves more than pure elements of taste or preferences. For instance, when selecting between stock A that pays out well during recessions and poorly during expansions, and stock B that pays out according to an opposite pattern, it is essential to forecast the probabilities of recessions and expansions, respectively. Disentangling pure preferences from probability assessments is a complex problem that simplifies to a manageable maximization problem only under special assumptions.

All these desiderata as to what we would need to perform rational choices over uncertain payoffs, are accomplished by one of the most important and useful results offered by modern microeconomics: the *expected utility theorem* (henceforth, EUT).

The EUT provides a set of hypotheses under which an investor's ranking over assets with uncertain monetary payoffs may be represented by an index combining, in the most elementary way (i.e., *linearly*), the two ingredients just discussed above:[2]

   I. a preference ordering on the state-specific payoffs, and
   II. the state probabilities associated to these payoffs, which at least initially, we set to be *objectively defined*.[3]

Here we need to emphasize strongly the incise "in the most elementary way" claimed above: what the EUT delivers is not only a method to select

---

[2] With regard to the axioms, a review of the literature reveals that alternative sets may be formulated that will look slightly different to a trained eye. However, their exact formulation hardly matters for practical application and for a solid grasp of the importance of EUT.

[3] The alternative is represented by the case in which probabilities are *subjectively defined*. In this case, both preferences (as represented by the utility of monetary payoffs) and subjective probability assessments will be representative of an individual investor's personality traits. See, for instance, Bailey (2005) for a readable derivation.

among risky payoffs, but also a simple one! To first appreciate the benefits and great simplicity of the EUT, we start by stating the result.

Result 2.3 (EUT): Under the five axioms specified below, there exists a *cardinal*, continuous, time-invariant, real-valued *Von Neumann-Morgenstern (VNM) felicity function* of money $U(\cdot)$, such that for any two lotteries/gambles/securities (i.e., probability distributions of monetary payoffs) x and y,

$$x \succsim y \quad \text{if and only} \quad \text{if } E[U(x)] \geq E[U(y)].$$

where for a generic lottery z (e.g., one that pays out either x or y),

$$\mathbb{U}(z) \equiv E[U(z)] = \sum_{s=1}^{S} Prob(state = s)U(z(s)) \qquad (2.1)$$

and $z(s)$ denotes the payoff lottery z in state s. $\mathbb{U}(\cdot)$ is called a *VNM expected utility function*.

The EUT simply states that uncertain payoff streams may be ranked based on the expectation of the happiness (*felicity*) they provide in each possible state of the world. It is difficult to underestimate the enormous simplification that EUT implies: instead of combining probabilities and preferences over possible state-contingent payoffs in complicated ways, the probabilities are used to take the expectation of an index of preferences applied to such payoffs. Therefore, EUT makes us step towards simple applications of averaging: the perceived, cardinal (measureable) happiness of a complex and risky menu of options, is given by the weighted average of the satisfaction derived from each such individual option, weighted by the associated probability. Averaging is a powerful criterion of aggregation of heterogeneous inputs, well-known and attractive to finance scholars and practitioners alike.

Note that the EUT implies that investors are concerned only with an asset's final payoffs and the cumulative probabilities of achieving them, while the temporal structure of the resolution of the uncertainty—for instance, whether the probability, $Prob(state = s)$, of a given payoff $z(s)$ is obtained for a sure amount z or through a complex web of lotteries— is irrelevant. For instance, we may assume one felicity function that, as we shall see later, plays an important role also in the development of modern portfolio choice theory, i.e., logarithmic utility of monetary payments (here gross, total payoffs) $U(R_i) = lnR_i$. Now, if we examine again the example proposed in chapter 1 (1.3), we are able to determinate a ranking of securities A, B, C, and D.

Example 2.1 Going back to the same payoffs proposed in example 1.3 (extended to a new security D) and assuming that $U(R_i) = lnR_i$, we have:

State	Security A		Security B		Security C		Security D	
	Payoff	Prob.	Payoff	Prob.	Payoff	Prob.	Payoff	Prob.
i	20	3/15	18	3/15	18	3/15	5	3/15
ii	18	5/15	18	5/15	16	5/15	14	4/15
iii	14	4/15	10	4/15	12	4/15	14	4/15
iv	10	2/15	5	2/15	12	2/15	18	2/15
v	6	1/15	5	1/15	8	1/15	18	1/15
$E[R_i]$	15.47		13.27		14.27		13.00	
Stdev$[R_i]$	4.10		5.33		2.91		4.29	
$E[lnR_i]$	2.693		2.477		2.635		2.483	

By construction, security B and D have similar means, standard deviations, and expected utility. However, we can say that security B is a sort of reverse of security D. Indeed, security D pays out well in states *iv* and *v*, when security B performs poorly. Conversely, security B outperforms security D in states *i* and *ii*.

Interestingly, the ranking provided by the expected utility criterion differs from the mean-variance dominance criterion: while, according the latter, only securities B and D are dominated (both B and D are dominated by both assets A and C), and hence securities A and C cannot be ranked, according to the expected log-payoff criterion, security A ranks above security C (and of course B and D). Importantly, we have to recognize that no special meaning should be derived from the fact that the differences in expected log-payoffs are generally small, as per result 2.3 the utility values represent state-contingent happiness and there is no recognized measurement standard for this feeling.

As for the equivalence of assets B and D, let's consider what happens when we hold an equally weighted portfolio (with 50-50% weights) of securities A and C and we are asked to choose between security B and D. The following table summarizes the relevant calculations.

State	Security A + C		Security A + C + B		Security A + C + D	
	Payoff	Prob.	Payoff	Prob.	Payoff	Prob.
i	38	3/15	56	3/15	43	3/15
ii	34	5/15	52	5/15	48	5/15
iii	26	1/5	36	1/5	40	1/5
iv	22	1/5	27	1/5	40	1/5
v	14	1/15	19	1/15	32	1/15
$E[R_i]$	29.73		43.00		42.73	
Stdev[R_i]	6.92		12.10		4.46	
$E[lnR_i]$	3.360		3.713		3.749	

Surprisingly, even though adding security D to the initial (A+C) portfolio does not increase the mean payoff by much more than adding security B (42.7 vs. 43.0), the properties of security D greatly stabilize the payoffs of the (A+C) portfolio, with the result that standard deviation declines only from 12 to 4.5. Note that, implicitly, the portfolio built this way features 25% in securities A and C, and 50% in the latter security that is added. As we shall see, an investor with logarithmic felicity function is risk-averse (i.e., she dislikes the variance), and as a result the expected log-payoff from combining securities A, C, and D (3.75) is higher than that of security A, C, and B (3.71). As commented above, security D yields lousy payoffs in general, but strong payoffs in states *iv* and *v* when positive payouts are most needed. Hence, adding asset D yields stabilizing, smoothing effects that a log-felicity investor appreciates. In practice, security D can be seen as a sort of insurance that pays out well when the other assets fails to deliver a good performance.

This example, through the assessment of a range of securities and the resulting portfolios, also alerts us to one fundamental advantage of EUT-based criteria over the dominant ones illustrated in chapter 1: its completeness, in the sense that all securities and/or portfolios can always be consistently ranked.

At this juncture, we have stated the EUT in a simple context where the objects of choice take the form of *lotteries*. The generic lottery is denoted $(x, y; \pi)$; it means that the lottery offers payoff x with probability π and payoff y with probability $1 - \pi$. This notion of a lottery is actually very general and

encompasses a huge variety of possible payoff structures.[4]
It is now time to dig deeper into the seven axioms that support the EUT.

Lottery reduction and consistency: (i) $(x, y; 1) = x$; (ii) $(x, y; \pi) = (y, x; 1 - \pi)$; (iii) $(x, z; \pi) = (x, y; \pi + (1 - \pi)q)$ if $z = (x, y; q)$.

This axiom means that investors are concerned with the net cumulative probability of each outcome and are able to see through the way the lotteries are set up and presented to them. For instance, if we consider the lottery $(x, z; \pi)$ and $z = (x, y; q)$, there is a probability $\pi + (1 - \pi)q$ to win x; in the expression $\pi + (1 - \pi)q$, π derives from the chance to win x directly from $(x, z; \pi)$ and $(1 - \pi)q$ from the chance to win the lottery $z = (x, y; q)$ times the probability of this second lottery paying out the first prize. Therefore, because of the axiom, only the utility of the final payoff matters to decision makers. The exact mechanism for its award is irrelevant. Of course, this is rather demanding in terms of the computational skills required of our investors.

Completeness and transitivity: The investor is always able to decide whether she prefers z to l, l to z, or both, in which case she is indifferent with respect to the two lotteries. There exists a best, most preferred lottery, b, as well as a worst, least desirable, lottery w. Moreover, for any lotteries z, l, and h, if $z \gtrsim l$ and $l \gtrsim h$, then $z \gtrsim h$.

Continuity: The preference relation is continuous in the sense established in section 1.1, appropriately adapted to fit the choice among lotteries (see Ingersoll, 1987).

By these three axioms alone, we know from result 2.1 that there exists a utility function, which we will denote by $\mathbb{U}(\cdot)$, defined both on lotteries and on fixed, one-time payments because, by the first axiom above, a payment may be viewed as a (degenerate) lottery. Our remaining assumptions are thus necessary only to guarantee that this function assumes the expected utility form, $\mathbb{U}(z) \equiv E[U(z)] = \sum_{s=1}^{S} Prob(state = s)U(z(s))$, so that, for

---

[4] For example, x and y may represent specific monetary payoffs or x may be a payment while y is a lottery, or even x and y may both be lotteries. Note that also riskless, one-time payments, are lotteries where one of the possible monetary payoffs is certain, say, $(x, y; \pi) = x$ if and only if $\pi = 1$. Although the technicalities become rather complex, the EUT also holds for assets paying a continuum of possible payoffs.

instance, $U(z) = U(x) \pi + U(y)(1 - \pi)$.[5]

Independence of irrelevant alternatives: Let $(x, y; \pi)$ and $(x, z; \pi)$ be any two lotteries; then, $y \succsim z$ if and only if $(x, y; \pi) \succsim (x, z; \pi)$. This implies that $(x, y; \pi_1) \succsim (x, z; \pi_2)$ if and only if $\pi_1 \geq \pi_2$, i.e., *preferences are independent of beliefs*, as summarized by state probabilities. This last implication is sometimes called dominance axiom and stated independently of others (see Ingersoll, 1987).

This means that a given bundle of goods or monetary amount remains preferred even though this bundle or sum is to be received under conditions of uncertainty, through a lottery. If two bundles are equally satisfying, then they are also considered equivalent as lottery prizes. In addition, there is no thrill or aversion towards suspense or gambling per se. In other words, we need investors smart enough to see through lotteries characterized by the same probability weighting, π. The final condition has a technical nature:

Certainty equivalence: Let x, y, z be payoffs for which $x > y > z$. Then there exists a fixed monetary amount CE (which stands for *certainty equivalent*) such that $(x, z; \pi) \sim CE$.

Pulling these five axioms together, one obtains the EUT and therefore concludes that for any pair of lotteries x and y, $x \succsim y$ if and only if $E[U(x)] \geq E[U(y)]$. Importantly, the function $U(\cdot)$ is assumed to be the same for all states, though the values of its arguments generally differ across states. However, both the probabilities and the VNM felicity function are allowed to differ across investors.

The VNM utility function is a "cardinal" measure, i.e., unlike the ordinal utility function $u(\cdot)$, the numerical value of utility has a precise meaning (up to a scaling) over and above the simple rank of the numbers. This can be easily demonstrated as follows. Suppose there is a single good. Now compare a lottery paying 0 or 9 units with equal probability to one guaranteed to pay 4 units. Under the utility function $v(x) = x$, the former, with an expected utility of 4.5, would be preferred. But if we apply the increasing transformation (over positive payoffs) $w(v(x)) = x^{1/2}$ the lottery has an expected utility of 1.5, whereas the certain payoff's utility is 2. These two

---

[5] Note that the VNM utility function ($\mathbb{U}(\cdot)$) and its associated utility of money ($U(\cdot)$) function are not the same. The former is defined over uncertain asset payoff structures while the latter is defined over individual monetary payments.

rankings are contradictory, so arbitrary monotone transformations of cardinal utility functions do not preserve ordering over lotteries. More generally, it is natural to ask whether also VNM felicity functions are unique up to some kind of transformations so to obtain some class of equivalence across utility functions as we did in section 1.1 for ordinal utility functions. It turns out that the VNM representation is preserved under a certain class of linear transformations. If $\mathbb{U}(\cdot)$ is a VNM felicity function, then

$$\mathbb{V}(\cdot) = a + b\mathbb{U}(\cdot). \tag{2.2}$$

where $b > 0$, is such a function. To see it, let $(x, y; \pi)$ be some uncertain payoff and let $U(\cdot)$ be the utility of money function associated with $\mathbb{U}$. Then:

$$\begin{aligned}
\mathbb{V}\big((x, y; \pi)\big) = a + b\mathbb{U}\big((x, y; \pi)\big) &= a + b[\pi U(x) + (1 - \pi)U(y)] \\
&= \pi[a + bU(x)] + (1 - \pi)[a + bU(y)] \\
&= \pi V(x) + (1 - \pi)V(y).
\end{aligned} \tag{2.3}$$

This shows that with every linear, monotone increasing (as implied by $b > 0$) transformation of an expected utility function, there is also an expected utility function. The utility of money function associated with $\mathbb{V}$ is $a + bU\big((x, y; \pi)\big)$; $\mathbb{V}(\cdot)$ represents the same preference ordering over uncertain payoffs as $\mathbb{U}(\cdot)$. Therefore, if John's felicity function is $U^{John}(R_i) = lnR_i$ and Mary's felicity is instead $U^{Mary}(R_i) = 2 + 4lnR_i$, Mary and John will share the same preferences. However, when $U^{Mary}(R_i) = +1000 - lnR_i$ or $U^{Mary}(R_i) = (lnR_i)^3$, this will not be the case because the first transformation is linear but monotone decreasing, the second transformation monotone increasing but non-linear. We summarize the result above as follows:

Result 2.4: Given a VNM utility function of money $U(\cdot)$ and a generic monotone increasing linear transformation $V(z) = a + bz$ with $b > 0$, the function $V(U(\cdot)) = a + bU(\cdot)$ represents the same preferences for risky lotteries as the original utility of wealth function $U(\cdot)$.

Each VNM cardinal utility function embodies a specific ordinal utility function. Since the latter are distinct only up to a monotone increasing transformation, two very different cardinal functions may display the same ordinal properties. Thus, two consumers who always make the same choice under certainty may choose among lotteries differently. For example, the two Cobb-Douglas utility functions $u(x, z) = (xz)^{1/2}$ and $v(x, z) = -1/(xz)$ are equivalent for ordinal purposes since $v(x, z) = [-u(x, z)]^{-2}$, which is monotone increasing. Here x and z are two consumption goods. Faced by choosing between (2, 2) for sure or a 50-50 chance at (4, 4) or (1, 1), the first agent will select the lottery with an expected utility of 2.5 over the sure thing with utility of 2. In the same situation, the second decision maker will select the safe alternative with utility -1/4 over the lottery with expected utility -17/32.

We close with one example that shows that the type of felicity function assumed for an investor may matter a lot. This justifies our investigation of the properties and shapes of felicity functions of monetary payoffs that we undertake in the following section.

Example 2.2. Using the same inputs as in example 2.1, and assuming that $U(R_i) = -1(R_i)^{-1} = -1/R_i$ we have:

State	Security A		Security B		Security C		Security D	
	Payoff	Prob.	Payoff	Prob.	Payoff	Prob.	Payoff	Prob.
i	20	3/15	18	3/15	18	3/15	5	3/15
ii	18	5/15	18	5/15	16	5/15	14	4/15
iii	14	4/15	10	4/15	12	4/15	14	4/15
iv	10	2/15	5	2/15	12	2/15	18	2/15
v	6	1/15	5	1/15	8	1/15	18	1/15
$E[R_i]$	15.47		13.27		14.27		13.00	
Stdev[R_i]	4.10		5.33		2.91		4.29	
-E[1/(R_i)]	-0.073		-0.096		-0.074		-0.094	

While under a logarithmic utility function, security A was ranked highest, now security A and C are basically on a par. We shall learn that $U(R_i) = \ln(R_i)$ and $U(R_i) = -1/R_i$ are related felicity functions but that the second implies larger aversion to risk. This justifies the current tie between the high-mean return but risky portfolio A and the less risky but also slightly less performing portfolio C.

As already commented with reference to example 2.1, the expected utility criterion based on the EUT result and made possible by the state-preference framework, offers one considerable advantage: it is a *complete*, flexible criterion to rank alternative lotteries, securities, and portfolios thereof in conditions of uncertainty. Even though this does not guarantee that the resulting optimal portfolio decisions will always be the most sensible or promising ones—as we shall see, this will mostly hinge on the nature and mathematical properties of the assumed utility of wealth function, the topic of the next section—these will be optimal and in general well-defined.

2 - Measuring Risk Aversion and Its Economic Implications

In this section, we put the notion of utility function to work. On the one hand, we ask whether and how the abstract notion of an individual's preference index may be linked to her actual decisions under conditions of risk. Naturally, we shall predict patterns of behaviors when faced with lotteries and in security portfolio decisions. On the other hand, we resort to the mathematical properties of utility functions to try and pin down whether investors dislike or like payoff-relevant, monetary risks.

2.1 Risk aversion and the concavity of the utility function

Given our objective specification of probabilities, it is the utility function of monetary payoffs (wealth) $U(\cdot)$ that uniquely characterizes an investor. This derives from the fact that in financial applications, it is common to express outcomes with a utility index measuring the satisfaction associated with a particular level of wealth. If there is a single consumption good, then this can be the numeraire for wealth; if there are a number of consumption goods, then utility can be expressed as a function of wealth and the vector of M consumption goods prices $(p_1, p_2,..., p_M)$ as:

$$U(W; p_1, p_2,..., p_M) \equiv \max_{x_1, x_2,..., x_M} u(x_1, x_2, ..., x_M) \;\; s.t. \;\; \sum_{i=1}^{M} p_i x_i = W \;\; (2.4)$$

As we shall examine in this section, a range of alternative additional assumptions on $U(\cdot)$ will identify an investor's tolerance or aversion to risk. If the utility function $u(\cdot)$ that depends on the quantities purchased and consumed of the M goods, $u(x_1, x_2, ..., x_M)$, is increasing, and all prices are strictly positive, then it can be shown that the utility of wealth will be strictly increasing in total wealth W; when $U(W; p_1, p_2,..., p_M)$ is differentiable, we shall write $U'(W) > 0$. Therefore in what follows therefore, we will always impose the maintained requirement that $U(\cdot)$ be increasing for all candidate utility functions (more wealth is preferred to less). This is called the *non-satiation hypothesis*.

Figure 2.1 shows the implication of this assumption in the case of a continuous felicity function that has stochastic wealth (because this will have realization at time *t+1*) as its argument. In the picture, one can see three different functions, all monotone increasing but with different shapes, i.e., types of concavity. We shall momentarily analyze their meanings and implications.

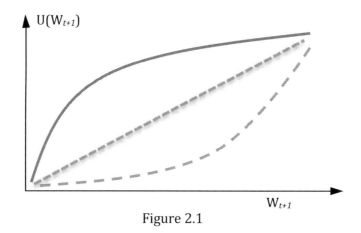

Figure 2.1

In example 2.1 we claimed that investors are likely to show a preference for smoothing consumption across states of nature through avoidance of variations in the value of their portfolio holdings. This is linked to the concept of risk aversion and to the postulate of *decreasing marginal utility* (henceforth, DMU), which are closely related. Because the state probabilities are objectively given in our construction, such DMU feature must derive from further restrictions placed on the utility-of-money function $U(\cdot)$. To understand the type of characterization involved, consider a financial contract where the potential investor either receives an amount h with probability ½, or must pay an amount h with probability ½. The intuitive notion of "being averse to risk" is that for any level of personal wealth W, an investor would not wish to own such a security. In utility terms this must mean:

$$U(W) > \frac{1}{2}U(W + h) + \frac{1}{2}U(W - h) = E[U(W + H)], \qquad (2.5)$$

where H is a zero-mean random variable that takes value h with probability ½ and $-h$ with probability ½. This inequality can be satisfied *for all wealth levels* W if the agent's utility function has the form suggested in figure 2.2. When this is the case we say the utility function is *strictly concave.*[6]

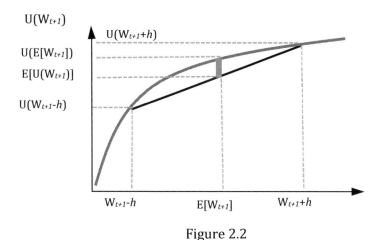

Figure 2.2

The important feature implied by this and similarly shaped felicity functions is that their slope decreases as the investor becomes wealthier (as W increases); that is, the marginal utility (MU), represented by the derivative $U'(W) \equiv d(U(W))/dW$ decreases as W grows larger. Equivalently, for any twice differentiable utility function,

$$U''(W) \equiv \frac{d^2U(W)}{dW^2} = \frac{dU'(W)}{dW} = \frac{dMU(W)}{dW} < 0, \qquad (2.6)$$

where $MU(W)$ is marginal utility as a function of wealth, which shows that risk aversion is equivalent to a declining marginal utility when the felicity function is twice differentiable.

As the earlier discussion indicates, both consumption smoothing and risk aversion are directly related to the notion of decreasing MU. Whether this

---

[6] In technical terms, a function $f(x)$: $\mathbb{R} \to \mathbb{R}$ is (strictly) concave if and only if $\forall \alpha \in (0,1)$ and a pair of points in the domain of the function, $f(\alpha x + (1-\alpha)y) > \alpha f(x) + (1-\alpha)f(y)$. Equation (2.5) specializes this definition to the case of $\alpha = $ ½. Strict convexity obtains when $f(\alpha x + (1-\alpha)y) > \alpha f(x) + (1-\alpha)f(y)$. A linear function is such that $f(\alpha x + (1-\alpha)y) = \alpha f(x) + (1-\alpha)f(y)$. A linear function is obviously both concave and convex.

is envisaged across time or states, decreasing MU basically implies that wealth (or consumption) variations caused by deviations from a fixed, average level diminish rather than increase expected utility. Essentially, the *positive deviations from the fixed average do not help as much as the negative ones hurt.* Figure 2.2 graphically shows the effect of declining marginal utility. The segment connecting W – h and W + h reveals what all possible levels of expected wealth are (as a function of the probabilities of the different outcomes, in this case set to be ½ and ½ from equation (2.5)). The fact that everywhere in correspondence to this segment the utility function lies above it, due to its concavity, indicates that a risk-averse investor shall prefer the utility of the sure thing to the expectation of the utility of the random variable with outcomes W – h and W + h.

At this point, it is natural to ask what the other shapes shown in figure 2.1 may imply in terms of risk aversion. The case of

$$U(W) < \frac{1}{2}U(W + h) + \frac{1}{2}U(W - h) = E[U(W + H)], \qquad (2.7)$$

delivers the intuitive notion of an investor that in fact *likes risk*, i.e., she prefers the expected utility of a gamble to the sure thing certainty equivalent to the same gamble. This inequality can be satisfied *for all wealth levels W* if the agent's utility function has the form suggested in figure 2.3. When this is the case, we say the utility function is *strictly convex*. The important feature implied by this and similarly shaped felicity functions is that their slope/gradient increases as the investor becomes wealthier (as W increases); that is, the marginal utility (MU), represented by the derivative $U'(W) \equiv d(U(W))/dW$ increases with greater W. Equivalently, for any twice differentiable utility functions,

$$U''(W) \equiv \frac{d^2U(W)}{dW^2} = \frac{dU'(W)}{dW} = \frac{dMU(W)}{dW} > 0, \qquad (2.8)$$

Figure 2.3 shows that when an investor is a *risk lover*, the *positive deviations from the fixed average increase the index of satisfaction more than the negative ones hurt it.* Therefore, the investor will aggressively bet to try and achieve gains (positive deviations) even accepting an increasing risk of negative ones. Finally, the knife-edge case of a *risk neutral* investor obtains when positive deviations from a fixed average carry the same importance as negative deviations. In this case, $U(W) = \frac{1}{2}U(W + h) + \frac{1}{2}U(W - h) = E[U(W + H)]$, and this is equivalent to establishing that marginal utility, represented by the derivative $U'(W) \equiv d(U(W))/dW$ is constant as wealth changes, $U''(W) \equiv dMU(W)/dW = 0$. Interestingly, from standard integration of the marginal utility function, it follows that

$$U'(W) = b \Longrightarrow U(W) = bW + a, \tag{2.9}$$

i.e., a risk-neutral investor will possess a linear utility function.[7]

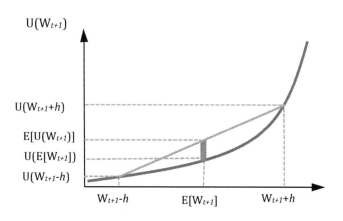

Figure 2.3

2.2 Measuring risk aversion

At this point, and assuming that all investors are risk averse, we ask how can we manage to measure risk aversion and hence compare the risk aversion of different decision makers. Given that under fairly mild conditions, risk aversion is equivalent to $U''(W) < 0$ for all wealth levels, one intuitive but simplistic idea is to establish that—for instance—John is more risk-averse than Mary is, if and only if $|U''_{John}(W)| > |U''_{Mary}(W)|$.[8] Unfortunately, this approach leads to the following inconsistency. Recall that from re-

---

[7] (2.9) simply exploits the fact that the primitive function of a constant MU function must be a linear affine function.

[8] We take absolute values so that the sign of the (negative) second derivatives can be dropped from the analysis.

sult 2.4, the preference ordering described by a utility function is invariant to linear increasing transformations. Suppose now that by chance, $U_{John}(W) = a + bU_{Mary}(W)$, where, say, $b > 1$. On the one hand, we know by construction that John and Mary have the same preferences for taking risks and therefore that it makes no sense to state the John is more risk averse than Mary, because this would be equivalent to claim that John is more risk averse than himself. On the other hand, note that $U''_{John}(W) = bU''_{Mary}(W) > U''_{Mary}(W)$, and this represents a contradiction.

Therefore the absolute value of the second derivative hardly represents a viable measure of risk aversion. We need instead a measure of risk aversion that is invariant to linear transformations. Two widely used measures of this sort have been proposed by, respectively, Pratt (1964) and Arrow (1971). Pratt's measure of *local absolute risk aversion* is:

$$ARA(W) \equiv -\frac{U''(W)}{U'(W)}. \tag{2.10}$$

By construction, $ARA(W) > 0$ for a risk-averse investor (note that $U''(W) < 0$) and the index is a function of wealth, because both its numerator and denominator are generally a function of wealth. If nonzero, the reciprocal of the measure of absolute risk aversion, $T(W) \equiv 1/ARA(W)$ can be used as a measure of *risk tolerance*.

Arrow's measure of *local relative risk aversion* is instead:

$$RRA(W) \equiv -\frac{U''(W)}{U'(W)}W = ARA(W) \cdot W \tag{2.11}$$

Also $RRA(W)$ is positive by construction in the case of risk-averse investors and it is a function of wealth. Note that when ARA happens to be constant, then $RRA(W)$ must be a linear (increasing) function of wealth; when RRA is constant, then it must be the case that $ARA(W) = RRA/W$, a simple inverse function of wealth.

Interestingly, both $ARA(W)$ and $RRA(W)$ are invariant to linear monotonic transformations. This occurs because both are "scaled" at the denominator (i.e., divided by) $U'(W)$. For instance, in the case of $ARA(W)$:

$$ARA_{John}(W) \equiv -\frac{U''_{John}(W)}{U'_{John}(W)} = -\frac{bU''_{Mary}(W)}{bU'_{Mary}(W)} = -\frac{U''_{Mary}(W)}{U'_{Mary}(W)} = ARA_{Mary}(W).$$

$$(2.12)$$

This shows that if the only difference between John and Mary were to be represented by a linear increasing transformation, then $ARA(W)$ would correctly reveal that their risk aversion is identical. A similar proof obviously applies to $RRA(W)$. As a result, to rank John and Mary's risk aversion, one will simply need to either verify whether $ARA_{John}(W) > ARA_{Mary}(W)$ (or $RRA_{John}(W) > RRA_{Mary}(W)$) for all wealth levels. Importantly, it is possible that for some intervals of wealth it may be $(R)ARA_{John}(W) > (R)ARA_{Mary}(W)$ but that for other levels or intervals the inequality be reversed.

Both measures represent local measures of risk aversion in the sense that economically, they usefully characterize the behavior of investors only when the risks (lotteries) considered are small. In the next section, we indeed discuss such economic characterizations implied by the $ARA(W)$ and $RRA(W)$ measures (functions). It turns out that these measures reflect the attitude of risk-averse investors towards how particular they become when deciding whether to accept a gamble and how much to invest in risky assets. While the ARA index concerns such choices when expressed in absolute monetary terms, the RRA index deals with characterizing such choices when expressed in relative, percentage terms.

2.3 Absolute and relative risk aversion and the acceptable odds of a bet

Consider an investor with wealth level W who is offered—at no charge—a bet involving winning or losing an amount h, with probabilities π and $1-\pi$, respectively. Any investor will accept such a bet if π is high enough and reject it if π is small enough (surely if $\pi = 0$, because the bet turns into a lump-sum tax of h on the initial wealth). Such a bet is defined as a *fair* bet when $\pi = \frac{1}{2}$ because it costs nothing and its expected payoff is $(1/2)h + (1/2)(-h) = 0$. When π differs from $\frac{1}{2}$, the bet is not fair and when $\pi > \frac{1}{2}$ the bet is clearly tilted in favor of the investor. However, the bet is intrinsically risky: for instance, even though $\pi = 0.6$ and the expected value of the bet is $0.2h$, it remains true that with probability $1-\pi = 0.4$, our investor can still lose h. Intuitively, we expect all risk-averse investors to demand a minimum $\pi > \frac{1}{2}$ for them to accept a bet. The positive expected payoff of the bet simply compensates the investor for the risk they are exposing themselves to. Moreover, her willingness to accept the bet will generally also be related to her level of current wealth, W.

Let $\pi = \pi(W; h)$ be that probability at which the agent is indifferent between accepting or rejecting the gamble/security. By definition, $\pi(W; h)$ must satisfy

$$U(W) = \pi(W; h)U(W + h) + [1 - \pi(W; h)]U(W - h), \qquad (2.13)$$

which means that the sure-thing utility she derives in the absence of the bet must equal the expected utility of taking part in the bet. Applying a Taylor's expansion around $h = 0$ (the case of no bet) to equation (2.13), in Appendix A, we obtain the following:

Result 2.5: Given a zero-cost bet with two possible outcomes h and $-h$, as $h \rightarrow 0$ (i.e., for small gambles), there is a precise link between Pratt's coefficient of absolute risk aversion and the minimum odds required by an investor to enter in the bet:

$$\pi(W; h) \cong \frac{1}{2} + \frac{1}{4}ARA(W)h. \qquad (2.14)$$

The higher is the coefficient of absolute risk aversion, the larger will be the difference $\pi(W; h) - \frac{1}{2} > 0$, i.e., the "mark-up" in the odds of the bet that the investor requires to tolerate it, given that she is risk-averse, i.e., $ARA(W) > 0$. Interestingly, the expression for $\pi(W; h)$ depends on the size of the bet, h, in a very simple way, i.e., linearly. However, this is due only to the fact that we are considering a second-order approximation that applies for $h \rightarrow 0$, i.e., small vanishing risks.

This finding is interesting because it casts new light onto the claim that to rank John and Mary's risk aversion, one will simply need to either verify whether $ARA_{John}(W) > ARA_{Mary}(W)$ for all wealth levels. If one accepts a characterization in which John is more risk averse than Mary if and only if $\pi_{John}(W; h) > \pi_{Mary}(W; h)$—which appears to be a sensible and economically grounded claim—now we know that as a first approximation (i.e., locally), this is equivalent to stating that $ARA_{John}(W) > ARA_{Mary}(W)$ for all wealth levels.[9]

---

[9] One can also prove that to state that $\pi_{John}(W; h) > \pi_{Mary}(W; h) \Leftrightarrow ARA_{John}(W) > ARA_{Mary}(W)$ for all wealth levels is equivalent to state that $U_{John}(W)$ may be written

Starting from (2.16) and exploiting the fact that from (2.13), we have $ARA(W) \equiv RRA(W)/W$, it is possible to re-write this result as $\pi(W; h) \cong 1/2 + 1/4\, RRA(W)(h/W)$, which can be interpreted as an approximate relationship between the minimum odds required to enter a symmetric bet and the coefficient of relative risk aversion. Interestingly though, in this case the expression for $\pi(W; \varpi)$ depends not on the *absolute size* of the bet, h, but on its relative size, say $\varpi \equiv h/W$, the potential loss or gain from the bet expressed as a percentage of the total initial wealth. With a derivation almost identical to the one shown before, it is possible to establish:[10]

Result 2.6: Given a zero-cost bet with two possible outcomes expressed in percentage of the initial wealth of the investor, ϖ and $-\varpi$, as $\varpi \to 0$ (i.e., for small gambles in relative terms), there is a precise link between the Arrow-Pratt's coefficient of relative risk aversion and the minimum odds required by an investor to enter in bet:

$$\pi(W; \varpi) \cong \frac{1}{2} + \frac{1}{4} RRA(W)\varpi. \tag{2.15}$$

For the same reasons illustrated above, if one accepts a characterization in which John is more risk averse than Mary if and only if $\pi_{John}(W; \varpi) > \pi_{Mary}(W; \varpi)$, now we know that, as a first approximation (i.e., locally), this is equivalent to stating that $RRA_{John}(W) > RRA_{Mary}(W)$ for all wealth levels.

Example 2.3. John is characterized by a negative exponential utility function of wealth,

$$U_{John}(W) = 1 - e^{-\theta W} \quad \text{with } \theta > 0.$$

Therefore $U'(W) = \theta e^{-\theta W} > 0$, $U''(W) = -\theta^2 e^{-\theta W} < 0$, so that

$$ARA_{John}(W) = -\frac{-\theta^2 e^{-\theta W}}{\theta e^{-\theta W}} = \theta,$$

which is clearly constant. As a result, in the face of a two-outcome symmet-

---

as a (strictly) concave and increasing transformation of $U_{Mary}(W)$. See Huang and Liztenberger (1988) for a proof.

[10] This proof will require not that the bet be small per se, but that it becomes small as a percentage of wealth. This means that for a given absolute size h, the approximation may become increasingly accurate simply because the investor grows wealthier.

ric bet with size h, we have:

$$\pi_{John}(W;\, h) = \pi(h) \cong \frac{1}{2} + \frac{1}{4}\theta h.$$

This implies that an increase in either absolute risk aversion or in the size of the bet have identical effects. Moreover, the minimal odds $\pi(W;\, h)$ turns out to be independent of wealth. Because

$$RRA_{John}(W) = ARA_{John}(W) \cdot W = \theta W,$$

the same minimum odds ratio may be written as:

$$\pi_{John}(W;\, \varpi) = \pi(h) \cong \frac{1}{2} + \frac{1}{4}\theta W \frac{h}{W} = \frac{1}{2} + \frac{1}{4}\varpi\theta W.$$

Mary is instead characterized by an isoelastic, power utility function of wealth

$$U_{Mary}(W) = \frac{W^{1-\gamma}}{1-\gamma} \quad \text{with } \gamma > 0.$$

Therefore $U'(W) = W^{-\gamma} > 0, U''(W) = -\gamma W^{-\gamma-1} < 0$, so that

$$RRA_{Mary}(W) = -\frac{-\gamma W^{-\gamma-1}}{W^{-\gamma}} W = \gamma,$$

which is clearly constant. As a result, in the face of a two-outcome symmetric bet with relative size ϖ, we have:

$$\pi_{Mary}(W;\, \varpi) = \pi(\varpi) \cong \frac{1}{2} + \frac{1}{4}\gamma\varpi.$$

This implies that an increase in either relative risk aversion and in the percentage size of the bet have identical effects. Moreover, the minimal odds $\pi(\varpi)$ turns out to be independent of wealth and to depend only in the fraction parameter ϖ. The same minimum odds ratio may be written as:

$$\pi_{Mary}(W;\, h) = \pi(h) \cong \frac{1}{2} + \frac{1}{4}\frac{\gamma}{W}h.$$

2.4 Absolute and relative risk aversion coefficients and the size of the risk premium

One distinguishing feature of risk averse investors is that they always value a risky asset less than the expected value of its payoffs. The difference between the valuation and the expected payoff is called *risk premium*. This derives from the very definition of risk aversion and it is simply an application of the standard *Jensen's inequality*:

$$U(E[W + H]) = U\left(W + \sum_{s=1}^{S} \pi_s h_s\right) > \sum_{s=1}^{S} \pi_s U(W + h_s)$$
$$= E[U(W + H)], \tag{2.16}$$

where H is a discrete random variable with S outcomes, each with probability $\pi_s \geq 0$. Of course, this is just a generalization of (2.7) to the case of S states. In fact, Jensen's inequality states that if $U(\cdot)$ is a concave function on the interval (a, b), and H a random variable such that Prob$\{H \in (a, b)\} = 1$, then assuming all expectations exist, $U(W+E[H]) > E[U(W+H)]$.[11]

Equation (2.18) leads to two useful definitions. The (maximum) certain sum of money a person is willing to pay to acquire a risky opportunity defines his *certainty equivalent* (CE) for that risky lottery:[12]

$$U(CE(W, H)) = \sum_{s=1}^{S} \pi_s U(W + h_s) = E[U(W + H)] \tag{2.17}$$

or $CE(W, H) = U^{-1}(E[U(W + H)])$. The difference between the expected value of a risky prospect and its CE is a measure of the risky payoff's risk premium, $\Pi(W, H)$:

$$\Pi(W, H) \equiv E[W + H] - CE(W, H). \tag{2.18}$$

It represents the maximum amount the agent would be willing to pay to avoid the gamble implied by the risky asset. Equivalently, $\Pi(W, H)$ must be such that:

---

[11] When $U(\cdot)$ is a convex function, the inequality is reversed, $U(W+E[H]) < E[U(W+H)]$. By the linear property of expectations, when $U(\cdot)$ is linear, we have that $a + b(W+E[H]) = E[a + b(W+H)]$ and the equality holds. Many readers will object that often in applied finance the risk premium is interpreted an additional compensation required by a risk averse investor to bear risk, while here we are emphasizing a lesser valuation of a risky stream of cash flow. However, notice now that given a realized payoff h_s, (2.16) implies that the realized return is higher for a risk-averse investor because she currently pays less to purchase the risky asset.

[12] Because utility cannot be measured in any meaningful way, natural units (a meter of utility? A watt of utility?), to practitioners it is more intuitive to measure satisfaction in terms of monetary equivalents. In order to satisfy this requirement, we may consider the certainty equivalent of an allocation, the risk-free amount of money that would make the investor as satisfied as the risky allocation. The certainty-equivalent has the advantage to be measured in the same units as the wealth objective.

$$U\big(E[W+H] - \Pi(W,H)\big) = E[U(W+H)]. \qquad (2.19)$$

When expected wealth and the risk premium are known, computing the certainty equivalent is trivial, and viceversa. The algebra is tedious, almost a tautology, but because $E[W+H] = W + E[H]$, given that initial wealth is given, and that equation (2.18) implies $CE(W,H) = E[W+H] - \Pi(W,H)$, it must be $W+CE(H) = W + E[H] - \Pi(W,H)$ or $CE(H) = E[H] - \Pi(H)$. Note that while lower case $\pi(W,h)$ for a two-point gamble represents the break-even odds required by a risk averse investor, a capital $\Pi(W,H)$ is the risk premium for any gamble H.

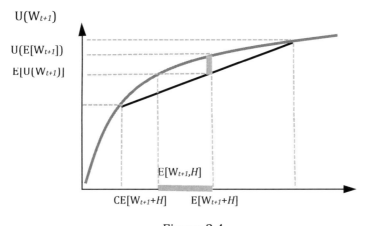

Figure 2.4

These concepts are illustrated in figure 2.4. Already graphically, the fact that $U(W + E[H])$ exceeds $E[U(W + H)]$, as measured on the vertical axis, gives an indication that aversion to risk exists. On the horizontal axis, we measure $\Pi(W,H)$ as the difference between $E[W+H]$ and the certainty equivalent $CE(W,H)$. Clearly, the length of both of the boldfaced, red segments in figure 2.4 depends on the concavity of the utility of money function. If one were to re-draw the picture, making $U(\cdot)$ "more concave", the size of both red segments would increase. Interestingly, the same would occur if—for fixed utility function $U(\cdot)$—one were to increase h, thus making the random bet H riskier.

In the case of $CE(W,H)$, one of the consequences of restricting the utility of wealth to the set of increasing, non-satiated functions, is that if the utility function $U(\cdot)$ is increasing, its inverse $U^{-1}(\cdot)$ is well-defined and increasing. Therefore, from the definition $CE(W,H) = U^{-1}(E[U(W+H)])$, the certainty-equivalent is an increasing function of expected utility and a portfolio allocation, or security A gives rise to a larger expected utility than an allocation B if and only if the former allocation implies a larger certainty-equivalent than B does, $CE(W, H_A) \equiv U^{-1}(E[U(W + H_A)]) \geq U^{-1}(E[U(W + H_B)]) \equiv CE(W, H_B)$. Hence, if the utility function is increasing, the certainty equivalent is also increasing. Interestingly, however, $CE(W, H)$ fails to inherit the concavity or convexity properties of the utility of wealth function. This derives from the fact that even though $U(\cdot)$ may be concave (say), $U^{-1}(\cdot)$ is not guaranteed to be so.

We now ask what mathematical relationship can be found between the size of the risk premium and the certainty equivalent as defined above, and the degree of risk aversion, for instance as measured by $ARA(W, h)$ or $RRA(W, h)$. Using Taylor series approximations, Appendix B shows that for small risks, i.e., when $H \to 0$:

Result 2.7: Given a zero-cost, fair bet with E[H] = 0, as $H \to 0$ (almost surely, i.e., for small gambles), there is a precise link between Pratt's coefficient of absolute risk aversion and the risk premium:

$$\Pi(W, H) \cong \frac{1}{2} ARA(W, H) Var[H]. \tag{2.20}$$

This result carries a flavor that will cut across many other portions of this book and that more generally plays a key role in all modern theory of finance:

Risk premium $\propto$ (Subjective risk aversion) $\times$ (Quantity of risk), (2.21)

where $\propto$ indicates that the LHS is proportional (but not strictly identical to) the RHS. Here the quantity of risk is (objectively, based on our construction of the EUT result) measured by the variance of the gamble/asset. As usual, because $ARA(W) \equiv RRA(W)/W$, it is possible to re-write this result as:

$$\frac{\Pi(W,H)}{W} \cong \frac{1}{2} RRA(W, H) \frac{Var[H]}{W^2} = \frac{1}{2} RRA(W, H) Var[\varpi], \tag{2.22}$$

which connects the percentage risk premium to the risk of the gamble measured in relative terms vs. initial wealth, W.

Example 2.4. John is characterized by a negative exponential utility function of wealth

$$U_{John}(W) = 1 - e^{-\theta W} \quad \text{with } \theta > 0.$$

We have seen in example 2.5 that

$$ARA_{John}(W) = -\frac{-\theta^2 e^{-\theta W}}{\theta e^{-\theta W}} = \theta,$$

is a constant. As a result, in the face of a two-outcome symmetric bet with size h (i.e., the possible outcomes are h and –h with fixed, objective probabilities π and 1- π, respectively), we have that $Var[H] = h^2 = \pi(h)^2 + (1 - \pi)(-h)^2$ and:

$$\Pi_{John}(W; h) \cong \frac{1}{2}\theta h^2.$$

This implies that while an increase in absolute risk aversion has a linear effect on the risk premium, the standard deviation of the gamble has a non-linear, quadratic one. Also in this case, the risk premium turns out to be independent of wealth.

If θ = 0.1, W = 100 euros and h = 10 euros with equally likely outcomes, then $\Pi_{John}(W; h) \cong \frac{1}{2}(0.1)(10)^2 = 5$ euros, i.e., an investor is ready to pay a considerable amount to avoid risk. In practice, as much as 5 euros to avoid a maximum risk of losing 5 euros that occurs with a ½ probability only? This seems rather unlikely, in fact. Let's now check what the exact definition yields in this case:

$$1 - e^{-0.1 \times CE} = 0.5\left(1 - e^{-(100-10)0.1}\right) + 0.5\left(1 - e^{-(100+10)0.1}\right)$$
$$e^{-0.1CE} = 1 - 0.5\left(1 - e^{-(100-10)0.1}\right) - 0.5\left(1 - e^{-(100+10)0.1}\right)$$
$$= 1 - 0.5(0.99987659) - 0.5(0.99998330)$$
$$= 7.0055000 \cdot 10^{-5} \Rightarrow CE = -\frac{1}{0.1}\ln(7.0055000 \cdot 10^{-5})$$
$$= 95.6623.$$

This means that $\Pi\left(100, \left\{-10, 10; \frac{1}{2}, \frac{1}{2}\right\}\right) \equiv 100 - 95.6623 = 4.3377$, which is less than the 5 euros found using the approximation. Of course, the unlikely result that an investor would be ready to pay as much as 5 euros to avoid a maximum risk of losing 5 euros that occurs with a ½ probability, only occurs because if we set h = 10 euros, the bet is far from small and the approximation will be a poor one. In fact, let's repeat the exercise when h = 2 euros: $\Pi_{John}(W; h) \cong \frac{1}{2}(0.1)(2)^2 = 0.2$ euros; the definition yields instead

$$e^{-0.1CE} = 1 - 0.5\left(1 - e^{-(100-2)0.1}\right) - 0.5\left(1 - e^{-(100+2)0.1}\right)$$
$$= 1 - 0.5(0.99994455) - 0.5(0.0.99996283)$$
$$= 4.6310 \cdot 10^{-5} \Rightarrow CE = -\frac{1}{0.1}\ln(4.6310 \cdot 10^{-5}) = 99.8015$$

which implies $\Pi\left(100, \left\{-2, 2; \frac{1}{2}, \frac{1}{2}\right\}\right) \equiv 100 - 99.8015 = 0.1985$, which is now very close to the 0.2 euros found using the approximation. This shows that the approximation works indeed for small risks.

Mary is instead characterized by an isoelastic, power utility function of wealth,

$$U_{Mary}(W) = \frac{W^{1-\gamma}}{1-\gamma} \quad \text{with } \gamma > 0.$$

and, as we have seen in example 2.6, this implies $RRA_{Mary}(W) = \gamma$, which is constant. As a result, in the face of a two-outcome bet with size h, we have:

$$\frac{\Pi_{Mary}(W; h)}{W} \cong \frac{1}{2}\gamma Var[\varpi] = \frac{1}{2}\gamma\varpi^2.$$

This implies that an increase in either relative risk aversion and in the variance percentage size of the bet have identical effects. In particular, $Var[\varpi] = \pi(h/W)^2 + (1-\pi)(-h/W)^2 = (h/W)^2 = \varpi^2$. Moreover, the percentage risk premium turns out to be independent of wealth.

For instance, if $\gamma = 5$, $W = 100$ euros and $h = 10$ euros with equally likely outcomes, this implies $\varpi = -0.1$ and $+0.1$, so that $\Pi_{Mary}(W; h)/W \cong \frac{1}{2}5(0.1)^2 = 0.025$, i.e., 2.5% of the investor's initial wealth.

It is also possible to convert these ideas into statements about the classical definition of a percentage risk premium to be added to asset returns in order to compensate a decision-maker for the risk she runs. Note that any risky gamble H, generates a gross return $H/W = 1 + \tilde{R}^H$ (the tilde emphasizes that this return is random depending on the realized outcome of the gamble) so that if we call CER the riskless, *certainty equivalent rate of return*, then:

$$U\left((1 + CER)W\right) = E[U\left((1 + \tilde{R}^H)\right)W)]$$
$$\Rightarrow CER = \frac{U^{-1}\left(E\left[U\left((1 + \tilde{R}^H)W\right)\right]\right)}{W} - 1. \qquad (2.23)$$

Of course, equation (2.23) defines CER only implicitly and the exact formula to be applied depends on the specific utility function of monetary wealth that one has assumed. However, the very definition of risk aversion, shows that because $U(E[(1 + \tilde{R}^H)]W) > E[U((1 + \tilde{R}^H))W)] = U((1 + CER)W)$, it must be $E[\tilde{R}^H] > CER$. The difference $E[\tilde{R}^H] - CER$ is often interpreted as a *percentage risk premium* associated to the risky asset/gamble H. It is the percentage extra return that an investor requires to accept the risky gamble instead of settling for the riskless CER. Of course, this rate of return risk premium does not represent a market or equilibrium premium. Rather it reflects personal preferences and it corresponds to the premium over the risk-free rate necessary to compensate, utility-wise, a specific individual with some postulated preferences and initial wealth, for engaging in the risky investment.

Example 2.4 (continued). Consider again Mary, who is characterized by an isoelastic, power utility function of wealth, $U_{Mary}(W) = \frac{W^{1-\gamma}}{1-\gamma}$ with $\gamma > 0$. In this case, because

$$U = \frac{v^{1-\gamma}}{1 - \gamma} \Rightarrow (1 - \gamma)U = v^{1-\gamma} \Rightarrow v = [(1 - \gamma)U]^{\frac{1}{1-\gamma}}$$

is the inverse function,

$$CER = \frac{\left[(1 - \gamma)E\left[U\left((1 + \tilde{R}^H)W\right)\right]\right]^{\frac{1}{1-\gamma}}}{W} - 1.$$

If we assume that $\gamma = 5$, and considering $\varpi = 0$ and 0.2,

$$E\left[U\left((1 + \tilde{R}^H)W\right)\right] = 0.5\frac{100^{-4}}{-4} + 0.5\frac{120^{-4}}{-4} = -1.8528163 \cdot 10^{-9}$$

$$CER = \frac{[(-4)(-1.8528163 \cdot 10^{-9})]^{\frac{1}{-4}}}{100} - 1 = \frac{107.7772}{100} - 1 = 0.077772,$$

Or 7.78%. Clearly, this value is below the 10% expected rate of return (obtained by equally probability-weighting the 0 and +20% returns). The difference of 2.2228% represents percentage risk premium associated to the risky asset/gamble H.

Because, from equation (2.18), we know that $\Pi(W, H) \equiv E[W + H] - CE(W, H)$, while from (2.20) we have shown that $\Pi(W, H) \cong$

$\frac{1}{2}ARA(W,H)Var[H]$, it must be the case that at least in approximation, for small gambles:

$$CE(W,H) \equiv E[W+H]\text{-}\Pi(W,H) \cong E[W+H] - \frac{1}{2}ARA(W,H)Var[H] \quad (2.24)$$

which is akin to a sort of approximate mean-variance objective in which for small risks, gambles/securities are ranked on the basis of their certainty equivalent, as formally advocated, for instance, by Meucci (2009, chapter 5).

3 – A Review of Commonly Used Utility of Wealth Functions

In this short section, we briefly review a few commonly employed VNM felicity functions that often appear in practice and that therefore represent a benchmark in applied work. Because this section will involve a certain amount of sophisticated functions, the less technical reader that is only interested in the intuition may skip it and move on to chapter 3. Two functions have been already examined in examples 2.3 and 2.4. With an initial level of wealth W_0, a utility of money function, which relative to the starting point has the property $U(W)/U(W_0) = h(W - W_0)$, so that utility reacts only to the absolute difference in wealth, is of the absolute risk aversion type. The only (non-satiated) function meeting this requirement is the (negative) exponential, where the response of utility to changes in $W - W_0$ is constant. A negative exponential utility function is represented as

$$U(W) = 1 - e^{-\theta W} \quad \text{with } \theta > 0, \quad (2.25)$$

and this is characterized by a constant coefficient of absolute risk aversion, $ARA(W) = -(-\theta^2 e^{-\theta W})/(\theta e^{-\theta W}) = \theta$, and by a monotone increasing, linear (in wealth) coefficient of relative risk aversion, $RRA(W) = ARA(W)W = \theta W$. Because $RRA(W)$ depends on the initial wealth level, relative quantities such as the percentage risk premium, will turn out to depend on the initial wealth level, which is often problematic in applications. In the case of a power utility function of wealth,

$$U(W) = \begin{cases} \frac{W^{1-\gamma}}{1-\gamma} & \gamma > 0, \gamma \neq 1 \\ lnW & \gamma = 1 \end{cases} \quad (2.26)$$

we have already established that $RRA(W) = \gamma$, a constant coefficient, so that $ARA(W) = RRA(W)/W = \gamma/W$, which is clearly an inverse function of wealth.[13]

Example 2.5. Interestingly, these insights are not purely theoretical. For instance, an investor with logarithmic utility of wealth, initial wealth of 100 euros, and faced with a fair gamble (the cost of which is its expected value) that pays out 150 euros with probability ½ and only 50 euros with probability ½, would be ready to pay a risk premium of 13.4 euros to avoid the gamble; equivalently, the certainty equivalent of this lottery is 86.60 euros.[14] Such a risk premium exceeds 13% of the investor's initial wealth. Now imagine that the same investor suddenly becomes richer, so that her initial wealth becomes 1,000 euros. The investor is faced with a fair gamble through which he receives 1,050 euros given a favorable outcome and 950 euros given an unfavorable outcome. The certainty equivalent would then equal 998.75 euros and this investor is ready to pay a risk premium of 1.25 euros only, i.e., just 1.23% of her initial wealth. Yet, because we are reasoning in relative terms, this is not surprising as the terms of the lottery (winning 50 with probability ½ and losing 50 with probability ½) are held fixed in absolute terms, while a log-utility investor shows declining absolute risk aversion. As a result, a wealthier person is still risk averse, but he is not nearly as disinclined as a poorer person to incur the risk of losing $50, because this amount represents a smaller fraction of her wealth. Of course, if the potential gain or loss from the risky prospect was $500—equivalently, if the size of the gamble were to be held fixed in relative terms—the investor would still express a 13% risk premium.

One utility function that will become useful later is the quadratic function:

$$U(W) = W - \frac{1}{2}\kappa W^2 \quad \text{with } \kappa > 0. \tag{2.27}$$

---

[13] In the case of $U(W) = \ln W$, $U'(W) = 1/W$, $U''(W) = -1/W^2$, so that $RRA(W) = -U''(W)W/U'(W) = -W(-1/W^2)/(1/W) = 1$. In fact, using l'Hopital's rule one can prove that $\lim_{\gamma \to 1} W^{1-\gamma}/(1-\gamma) = \ln W$.

[14] The required calculations and those that follow are similar to calculations presented above, and therefore left as an exercise for the reader.

Interestingly, note that expected utility is:

$$E[U(W)] = E[W] - \frac{1}{2}\kappa E[W^2] = E[W] - \frac{1}{2}\kappa[Var[W] + (E[W])^2]$$
$$= E[W]\left(1 - \frac{1}{2}\kappa E[W]\right) - \frac{1}{2}\kappa Var[W], \qquad (2.28)$$

which carries the same flavor as the certainty equivalence function in equation (2.23). Under quadratic utility, $U'(W) = 1 - \kappa W$, $U''(W) = -\kappa$, so that

$$ARA(W) = -\frac{-\kappa}{1-\kappa W} = \frac{\kappa}{1-\kappa W} = \frac{\kappa}{W[(1/W)-\kappa]} \qquad (2.29)$$

$$RRA(W) = -\frac{-\kappa W}{1-\kappa W} = \frac{\kappa}{[(1/W)-\kappa]}. \qquad (2.30)$$

Clearly, a quadratic utility investor is not always risk averse: $ARA(W)$ and $RRA(W)$ are positive if and only if $\kappa < 1/W$, or equivalently if $W < W^* = 1/\kappa$, the inverse of the coefficient κ trading-off the term $E[W]\left(1 - \frac{1}{2}\kappa E[W]\right)$ with variance in the expected utility representation in equation (2.28). $W^* = 1/\kappa$ is also called the *bliss point*. One can easily show that the issue we face with restricting wealth is even deeper than restricting the utility of wealth function to generate positive risk aversion. Indeed, because $U'(W) = 1 - \kappa W > 0$, it is clear that $W < W^* = 1/\kappa$, is also necessary and sufficient for the investor to be non-satiated, i.e., for the utility function to be monotone increasing. In fact, because $\kappa < 1/W$ is the same as $\kappa W < 1$ and this implies $0.5\kappa E[W] < 0.5 < 1$, note that $W < W^*$, also guarantees that $\left(1 - \frac{1}{2}\kappa E[W]\right) > 0$, which gives equation (2.28) an obvious mean-variance flavor that will be used later, see chapter 4.

While the three types of utility functions examined so far all imply—in the case of a quadratic function subject to the restriction that wealth does not exceed the bliss point, which is a decreasing function of the risk aversion coefficient κ—that the investor is risk-averse, we have already examined the case of a non-satiated, risk-neutral investor characterized by a linear utility function:

$$U(W) = a + bW \quad \text{with } b > 0. \qquad (2.31)$$

In this case, $U'(W) = b$ but $U''(W) = 0$, which implies that $ARA(W) = RRA(W) = 0$.

All these utility functions are strictly increasing, strictly concave, and have risk tolerance $T(W)$ that depends of wealth in a *linear affine* fashion:

$$T_{exp}(W) = \frac{1}{\theta} \quad T_{power}(W) = \frac{1}{\gamma}W \quad T_{quadr}(W) = \frac{1}{\kappa} - W \quad (2.32)$$

These utility functions are called *linear risk tolerance* (LRT) utility functions (alternatively, HARA utility functions, where HARA stands for *hyperbolic absolute risk aversion*, since $ARA(W)$ defines a hyperbola). LRT utility functions have many attractive properties. In general, the HARA class may be written as:

$$U(W) = \frac{\gamma}{1-\gamma}\left(\frac{\theta W}{\gamma} + \beta\right)^{1-\gamma} \quad \text{with } \gamma \neq 1, \frac{\theta W}{\gamma} + \beta > 0, \theta > 0. \quad (2.33)$$

(and $\beta = 1$ if $\gamma \to +\infty$). It is easy to check that

$$U'(W) = \theta\left(\frac{\theta W}{\gamma} + \beta\right)^{-\gamma} \quad U''(W) = -\theta^2\left(\frac{\theta W}{\gamma} + \beta\right)^{-\gamma-1}, \quad (2.34)$$

to get

$$ARA(W) = \left(\frac{W}{\gamma} + \frac{\beta}{\theta}\right)^{-1}. \quad (2.35)$$

This shows that when $\gamma \to +\infty$, $ARA(W) \to \theta$ (the CARA case, *constant absolute risk aversion*), and when $\beta = 0$, $ARA(W) = \gamma/W$ (the CRRA case, *constant relative risk aversion*). Correspondingly, the risk tolerance function is

$$T_{HARA}(W) = \frac{\beta}{\theta} + \frac{W}{\gamma} \quad (2.36)$$

and this is clearly linear affine and increasing in wealth, consistent with our premise. Moreover, equation (2.36) nests all cases reported in (2.32).[15]

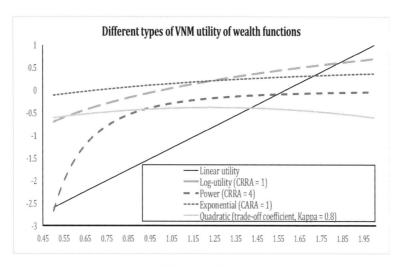

Figure 2.5

Figure 2.5 compares these very utility of wealth functions under a range of assumptions for the parameters θ, γ, κ and b. Visibly, the quadratic utility function fails to be monotonic even though it is concave everywhere. Because we set $\kappa = 0.8$, the bliss point W^* in this case equals 1.25 and in the plot the utility function declines for wealth that exceeds 1.25. However, all functions, apart from the linear, risk-neutral function, appear to be concave. The power utility function characterized by $\gamma = 4$ is clearly more concave than the other utility functions. As already emphasized, no special meaning (or lack therefore) ought to be attached to the fact that all utility functions are negative for some wealth

---

[15] For the linear risk tolerance utility functions, it can be shown (see LeRoy and Werner, 2000) that the optimal investment in each risky asset is given by ($j = 1, 2, ..., N$):

$$\hat{a}_j(W) = \left(\frac{\beta}{\theta} + \frac{W}{\gamma}R^f\right)b_j = \frac{\beta}{\theta}b_j + \frac{b_j R^f}{\gamma}W$$

where the b_js are coefficients independent of wealth and of the parameters β and θ. The optimal amounts invested are therefore a simple linear function of wealth. Consequently, optimal investments at different levels of wealth differ only by the amounts of wealth invested in risky securities, and not by the compositions of the portfolios of risky securities. In chapter 4, this result will be called Cass-Stiglitz's theorem.

levels (in fact, a few are always negative for all wealth levels, like in the case of power utility).

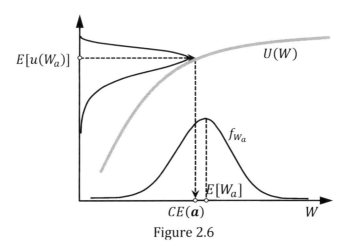

Figure 2.6

Finally, figure 2.6 shows how risk aversion, here captured by the concavity of $U(\cdot)$, changes the perception of the problem for an investor. On the horizontal axis, where wealth is measured, we plot the density function of portfolio outcomes. The distribution is symmetric and resembles a Gaussian density, even though f_{W_a} does not have to be necessarily normal. If one maps the probability distribution of wealth into a probability density function for the corresponding utility index, $f_{U(W_a)}$, it is clear that the concavity of the utility function makes for one asymmetric, fat tailed distribution that certainly deviates from a Gaussian benchmark and that has—at least in principle—important effects on an investor's optimal decisions.

References and Further Readings

Arrow, K., J., *Aspects of the Theory of Risk Bearing*. Helsinki: Yrjo Jahnssonin Saatio, 1965.

Bailey, R., E., *The Economics of Financial Markets*. Cambridge: Cambridge University Press, 2005.

Cass, D., and Stiglitz, J., E. The Structure of Investor Preferences and Asset Returns and Separability in Portfolio Allocation: A Contribution to the Pure Theory of Mutual Funds. *Journal of Financial Economics*, 2: 122-160, 1970.

Elton, E., J., Gruber, M., J., Brown, S., J., and Goetzmann, W., N., *Modern Port-*

folio Theory and Investment Analysis. Hoboken: John Wiley & Sons, 2009.

Huang, C.-f., and Litzenberger, R., H., *Foundations for Financial Economics.* Amsterdam: North-Holland, 1988.

Ingersoll, J., E., *Theory of Financial Decision Making.* Rowman & Littlefield, 1987.

LeRoy, S. F., and Werner, J., *Principles of Financial Economics.* Cambridge, New York: Cambridge University Press, 2000.

Mas-Colell, A., Whinston, M. D., and Green, J. R., *Microeconomic Theory* (Vol. 1). New York: Oxford University Press, 1995.

Meucci, A., *Risk and Asset Allocation.* Springer Science & Business Media, 2009.

Pratt, J., W. Risk Aversion in the Small and in the Large. *Econometrica*, 32: 122-136, 1964.

von Neumann, J., and Morgenstern, O., *Theory of Games and Economic Behavior.* Princeton: Princeton University Press, 1947.

Appendix A

Let $\pi = \pi(W; h)$ be that probability at which the agent is indifferent between accepting or rejecting the gamble/security. By definition, $\pi(W; h)$ must satisfy

$$U(W) = \pi(W; h)U(W + h) + [1 - \pi(W; h)]U(W - h), \qquad (A.1)$$

which means that the certain utility she derives in the absence of the bet must equal the expected utility of taking part in the bet. The notation $\pi(W; h)$ emphasizes that such a break-even probability takes the "size" of the bet h as a parameter, a given. Applying a Taylor's expansion around $h = 0$ (the case of no bet) to equation (A.1), we obtain:

$$U(W + h) = U(W) + hU'(W) + \frac{1}{2}h^2U''(W) + o(h^2)$$

$$U(W - h) = U(W) - hU'(W) + \frac{1}{2}h^2U''(W) + o(h^2), \qquad (A.2)$$

where the $o(h^2)$ terms are remainders of order higher than h^2 in the sense that they become smaller faster than h^2 does when $h \to 0$. Substituting these quantities into equation (A.1) gives

$$U(W) = \pi(W; h)\left[U(W) + hU'(W) + \frac{1}{2}h^2U''(W) + o(h^2)\right]$$
$$+ [1 - \pi(W; h)]\left[U(W) - hU'(W) + \frac{1}{2}h^2U''(W) + o(h^2)\right]$$

$$= U(W) + (2\pi(W; h) - 1)hU'(W) + \frac{1}{2}h^2U''(W) + o(h^2) \quad (A.3)$$

Solving for $\pi(W; h)$, yields:[16]

$$\pi(W; h) = \frac{1}{2} - \frac{1}{4}h\frac{U''(W)}{U'(W)} - \frac{1}{2}\frac{o(h^2)}{hU'(W)} = \frac{1}{2} + \frac{1}{4}h\left(-\frac{U''(W)}{U'(W)}\right) + o(h)$$

$$= \frac{1}{2} + \frac{1}{4}ARA(W)h + o(h) \xrightarrow{h \to 0^+} \frac{1}{2} + \frac{1}{4}ARA(W)h \quad (A.4)$$

This shows that the higher is the coefficient of absolute risk aversion, the larger will be the difference $\pi(W; h) - 1/2 > 0$, i.e., the "mark-up" in the odds of the bet that the investor requires to tolerate it, given that she is risk-averse, i.e., $ARA(W) > 0$. Of course, if the investor were not risk averse, i.e., $ARA(W) \leq 0$, then $\pi(W; h) \leq 1/2$: the investor would be ready to accept an unfair (or, in the case of $ARA(W) = 0$, exactly fair) bet because she likes to take on risk.

Appendix B

For simplicity, the derivation that follows applies to the case of an actuarially fair gamble, for which $E[H] = 0$. Differently from earlier results, H can take any number of values and in fact, it may even follow a continuous distribution. Using Taylor series approximations, we can develop the left-hand side (LHS) and right-hand side (RHS) of the definitional equation (2.18) as:

$$U(W + E[H] - \Pi(W, H)) = U(W - \Pi(W, H))$$
$$= U(W) - \Pi(W, H)U'(W) + o(\Pi^2(W, H)) \quad (B.1)$$

$$E[U(W + H)] = U(W) + E[HU'(W)] + \frac{1}{2}E[H^2U''(W)] + E[o(H^2)]$$
$$= E[U(W+H)] = U(W) + U'(W) \times 0 + 0.5U''(W)E[H^2] + E[o(H^2)]$$
$$= U(W) + \frac{1}{2}U''(W)Var[H] + E[o(H^2)], \quad (B.2)$$

---

[16] In the expression that follows, $-\frac{1}{2}\frac{o(h^2)}{hU'(W)}$ equals $o(h)$ because of the division by h. The presence of the term $-\frac{1}{2}\frac{1}{U'(W)}$ is irrelevant to the behavior of this term as $h \to 0$.

Because $Var[H] = E[H^2] - \{E[H]\}^2 = E[H^2]$. Both Taylor expansions are taken around $H = 0$, i.e., for the case of no gamble or, equivalently, a riskless asset or portfolio; clearly, when $H = 0$, $\Pi(W,H) = 0$, which explains the expansion in (B.1). Moreover, note that while (B.1) is a first-order expansion because based on the induced expansion point $\Pi(W,H) = 0$, (B.2) is a second order expansion.

At this point, equating the two expansions, we have

$$U(W) - \Pi(W,H)U'(W) \cong U\big(W - \Pi(W,H)\big) = E[U(W + H)]$$
$$\cong U(W) + \frac{1}{2}U''(W)Var[H]. \tag{B.3}$$

and ignoring the approximations involved, one can solve for:

$$\Pi(W,H) = -\frac{1}{2}\frac{U''(W)}{U'(W)}Var[H] = \frac{1}{2}\left(-\frac{U''(W)}{U'(W)}\right)Var[H]$$
$$\cong \frac{1}{2}ARA(W,H)Var[H]. \tag{B.4}$$

The approximation symbol emphasizes once more that the formula in (B.4) only holds for small risks, i.e., when $H \to 0$ (almost surely, meaning that H taking non-zero values becomes practically impossible) and therefore $\Pi(W,H) \to 0$.

3 Introduction to Mean-Variance Analysis

"A good portfolio is more than a long list of good stocks and bonds. It is a balanced whole, providing the investor with protections opportunities with respect to a wide range of contingencies" (H.M. Markowitz, "Portfolio selection: efficient diversification of investments", 1968)

Summary: – 1. The Opportunity Set and the Efficient Frontier (No Riskless Borrowing and Lending). – 2. The Opportunity Set and the Efficient Frontier (with Riskless Borrowing and Lending). – 3. Efficient Frontier under Short-Selling Constraints.

1 – The Opportunity Set and the Efficient Frontier (No Riskless Borrowing and Lending)

In chapter 2, we have introduced the key elements that characterized a portfolio decision problem under uncertainty. In this chapter, we shall restrict our analysis to the famous mean-variance model developed by Harry Markowitz more than half a century ago and still largely used in finance. We start our discussion by focusing only on risky assets. Indeed, as we shall see later on, even when riskless lending (and borrowing) is possible, the determination of the optimal weights on a set of risky assets can be treated separately from the decision about the amount of wealth that should be invested as whole in the optimal risky portfolio. Throughout this chapter, we will assume returns to be jointly normally distributed and, consequently, that their joint distribution is completely characterized by their means, variances, and covariances. Accordingly, it is common to represent each asset (and each portfolio of assets) in a two-dimensional diagram, where the expected portfolio return is plotted on the vertical axis and standard deviation is represented on the horizontal axis.[1]

Figure 3.1 shows how securities, for instance three stocks named A, B, and C, can be represented in this risk-return space (commonly known as mean-standard deviation diagram). Although it is possible to combine two or more assets into an infinite number of different portfolios, a rational risk-averse investor would generally consider only a subset of these possibilities. For instance, we already know from chapter 2 that stock C in figure 3.1 is dominated by the remaining two stocks in terms of mean-variance dominance criterion. You will recall that this states that the investor always prefers higher means and smaller variances. Therefore, a non-satiated, risk-averse investor who only cares for risk and return would never choose to hold stock C. According to the mean-variance criterion a portfolio shall be deemed efficient if and only if there is no other portfolio that allows the investor to achieve the same expected return with a lower level of risk or a higher level of expected return with the same level of risk. As an application of the MV criterion, we can distinguish among three different, useful concepts:

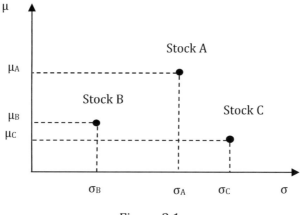

Figure 3.1

---

[1] It may seem surprising that, although we speak of mean-variance optimization and portfolio selection, the diagram we are about to describe reports portfolio standard deviation on its horizontal axis, instead of variance. However, given that standard deviation is the positive square root of variance, minimizing the latter is equivalent to minimizing the former. In addition, the standard deviation is comparable with mean returns as it is similarly expressed in percentage levels. In this chapter, we therefore use the term risk indifferently to indicate variance and standard deviation.

I.   The **opportunity set** (or *feasible region*), which includes all the portfolios (both efficient and inefficient) that the investor is able to build given the available securities (in her asset menu).

II.   The **mean-variance frontier**, which is a subset of the opportunity set containing only the portfolio with minimum variance for any target level of expected return.

III. The **efficient frontier**, which only includes the efficient portfolios, in the sense described above.

The efficient frontier is therefore just a portion of the mean-variance frontier. Indeed, the mean-variance frontier is obtained by minimizing the risk for a certain target expected return. However, it may still be possible that a portfolio exists which has a higher return than another portfolio with the same level of risk. Therefore, only portfolios that have a higher expected return than what we are about to define as the global minimum variance portfolio (GMVP) – i.e., the portfolio with the minimum possible level of risk – will be included in the efficient frontier. Noticeably, the preferences of the investor for risk are not relevant to the determination of the efficient frontier, while they will be essential to find the portfolio(s) (eventually unique) on the frontier that the investor will eventually decide to hold.

In the rest of this section, we will discuss how to determine the efficient frontier when only risky assets are available and risk-free lending and borrowing are not allowed. We start from the case of two risky assets, where the minimum-variance frontier and the opportunity set coincide. Then we generalize the resulting theory to the case of many risky assets. Risk-free borrowing and lending will instead be introduced in a subsequent section.

1.1 The efficient frontier with two risky securities

Before we derive the general formula of the efficient frontier, it is helpful to focus on a simple example where only two risky assets are available (let's call them securities A and B). Clearly, all the wealth that is not invested in the first security should be used to buy the second one, so that no money "shall be left on the table" and the weight assigned to the latter is defined as $\omega_B = 1 - \omega_A$. In practice, the weight of one of the two securities can be re-written as a function of the other. Consequently, the portfolio mean is equal to

$$\mu_P = \omega_A \mu_A + (1 - \omega_A)\mu_B \tag{3.1}$$

and the portfolio variance

$$\sigma_P^2 = \omega_A^2 \sigma_A^2 + (1 - \omega_A)^2 \sigma_B^2 + 2\omega_A(1 - \omega_A)\sigma_{AB}. \tag{3.2}$$

Obviously, recalling the definition of σ_{AB} from chapter 1, equation (3.2) is equal to

$$\sigma_P^2 = \omega_A^2 \sigma_A^2 + (1 - \omega_A)^2 \sigma_B^2 + 2\omega_A(1 - \omega_A)\rho_{AB}\sigma_A\sigma_B. \tag{3.3}$$

At this point, portfolio standard deviation is simply the square root of portfolio variance:

$$\sigma_P = \sqrt{\omega_A^2 \sigma_A^2 + (1 - \omega_A)^2 \sigma_B^2 + 2\omega_A(1 - \omega_A)\rho_{AB}\sigma_A\sigma_B}. \tag{3.4}$$

We skip the straightforward and yet tedious calculations, but it is possible to solve (3.1) for ω_A and plug the result into (3.3). Noticeably, we obtain a system of two equations that contain two unknowns. Because we have two equations and two unknowns, the system has in general a unique solution. Therefore, the opportunity set is a curve and it coincides with the mean-variance frontier (as there is only one possible level of risk for a given level of return). However, the shape of this line depends on the correlation between the two securities.

First of all, we consider two securities that are perfectly *positively* correlated ($\rho_{AB} = +1$). In this case portfolio variance has the form $X^2 + Y^2 + 2XY$, a perfect square factor that may be written as $(X + Y)^2$, so that

$$\sigma_P = \sqrt{[\omega_A\sigma_A + (1 - \omega_A)\sigma_B]^2} = \omega_A\sigma_A + (1 - \omega_A)\sigma_B \tag{3.5}$$

We can solve (3.5) to find ω_A, to get

$$\omega_A = \frac{\sigma_P - \sigma_B}{\sigma_A - \sigma_B}, \tag{3.6}$$

and then plug it into (3.1)

$$\mu_P = \frac{\sigma_P - \sigma_A}{\sigma_A - \sigma_B}\mu_A + \left(1 - \frac{\sigma_P - \sigma_A}{\sigma_A - \sigma_B}\right)\mu_B = \mu_B + \frac{\sigma_P - \sigma_A}{\sigma_A - \sigma_B}(\mu_A - \mu_B). \tag{3.7}$$

Remarkably, (3.7) is the equation of a straight line, with slope coefficient $(\mu_A - \mu_B)/(\sigma_A - \sigma_B)$. Figure 3.2 represents the opportunity set when the two securities are perfectly positively correlated. In particular, the solid line represents the opportunity set if *short-selling* is not allowed (i.e., $0 \leq \omega_A \leq 1$).[2] Instead, the dashed portion of the line corresponds to all portfolios that may be achieved only if a negative weight is assigned to one of the securities. It is evident that both the stocks are points on the mean-variance frontier. In addition, if short-selling is not allowed, the stock with the lowest risk also corresponds to the GMVP.[3] Consequently, in this (very) special case, the opportunity set not only coincides with the mean-variance frontier, but also with the efficient frontier, i.e., *any* combination of the two stocks is efficient and the investor's final decision will only depend on her preferences for risk, something that will be explored in chapter 4.

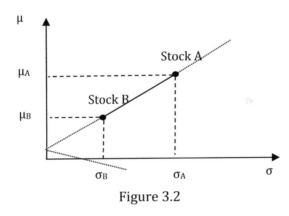

Figure 3.2

Consider next two securities that are perfectly negatively correlated $(\rho_{A,B} = -1)$. In this case, the variance has the form $X^2 + Y^2 - 2XY$ a per-

---

[2] Short-selling means that the investor borrows a security that she does not own and sells it in the market, earning proceeds that can be in turn invested in other securities. When it is not differently stated, we shall assume that short-selling is completely frictionless, i.e., the short-seller not only does not provide any collateral for any borrowed security, but also has immediate access to the proceeds from the naked short sale transaction. However, one should keep in mind that this definition hardly applies in reality: in reality, an investor that short-sells an asset has to post a (potentially large) part of the proceeds as collateral.

[3] Indeed, in the case of perfect positive correlation the standard deviation of the portfolio is simply equal to the weighted sum of the standard deviations of the two securities. Therefore, the minimum is reached when we assign weight equal to zero to the stock with the highest standard deviation and 100% weight to the one with the least risk.

fect square factor that may be written as $(X - Y)^2$ or $(-X + Y)^2$. Therefore, σ_P is either equal to

$$\sigma_P = w_A \sigma_A - (1 - w_A)\sigma_B \quad or\ to \quad \sigma_P = -w_A \sigma_A + (1 - w_A)\sigma_B. \quad (3.8)$$

However, since the square root of a negative number is imaginary and that would make the result hardly practical, each of the equations above only holds when the right-hand side is positive. As one equation is just equal to the other multiplied by -1, one of the two equations will always be positive while the other is negative (with the exception of the case in which $\sigma_P = 0$), so that there is always a unique solution. Also in this case, the opportunity set is represented as a straight line, but the coefficient will depend on which of the equations in (3.8) actually holds. Indeed, if the first equation applies, the opportunity set is equal to:

$$\mu_P = \frac{\sigma_P + \sigma_B}{\sigma_A + \sigma_B}\mu_A + \left(1 - \frac{\sigma_P + \sigma_B}{\sigma_A + \sigma_B}\right)\mu_B = \mu_B + \frac{\sigma_P + \sigma_B}{\sigma_A + \sigma_B}(\mu_A - \mu_B), \quad (3.9)$$

while if the second equation holds, the opportunity set is equal to:

$$\mu_P = \frac{\sigma_B - \sigma_P}{\sigma_A + \sigma_B}\mu_A + \left(1 - \frac{\sigma_B - \sigma_P}{\sigma_A + \sigma_B}\right)\mu_B = \mu_B + \frac{\sigma_B - \sigma_P}{\sigma_A + \sigma_B}(\mu_A - \mu_B). \quad (3.10)$$

The two alternative opportunity sets are represented in figure 3.3.

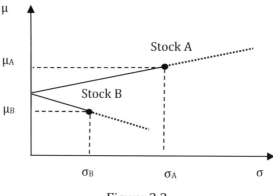

Figure 3.3

Again, the solid lines represent the combination that can be achieved when short-selling is not allowed, while the dashed line represents portfolios that can be obtained by only shorting one stock.

Since the formula of the variance of a portfolio of two perfectly negatively correlated stocks is of the form $X^2 + Y^2 - 2XY$, while the variance of the portfolio of two perfectly positively correlated stocks is of the form $X^2 + Y^2 + 2XY$, it appears evident that the former portfolio will always have a lower variance than the latter. In particular, the variance of a portfolio of perfectly positively correlated stocks is always higher than the weighted sum of the individual variances, while the variance of a portfolio of perfectly negatively correlated stocks is always lower than the weighted sum of the individual variances. In addition, when two stocks are perfectly negatively correlated, it is possible to find a combination of them that has zero variance, i.e., it is risk-free. Such a riskless portfolio is clearly the global minimum-variance portfolio for the special case of $\rho_{A,B} = -1$. Therefore, the weight of each stock in the GMVP can be simply found by solving:

$$\omega_A^{GMVP} \sigma_A - (1 - \omega_A^{GMVP})\sigma_B = 0 \ \ or \ -\omega_A^{GMVP} \sigma_A + (1 - \omega_A^{GMVP})\sigma_B = 0 \quad (3.11)$$

so that ω_A^{GMVP} is equal to

$$\omega_A^{GMVP} = \frac{\sigma_B}{\sigma_A + \sigma_B}. \quad (3.12)$$

Now that we have discussed the two extreme cases (perfect positive and negative correlation), we can discuss what happens when the correlation coefficient takes intermediate values. We know that variance and standard deviations can never take negative values. We also know that the lowest possible value of the variance (i.e., zero) is achieved when the stocks are perfectly negatively correlated. Therefore, the two equations in (3.9) - (3.10) represent a lower bound for the opportunity set and the mean-variance frontier.

The curved line in figure 3.4 is an example of one opportunity set when the correlation coefficient is between -1 and 1.

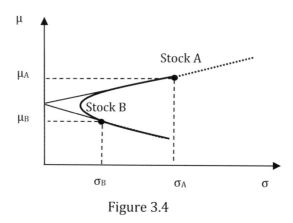

Figure 3.4

When ρ_{AB} assumes intermediate values in (-1, 1), the mean-variance frontier is non-linear. In particular, one can demonstrate that the relationship between portfolio variance and expected return is a *parabola* (i.e., a quadratic function), and that the relationship between portfolio standard deviation and expected return is a (branch of) *hyperbola*. However, because we conventionally express the expected return as a function of risk and not vi-ceversa—this derives from the sensible assumption that it is the quantity of risk that causes expected asset returns and not the vice versa—we cannot write this relationship as a function. Instead, we can just say that the mean-variance frontier is a "right-rotated *hyperbola*", as in figure 3.4.

Mathematically, the mean-variance frontier is in fact not a function, but a weaker mathematical object, a "correspondence". This derives from the fact that, visibly, to each fixed level of standard deviation on the horizontal axis, one can generally associate two distinct portfolios to which correspond different expected returns, for each of which given that standard deviation represents the minimum achievable level.

However, the efficient frontier (also known as the *efficient set*) is only a portion of the mean-variance frontier. In practice, the efficient frontier is the branch of the "rotated hyperbola" that lies above (and includes) the global minimum variance portfolio. Consequently, in order to distinguish the efficient frontier from the mean-variance one, we have to find the GMVP. This operation is quite simple when only two securities are involved. As already discussed, by definition, the GMVP is the combination of stocks with the lowest possible variance (and thus standard deviation). Therefore, the weight of security A (and, by difference, of security B) in the GMVP can be retrieved by minimizing portfolio variance, i.e., by taking the first derivative of (3.3),

$$\frac{\partial \sigma_P^2}{\partial \omega_A} = 2\omega_A \sigma_A^2 - 2(1 - \omega_A)\sigma_B^2 + 2(1 - 2\omega_A)\rho_{AB}\sigma_A\sigma_B, \qquad (3.13)$$

setting it equal to zero, and solving for ω_A:

$$2\omega_A^{GMVP}\sigma_A^2 - 2(1 - \omega_A^{GMVP})\sigma_B^2 + 2(1 - 2\omega_A^{GMVP})\rho_{AB}\sigma_A\sigma_B = 0$$

$$\Rightarrow \omega_A^{GMVP}(\sigma_A^2 + \sigma_B^2 - 2\rho_{AB}\sigma_A\sigma_B) = \sigma_B^2 - \rho_{AB}\sigma_A\sigma_B$$

$$\Rightarrow \omega_A^{GMVP} = \frac{\sigma_B^2 - \rho_{A,B}\sigma_A\sigma_B}{\sigma_A^2 + \sigma_B^2 - 2\rho_{A,B}\sigma_A\sigma_B}. \qquad (3.14)$$

Once the composition of the GMVP has been obtained, it is straightforward to compute the corresponding expected returns and variance. The following example shows what steps have to be followed in practice:

Example 3.1. Consider stock A with $\mu_A = 5.5\%$ and $\sigma_A = 10\%$, and stock B with $\mu_B = 2.5\%$ and $\sigma_B = 3\%$. To better clarify what happens when the correlation coefficient takes intermediate values, we consider three different examples, with $\rho_{AB} = 0, \rho_{A,B} = 0.5, \rho_{AB} = -0.5$.
The formula for expected portfolio returns is identical in all the three examples and equal to

$$\mu_P = \omega_A \times 5.5\% + (1 - \omega_A) \times 2.5\%,$$

which, after rearranging, can be written as:

$$\mu_P = 2.5\% + \omega_A \times 3\%.$$

Instead, the formula for portfolio standard deviation depends on the correlation coefficient. When $\rho_{A,B} = 0$, then

$$\sigma_{P_1} = \sqrt{\omega_A^2 \times 0.01 + (1 - \omega_A)^2 \times 0.0009}.$$

When $\rho_{A,B} = 0.5$, we have

$$\sigma_{P_2} = \sqrt{\omega_A^2 \times 0.01 + (1 - \omega_A)^2 \times 0.0009 + 2\omega_A(1 - \omega_A) \times 0.5 \times 0.1 \times 0.03}.$$

Finally, when $\rho_{A,B} = -0.5$, we find

$$\sigma_{P_3} = \sqrt{\omega_A^2 \times 0.01 + (1 - \omega_A)^2 \times 0.0009 - 2\omega_A(1 - \omega_A) \times 0.5 \times 0.1 \times 0.03}.$$

At this point, to draw the opportunity set for each of the three examples, we find a certain number of points in the mean-variance reference diagram by setting $\omega_A = -1, -0.9, \ldots, 0, 0.10, 0.20, \ldots, 1$, plotting and then connecting adjoining points (which by necessity represents a rough but usually not very visible interpolation between points). The figure shows the results of this experiment. It is evident what we have already discussed earlier in the chapter: when the correlation coefficient is negative it is possible to achieve portfolios that have a lower risk than each of the two assets. In fact, it is easy to see that some points on the dotted line ($\rho_{AB} = -0.5$) lie on the left of the asset with the lowest standard deviation, in this case stock B, to indicate how a negative correlation between stocks makes it possible to exploit obvious diversification opportunities/payoffs.

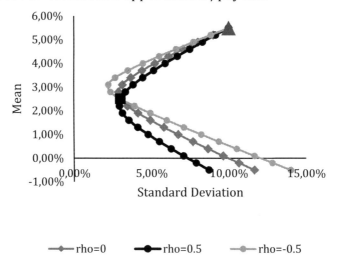

We also know that only a portion of the portfolios lying on the opportunity set are efficient, i.e., the ones with expected return higher than the GMVP. Therefore, we compute the composition of the GMVP by plugging the values from this example in (3.14). We find that in the case of $\rho_{AB} = 0$, the GMVP has a mean return equal to 2.75% and a standard deviation equal to 2.87%; its composition is $\omega_A = 0.083$ and $\omega_B = 0.917$. In the case $\rho_{AB} = 0.5$, the GMVP has a mean return of 2.27% and a standard deviation equal to 2.92%; its composition is $\omega_A = -0.075$ and $\omega_B = 1.075$. Finally, in the case of $\rho_{AB} = -0.5$, the GMVP has a mean equal to 3.02%, a standard deviation equal to 2.20%, and its composition is characterized by $\omega_A = 0.170$ and $\omega_B = 0.830$. Again, it appears that the lower the correlation between the stocks is, the lower the total risk of the portfolio.

Importantly, (3.14) only holds when we do not impose *any restrictions* on the weights that can be assigned to the securities. Instead, if short-selling is not allowed, i.e., $1 \geq w_A \geq 0$ and $1 \geq (1 - w_A) \geq 0$, we have to perform a *constrained* optimization, as we will discuss in section 3.

When short-selling is not allowed it is possible to restrict the area where the opportunity set has to lie to the triangle defined by the two stocks and a point H on the vertical axis.

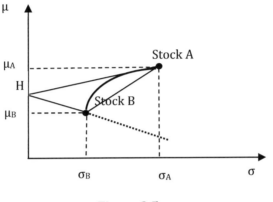

Figure 3.5

The following lemma formally states this useful property:

Portfolio diagram lemma: In mean-variance space, the curve defined by non negative combinations of two assets A and B must lie within the triangular region defined by the two original asset coordinates and the point on the vertical axis with coordinates $(0, H)$, where

$$H = \frac{\mu_A \sigma_B + \mu_B \sigma_A}{\sigma_A + \sigma_B}. \tag{3.15}$$

The interested Reader can find a formal proof of this lemma in Luenberger, (1997, chapter 6).

We conclude the analysis of our simplified framework where the investor can only choose between two assets with the presentation of key results for a classical problem, the stock and bond allocation. This problem represents the key to tactical asset allocation and to active money management that exploits any market timing skills. Figure 3.6 shows the opportunity set that a French, an Italian, and a German investor would face if they had to allocate their wealth to the 10-year government bonds issued by their countries and an index representing their main national stock market (i.e., the CAC 40, the FTSE MIB, and the DAX, respectively). Importantly, we approach the domestic diversification problem of each of the investors and do not allow them to diversify outside their national borders, so that each investor faces a two-asset menu.

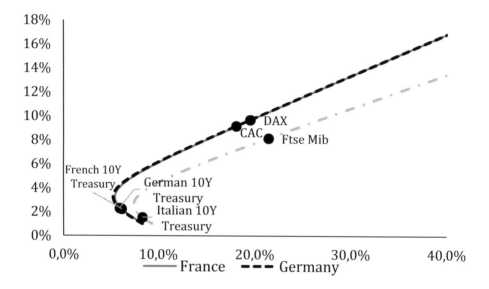

Figure 3.6

As stocks and bonds usually display negative correlations, it is possible to build mixed stock-bond portfolios that have a lower risk than each of the asset classes in isolation. For instance, the DAX index and the German 10-year Government bond have a correlation coefficient equal to −0.21. Similarly, the CAC and the French 10-year Government bond have a correlation coefficient equal to −0.18. The opportunity sets faced by French and German investor are almost identical and feature GMV portfolios that have minimum standard deviations of 0.5-1.0% less than 10-year government bonds. Instead, the correlation between the FTSE MIB index and 10-year Italian government bonds is higher (−0.11) and, more generally, the mean-variance frontier facing an Italian investor who diversifies domestically is much less favorable than in the case of German and French investors, i.e., the Italian frontier is located inward, to the right of the other two frontiers.

1.2 The efficient frontier with N risky securities

In the previous paragraph, we have devoted some time to analyze a simplistic, and yet useful, framework with only two risky assets. This has been very helpful to understand the main properties of the mean-variance and of the efficient frontiers, and the way in which their shape depends on the correlation among the assets. For instance, we learnt that the lower the correlation coefficient, the better the achievable risk-return payoff. However, usually the investor chooses among a large number of risky securities. Just to think of an example, she may be willing to allocate her wealth among the 500 US stocks composing the S&P 500 Index. Therefore, we now extend our simplified framework to the general case, where N risky assets are available.

As already discussed in the previous section, an investor choosing between two risky securities has an easy task at identifying the efficient frontier, as it only has to avoid portfolios that imply a lower expected return than the GMVP does. However, when $N > 2$ risk assets are included in the asset menu, the MV frontier no longer coincides with the opportunity set, which now becomes a region and not a line.[4]

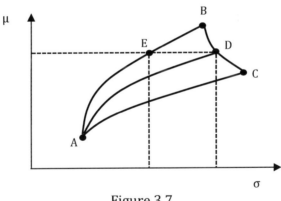

Figure 3.7

For instance, suppose that there are three uncorrelated assets: A, B, and C. We already know that we can draw a segment connecting any pair of assets and that this will represent all possible combinations of the two. Fig-

---

[4] Indeed, the mean and variance of a portfolio are computed according to the general formulas discussed in chapter 1, equations (1.12) and (1.15). These two equations form a system that has $N > 2$ unknowns, which in general implies an infinite number of solutions, i.e., there is an infinite number of weight combinations that give identical means—for a given variance—or identical variance, for a given mean.

ure 3.7 shows the three lines that represents the combination between the pairs A and B, B and C, A and C. Clearly, we can then connect any asset with any combination of the other two (e.g., see portfolio D in figure 3.7). There is no end to how often and frequently (as the portfolios get progressively closer) this process may be repeated. Therefore, the result is that the feasible region is now a *solid* two-dimensional area.

Obviously, portfolio D, despite being feasible as a combination of assets B and C, is not efficient according to the MV criteria. Indeed, it is characterized by the same mean return as portfolio E (which is a combination of asset A and B) but it implies a higher standard deviation. Therefore, as our investor is risk-averse and always prefers more to less, when all the rest is kept to be the same, she would never hold portfolio D. In order to exclude all the inefficient securities and portfolios, as a first step the investor needs to trace out the mean-variance frontier, i.e., she has to select the portfolios that have minimum variance (and thus standard deviation) for each level of return. Practically, she is only interested in the upper bound of the feasible region. Mathematically, the investor has to solve the following quadratic programming problem:

$$\min_{\{\omega\}} \frac{1}{2} \omega' \Sigma \omega$$

$$\text{subject to} \qquad \iota' \omega = 1$$

$$\mu' \omega = \bar{\mu}, \qquad\qquad\qquad (3.16)$$

where ι is a N-vector of ones, and $\bar{\mu}$ is a given target level of expected returns.[5] Notice that, for the time being, we are not restricting the weights to be positive, meaning that we are considering the $N > 2$ assets as traded in a frictionless economy where unlimited short-selling and borrowing are allowed. Later we will discuss how to impose short-sale restrictions.

To be able to solve the quadratic program, we also assume that no pair or more general combination of asset returns are linearly dependent, i.e., the rate of return of each asset cannot be expressed as a linear combination of the others. Under this assumption the variance-covariance matrix Σ is nonsingular and generally speaking, it can be inverted. In fact, because it is a second moment matrix, it turns out that Σ is positive definite.

---

[5] Notice that the factor ½ before of the portfolio variance is there for computation convenience only and does not change the final result.

Under these conditions, (3.16) turns into a maximization program subject to equality constraints that represents analytically the principle that we have stated before, i.e., it minimizes portfolio variance subject to the constraint that the expected return is equal to $\bar{\mu}$, and the weights sum to one ("no money is left on the table"). Importantly, any $\bar{\mu}$ can be validly picked by the analyst building the mean-variance frontier, even though ex-post we know already that the efficient segment will involve only target means $\bar{\mu}$ that exceed the expected return on the GMVP.

Therefore, we face a constrained minimization problem that can be solved through the use of Lagrangian multiplier method. More precisely, the solution $\boldsymbol{\omega}^*$ (i.e., the vector containing the weights of the minimum-variance portfolio with return $\bar{\mu}$) is found by forming the Lagrangian, $L = \frac{1}{2}\boldsymbol{\omega}'\boldsymbol{\Sigma}\boldsymbol{\omega} + \lambda(\bar{\mu} - \boldsymbol{\omega}'\boldsymbol{\mu}) + \gamma(1 - \boldsymbol{\omega}'\boldsymbol{\iota})$, and minimizing it:

$$\min_{\{\omega,\lambda,\gamma\}} \frac{1}{2}\boldsymbol{\omega}'\boldsymbol{\Sigma}\boldsymbol{\omega} + \lambda(\bar{\mu} - \boldsymbol{\omega}'\boldsymbol{\mu}) + \gamma(1 - \boldsymbol{\omega}'\boldsymbol{\iota}), \qquad (3.17)$$

where λ and γ are two positive constants (also known as Lagrangian multipliers). If we define $A \equiv \boldsymbol{\mu}'\boldsymbol{\Sigma}^{-1}\boldsymbol{\iota}$, $B \equiv \boldsymbol{\mu}'\boldsymbol{\Sigma}^{-1}\boldsymbol{\mu}$, $C \equiv (\boldsymbol{\iota}'\boldsymbol{\Sigma}^{-1}\boldsymbol{\iota})$, and $D = BC - A^2$, the unique solution $\boldsymbol{\omega}^*$ is equal to

$$\boldsymbol{\omega}^* = \boldsymbol{g} + \boldsymbol{h}\,\bar{\mu},$$

where

$$\boldsymbol{g} = \frac{1}{D}[B(\boldsymbol{\Sigma}^{-1}\boldsymbol{\iota}) - A(\boldsymbol{\Sigma}^{-1}\boldsymbol{\mu})], \quad \boldsymbol{h} = \frac{1}{D}[C(\boldsymbol{\Sigma}^{-1}\boldsymbol{\mu}) - A(\boldsymbol{\Sigma}^{-1}\boldsymbol{\iota})]. \quad (3.18)$$

The derivation of this result can be found in Appendix A, and alternatively in Huang and Litzenberger, 1988 (chapter 3) or Ingersoll, 1987 (chapter 4).

Noticeably, if we consider that $\boldsymbol{\omega}^* = \boldsymbol{g}$ when $\bar{\mu} = 0$ and that $\boldsymbol{\omega}^* = \boldsymbol{g} + \boldsymbol{h}$ when $\bar{\mu} = 1$ we can claim that the whole mean-variance frontier can be generated as a linear combination of the weights of a portfolio with zero return and a portfolio with 100% return. More generally, one can demonstrate that the entire MV frontier (and thus also the efficient part of it) can be generated by *any* two portfolios that belong to it. Consider two generic frontier portfolios P_1 and P_2 with mean μ_{P_1} and μ_{P_2}, and assume that P_3 is a generic portfolio on the mean-variance frontier. Clearly, it is always possible to find a quantity x such that $\mu_{P_3} = x\mu_{P_1} + (1-x)\mu_{P_2}$, i.e. we can always find a portfolio of P_1 and P_2 that has the same expected return as P_3. The weights of this portfolio are:

$$\omega_{P_3} = x\omega_{P_1} + (1-x)\omega_{P_2} = x(g + h\mu_{P_1}) + (1-x)(g + h\mu_{P_2})$$
$$= g + h(x\mu_{P_1} + (1-x)\mu_{P_2}) = g + h\mu_{P_3}, \qquad (3.19)$$

which is exactly the formula for a mean-variance portfolio in (3.18). Therefore, the linear combination of P_1 and P_2 that has mean return equal to μ_{P_3} is exactly our frontier portfolio P_3. This leads us to the important result stated below.

Result 3.1 It is sufficient to know two points (portfolios) on the mean-variance frontier to generate all the others. In particular, the entire efficient portion of the MV frontier can be generated by any two portfolios on the same frontier.

Although this finding may seem trivial it has an important implication: all MV-optimizers who choose portfolios by examining only mean and standard deviation can be satisfied by holding a combination of *only two* mutual funds (provided these are MV efficient), regardless of their preferences (here, coefficient trading off expected return and risk). Indeed, their heterogeneous preferences will only impact the way in which they combine the two funds that they choose to hold, but will not have any influence on the choice of a specific pair of funds. Another important consequence of this theorem is that in equilibrium, if all investors are rational MV optimizers, the *market portfolio*, being a convex combination of the optimal portfolios of all the investor, has to be an efficient portfolio. This observation will be useful in chapter 5, when we will discuss applications of the Capital Asset Pricing Model to portfolio decisions.

Result 3.1 represents in fact an application of the more general two-fund separation theorem, which will be invoked again later. A formal statement of two-fund separation theorem is given below:

Two-fund separation theorem: A market model represented by the random vector of asset returns R is said to display two-fund separation if there exist two mutual funds – F_1 and F_2 – such that for any portfolio q formed as $q'R$ there exists a scalar x such that $E[u(xR_{F_1} + (1-x)R_{F_1})] \geq E[u(q'R)]$, for all concave utility functions $u(\cdot)$.

As for the shape of the mean-variance frontier when N assets are available, this is a rotated hyperbola as in the case of two assets. Indeed, the variance of a portfolio is simply obtained by substituting $\boldsymbol{\omega}^*$ into the standard portfolio variance formula obtained in the Appendix:

$$\sigma_P^2 = \frac{1}{D}[C(\mu_P)^2 - 2A\mu_P + B], \qquad (3.20)$$

which is the equation of a parabola. Therefore, if we want to represent the minimum-variance frontier in the classical mean-standard deviation space to which we are now familiar, the frontier will again consist of a "right-rotated hyperbola" as we have already observed in figure 3.4. Interestingly, such a hyperbola has a vertex at $(\sqrt{1/C}, A/C)$, which also represents the global minimum variance portfolio. Indeed, the weights of the global minimum variance portfolio are obtained by removing the constraint $\boldsymbol{\mu}'\boldsymbol{\omega} = \bar{\mu}$ from our previous minimization problem, i.e., by setting $\lambda = 0$. In fact, when $\lambda = 0$, in the objective (3.17) one finds herself just minimizing the variance subject to the constraint that the portfolios weights need to sum to one. Such a constraint removal leads to the expression

$$\boldsymbol{\omega}_{GMVP} = \frac{\Sigma^{-1}\iota}{C} = \frac{\Sigma^{-1}\iota}{\iota'\Sigma^{-1}\iota}, \qquad (3.21)$$

and therefore

$$\mu_{GMVP} = \boldsymbol{\mu}'\boldsymbol{\omega}_{GMVP} = \frac{\boldsymbol{\mu}'\Sigma^{-1}\iota}{C} = \frac{A}{C} \qquad (3.22)$$

$$\sigma_{GMVP}^2 = \frac{1}{D}(C(\mu_{GMVP})^2 - 2A\mu_{GMVP} + B) = \frac{1}{D}\left(C\left(\frac{A}{C}\right)^2 - 2A\cdot\frac{A}{C} + B\right)$$
$$= \frac{1}{D}\left(\frac{BC - A^2}{C}\right) = \frac{1}{D}\left(\frac{D}{C}\right) = \frac{1}{C}. \qquad (3.23)$$

As we already know from section 1, the GMVP is important to the investor as it defines the minimum return that an efficient portfolio may attain.[6] All

---

[6] The GMVP enjoys another interesting property: it has covariance $1/C$ (i.e., equal to its variance) with *any* portfolio or asset (not only those lying on the minimum vari-

portfolios that have a return lower than the GMVP, are considered ineffi-cient despite the fact they fall on the MV frontier. Therefore, as in the case of two assets only, the *efficient frontier* is the portion of the MV frontier ly-ing above (and including) the GMVP. Noticeably, for any inefficient portfo-lio in the feasible region, there exist one on the efficient frontier that has the same variance, but a higher expected return.

Example 3.2. Consider three assets (imagine, for example, treasury bonds, corporate bonds, and equity, respectively) characterized by the mean vec-tor and the variance-covariance matrix below for their percentage returns:

$$\mu = \begin{bmatrix} 6.00 \\ 7.50 \\ 9.00 \end{bmatrix}$$

$$\Sigma = \begin{bmatrix} 0.005 & 0.004 & -0.002 \\ 0.004 & 0.008 & 0.003 \\ -0.002 & 0.003 & 0.025 \end{bmatrix}.$$

We have learnt that once we find their weights the portfolios with 0% and 100% return, we can generate all the mean-variance frontier. Therefore, we need to compute portfolios **g** and **h**. As a first step, we compute the quantities A, B, C and D. In order to do so, we need to invert the variance-covariance matrix. This task usually requires a lot of computational effort, especially if Σ is of a large size. Fortunately, we can generally rely on the help of a Microsoft Excel spreadsheet. Excel can easily handle standard ma-trix computations, including the inversion of a matrix. Therefore, you just need to copy the variance-covariance matrix above in your spreadsheet and use the formula MINVERSE, making sure to:

- select the whole area where the resulting matrix will be placed (e.g., in our case you need to select a 3 × 3 matrix);
- pressing CTRL + ALT + SHIFT.

From this computation you obtain:

$$\Sigma^{-1} = \begin{bmatrix} 402.11 & -223.16 & 58.95 \\ -223.16 & 254.74 & -48.42 \\ 58.95 & -48.42 & 50.53 \end{bmatrix}.$$

---

ance frontier). This result is easy to prove: the covariance of two portfolios A and B is $\sigma_{AB} = \omega'_A \Sigma \omega_B$. Therefore, $\sigma_{GMVP,P} = \frac{\iota' \Sigma^{-1} \Sigma \omega_P}{C} = \frac{1}{C}$, where P is a generic portfolio (obvi-ously, the investment in a single asset is simply a portfolio with weight equal to one on that asset and weight equal to zero on all the others).

Now, we can use the MMULT function to perform the multiplications that are needed to compute A, B and C. In particular, if we name μ as "mean", Σ^{-1} as "invcov", and "one" a 3×1 vector of ones, to compute A we can write down the required formula as follows:

MMULT (TRANSPOSE (mean), MMULT(invcov, mean)),

where TRANSPOSE is the function that we use to transpose a vector or a matrix. Also this time we need to press CTRL + ALT + SHIFT, as we always do when dealing with matrixes, but we just select a cell to insert the output, as the result is a scalar.

$$A = \mu'\Sigma^{-1}\iota = \begin{bmatrix} 6.00\% \\ 7.50\% \\ 9.00\% \end{bmatrix}' \cdot \begin{bmatrix} 402.11 & -223.16 & 58.95 \\ -223.16 & 254.74 & -48.42 \\ 58.95 & -48.42 & 50.53 \end{bmatrix} \cdot \begin{bmatrix} 1 \\ 1 \\ 1 \end{bmatrix} = 18.5.$$

We repeat the exercise also for B and C:

$$B = \mu'\Sigma^{-1}\mu = \begin{bmatrix} 6.00\% \\ 7.50\% \\ 9.00\% \end{bmatrix}' \cdot \begin{bmatrix} 402.11 & -223.16 & 58.95 \\ -223.16 & 254.74 & -48.42 \\ 58.95 & -48.42 & 50.53 \end{bmatrix} \cdot \begin{bmatrix} 6.00\% \\ 7.50\% \\ 9.00\% \end{bmatrix} = 1.26$$

$$C = (\iota'\Sigma^{-1}\iota) = \begin{bmatrix} 1 \\ 1 \\ 1 \end{bmatrix}' \cdot \begin{bmatrix} 402.11 & -223.16 & 58.95 \\ -223.16 & 254.74 & -48.42 \\ 58.95 & -48.42 & 50.53 \end{bmatrix} \cdot \begin{bmatrix} 1 \\ 1 \\ 1 \end{bmatrix} = 282.11$$

$$D = BC - A^2 = 1.26 \times 282{,}11 - 18{,}51^2 = 14.21.$$

Finally, we are ready to compute **g** and **h**:

$$\mathbf{g} = \frac{1}{D}[B(\Sigma^{-1}\iota) - A(\Sigma^{-1}\mu)]$$

$$= \frac{1}{14.21}\left\{ 1.26 \cdot \begin{bmatrix} 402.11 & -223.16 & 58.95 \\ -223.16 & 254.74 & -48.42 \\ 58.95 & -48.42 & 50.53 \end{bmatrix} \cdot \begin{bmatrix} 1 \\ 1 \\ 1 \end{bmatrix} - 18.5 \right.$$

$$\left. \cdot \begin{bmatrix} 402.11 & -223.16 & 58.95 \\ -223.16 & 254.74 & -48.42 \\ 58.95 & -48.42 & 50.53 \end{bmatrix} \cdot \begin{bmatrix} 6{,}00 \\ 7{,}50 \\ 9{,}00 \end{bmatrix} \right\} = \begin{bmatrix} 4.63 \\ -3.27 \\ -0.37 \end{bmatrix}$$

$$\mathbf{h} = \frac{1}{D}[C(\Sigma^{-1}\mu) - A(\Sigma^{-1}\iota)]$$

$$= \frac{1}{14.21}\left\{ 282.10 \cdot \begin{bmatrix} 402.11 & -223.16 & 58.95 \\ -223.16 & 254.74 & -48.42 \\ 58.95 & -48.42 & 50.53 \end{bmatrix} \begin{bmatrix} 6.00 \\ 7.50 \\ 9.00 \end{bmatrix} \right.$$

$$\left. - 18.5 \cdot \begin{bmatrix} 402.11 & -223.16 & 58.95 \\ -223.16 & 254.74 & -48.42 \\ 58.95 & -48.42 & 50.53 \end{bmatrix} \cdot \begin{bmatrix} 1 \\ 1 \\ 1 \end{bmatrix} \right\} = \begin{bmatrix} -57.78 \\ 48.89 \\ 8.89 \end{bmatrix}$$

Importantly, all we need to learn in order to perform this computation in a spreadsheet is the formula for matrix multiplications that we have discussed above. We are now able to trace the whole mean variance frontier by applying (3.18) to calculate minimum-variance portfolio weights for a certain number of fixed target levels of $\bar{\mu}$, computing the corresponding standard deviations and then plotting them in Excel using a standard ("XY") dispersion chart.

We will show the computation for one level of $\bar{\mu}$, let's say 8% and leave the rest for you.

$$\boldsymbol{\omega}^* = \mathbf{g} + \mathbf{h}\,\bar{\mu} = \begin{bmatrix} 4.63 \\ -3.27 \\ -0.37 \end{bmatrix} + 8\% \cdot \begin{bmatrix} -57.78 \\ 48.89 \\ 8.89 \end{bmatrix} = \begin{bmatrix} 0.01 \\ 0.65 \\ 0.34 \end{bmatrix}.$$

Portfolio variance is therefore equal to:

$$\sigma_*^2 = (\boldsymbol{\omega}^*)'\Sigma\boldsymbol{\omega}^* = \begin{bmatrix} 0.01 \\ 0.65 \\ 0.34 \end{bmatrix}' \cdot \begin{bmatrix} 0.005 & 0.004 & 0.002 \\ 0.004 & 0.008 & 0.003 \\ -0.002 & 0.003 & 0.025 \end{bmatrix} \cdot \begin{bmatrix} 0.01 \\ 0.65 \\ 0.34 \end{bmatrix} = 0.007,$$

so that

$$\sigma_* = \sqrt{0.007} = 8.37\%.$$

You can also easily verify that (3.20) holds:

$$\sigma_*^2 = \frac{1}{D}(C\,(\mu_*)^2 - 2A\mu_* + B)$$

$$= \frac{1}{14.21} \cdot (282.11 \cdot 8\%^2 - 2 \cdot 18.5 \cdot 8\% + 1.26) = 0.007.$$

If we repeat the exercise for a sufficiently large number of levels of $\bar{\mu}$, we obtain the mean-variance frontier below.

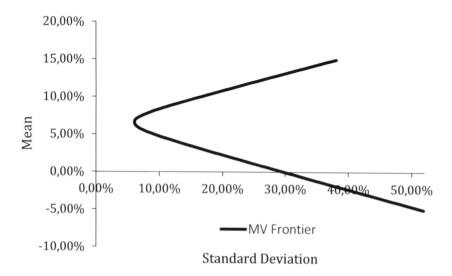

We know that all the points lying below the minimum-variance portfolio are inefficient. Therefore, we have to compute the global minimum variance portfolio to determinate which points on the MV frontier are also on the efficient frontier. From (3.21) we know that:

$$\boldsymbol{\omega}_{GMVP} = \frac{\Sigma^{-1} \iota}{C} = \frac{1}{282.11} \cdot \begin{bmatrix} 402.11 & -223.16 & 58.95 \\ -223.16 & 254.74 & -48.42 \\ 58.95 & -48.42 & 50.53 \end{bmatrix} \cdot \begin{bmatrix} 1 \\ 1 \\ 1 \end{bmatrix} = \begin{bmatrix} 0.84 \\ -0.06 \\ 0.22 \end{bmatrix}$$

and we can thus determinate the coordinates of the GMVP in the mean-standard deviation plan:

$$\mu_{GMVP} = \frac{A}{C} = \frac{18.5}{282.11} = 6.6\%$$

$$\sigma_{GMVP} = \frac{1}{\sqrt{C}} = \frac{1}{\sqrt{282.11}} = 5.97\%.$$

Noticeably, the GMVP has a lower standard deviation than the asset with the lowest risk, thanks to the effect of diversification.

To close our exercise, we proceed to demonstrate that it is easy to verify whether or not an asset or a portfolio lies on the efficient frontier. As an example, consider our first asset, Treasury bonds, which has mean of 0.06 and variance of 0.005. We compute the weights of the minimum-variance portfolio with expected return equal to 6% and we find:

$$\boldsymbol{\omega}^{**} = \mathbf{g} + \mathbf{h}\,\bar{\mu} = \begin{bmatrix} 4.63 \\ -3.27 \\ -0.37 \end{bmatrix} + 6\% \cdot \begin{bmatrix} -57.78 \\ 48.89 \\ 8.89 \end{bmatrix} = \begin{bmatrix} 1.17 \\ -0.33 \\ 0.16 \end{bmatrix}$$

and the variance of this portfolio is

$$\sigma_{**}^2 = (\boldsymbol{\omega}^{**})' \Sigma \boldsymbol{\omega}^{**} = \begin{bmatrix} 1.17 \\ -0.33 \\ 0.16 \end{bmatrix}' \cdot \begin{bmatrix} 0{,}005 & 0{,}004 & 0{,}002 \\ 0{,}004 & 0{,}008 & 0{,}003 \\ -0{,}002 & 0{,}003 & 0{,}025 \end{bmatrix} \cdot \begin{bmatrix} 1.17 \\ -0.33 \\ 0.16 \end{bmatrix} = 0.004$$

which is lower than 0.005. Therefore, this asset cannot be on the MV frontier. Indeed, differently from the case of two risky assets only, when $N > 2$ the securities do not have to lie on the MV frontier. In fact, the MV frontier may even be entirely composed of portfolios of assets, with no individual assets specifically falling on the frontier.

2 – The Opportunity Set and the Efficient Frontier (with Riskless Borrowing and Lending)

In the previous section, we have identified the efficient frontier when two or more risky assets are available, but we have ignored the existence of a risk-free asset (i.e., a security the return of which is known with certainty and therefore displays zero variance and zero covariance with all risky assets). Buying such a riskless asset (e.g., a short-term Treasury bond issued by a highly rated government or a deposit in a state-insured account, with a backing pledged on the tax power of central authorities) corresponds to lending at a risk-free rate to the issuer of the asset. For the time being, we will assume that the investor is able to borrow at the same rate she would receive if she were to lend, i.e., invest in the risk-free asset. In other words, we assume an abstract world in which the investor is able to obtain leverage funding by selling the risk-free asset short. In addition, there is no limit to the amount that the investor can borrow at the riskless rate. Obviously, although it simplifies the analysis a lot, these assumptions regarding risk-free borrowing and lending are quite unrealistic, at least for the majority of the investors. Just because such hypotheses are extreme, we shall relax them later in this section.

Consider now a fictional experiment in which the possibility to borrow and lend (without limits) at the risk-free rate is offered to an investor who was already allocating her wealth among N risky assets. This is similar to the problem that we faced in the previous section: the investor will still be holding a portfolio of risky securities on the efficient frontier but the total sum of the weights attributed to the risky assets does not have to be one any longer. Indeed, if $\sum_{i=1}^{N} \omega_i < 1$ the rest of the investor's wealth will be invested in the risk-free asset, while if $\sum_{i=1}^{N} \omega_i > 1$ wealth will be leveraged by borrowing at the risk-free rate, to be called R^f.

Therefore, if we consider that the investor invests a certain fraction X of her wealth in an efficient frontier, risky portfolio—let's call it portfolio A assumed to be characterized by mean and standard deviation equal to μ_A and σ_A, respectively—and a share $1 - X$ in the riskless asset with a certain return R^f, we obtain that her final portfolio has the mean and standard deviation expressed as:

$$\mu_P = X\mu_A + (1 - X)R^f = R^f + X(\mu_A - R^f) \tag{3.24}$$

$$\sigma_P = \sqrt{\sigma_P^2} = \sqrt{X^2 \sigma_A^2} = X\sigma_A. \tag{3.25}$$

If we solve (3.25) for X and substitute it in (3.24) we obtain that

$$\mu_P = R_F + \frac{\sigma_P}{\sigma_A}(\mu_A - R^f) = R^f + \frac{(\mu_A - R^f)}{\sigma_A}\sigma_P, \qquad (3.26)$$

which is the equation of a straight line with intercept R^f and slope coefficient $(\mu_A - R^f)/\sigma_A$. The line in (3.26) is sometimes referred to as *capital
transformation line*. The term $(\mu_A - R^f)/\sigma_A$ has a particular meaning in finance. Indeed, it is called Sharpe ratio (SR) from the name of one of its ear-
liest proponents and users, and represents the total reward for taking a
certain amount of risk, represented by the standard deviation, i.e. the mean
return in excess of the risk-free rate (called the *risk premium*) per unit of
volatility.

Figure 3.8 shows the line that represents an investor's possibilities for different portfolio choices of the risky benchmark A (A', A'', and A''') on the
efficient frontier. The points to the left of A involve lending at the risk-free
rate while the ones to the right involve borrowing at the risk free rate. It is
evident that

$$\frac{(\mu_{A'} - R^f)}{\sigma_{A'}} < \frac{(\mu_{A'''} - R^f)}{\sigma_{A'''}} < \frac{(\mu_{A''} - R^f)}{\sigma_{A'}} \qquad (3.27)$$

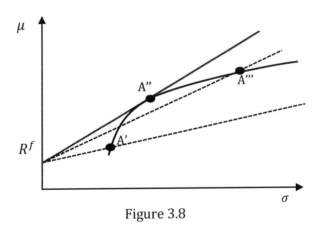

Figure 3.8

As we have assumed that an investor always prefers more to less, she
would not be willing to hold A''' and A', because they lead to a lower compensation for a unit of risk. Intuitively, the investor will welcome a "rota-

tion" of the straight line passing by R^f as far as possible in a counterclock-wise direction, until she reaches the point of tangency. To welcome a rotation will mean in practice that the investor will progressively replace the benchmark portfolio A' with A''' and so forth, until A'' is achieved. The rotation goes as far as possible in the sense that all these portfolios that are tried out by the investor must necessarily belong to the efficient sub-set of the MV frontier.

Therefore—at least assuming that beliefs are homogeneous, there are no frictions or taxes, and that individuals face the same riskless rate and identical asset menus—all rational, non-satiated investors will only hold the *tangency portfolio* (which may be then shown to eventually morph into the "market" portfolio), in combination with a certain share of risk-free lending or borrowing. In other words, while the quantity of money that the investor lends or borrows at the risk-free rate depends on the investor's preference for risk, the risky portfolio should be the same for all the investors, regardless of their level of risk aversion. In practice, when riskless lending and borrowing are possible, the investor always chooses a point situated on the straight line that connects the coordinate $(0, R^f)$ with the tangency portfolio. This line is usually called *Capital Market Line* (CML) and its role will be emphasized again in chapter 5. Summing up, we can formulate the claim below, which is just another special application of the two fund separation theorem discussed in the previous section.

Result 3.2 When riskless borrowing and lending are possible, there exists a unique portfolio T of risky assets such that any efficient portfolio can be constructed as a combination of T and the risk-free rate. Consequently, the optimal portfolio of risky asset can be identified separately from the knowledge of the risk preferences of the investor.

We now discuss how the tangency portfolio can be identified. We have already seen that it is the point of tangency between the efficient frontier of the risky-asset problem and the ray passing through R^f. Let's define as ϑ the angle between each ray passing through R^f and the horizontal axis, such that:

$$\tan \vartheta = \frac{(\mu - R^f)}{\sigma} = \frac{(\omega' \mu - R^f)}{(\omega' \Sigma \omega)^{1/2}}, \tag{3.28}$$

where μ and σ are mean and standard deviation of a generic portfolio located on the risky-asset efficient frontier. The tangency portfolio is the feasible point that maximizes $\tan \vartheta$, which is equal to the SR:

$$\max_{\{\omega\}} \frac{(\omega'\mu - R^f)}{(\omega'\Sigma\omega)^{\frac{1}{2}}}$$

$$subject\ to \quad \omega'\iota = 1 \tag{3.29}$$

The problem above can be solved using the standard Lagrangian method presented in the previous section, but there is also an alternative: to simply substitute the constraint into the objective function.

Indeed, because we can re-write R^f as $1 \cdot R^f$ and considering that our constraint is $1 = \omega'\iota$, we can re-write our maximization problem as

$$\max_{\{\omega\}} \frac{\omega'(\mu - R^f\iota)}{(\omega'\Sigma\omega)^{1/2}}. \tag{3.30}$$

This is now a simple unconstrained maximization problem that we can solve by equating the first derivative of the objective function to zero. The formal solution to this problem can be found in Appendix B. The weights of the unique tangency portfolio T are then:

$$\omega_T = \frac{\Sigma^{-1}(\mu - R^f\iota)}{A - CR^f}. \tag{3.31}$$

Example 3.2. (continued) Consider again the three securities that we analyzed in section 1. Imagine that now the investor is allowed to borrow and lend at the riskless rate without any limits and assume that $R^f = 2.50\%$. Now the investor will be interested in a unique risky portfolio with weights ω_T:

$$\omega_T = \frac{\Sigma^{-1}(\mu - R^f\iota)}{A - CR^f}$$

$$= \frac{1}{18.5 - 282.11 \cdot 2.5\%} \begin{bmatrix} 402.11 & -223.16 & 58.95 \\ -223.16 & 254.74 & -48.42 \\ 58.95 & -48.42 & 50.53 \end{bmatrix} \begin{bmatrix} 3.50\% \\ 5.00\% \\ 6.50\% \end{bmatrix} = \begin{bmatrix} 0.59 \\ 0.16 \\ 0.25 \end{bmatrix}.$$

If you cannot recall formula (3.29) off the top of your head but you can use Microsoft Excel, there is also a different method that you can use to compute the weights of the tangency portfolio. Indeed, both constrained and unconstrained optimization programs can be tackled using the Microsoft Excel Solver®. In practice, you just need the following inputs:

- the vector of mean returns on the risky assets;
- the variance-covariance matrix of the returns on the risky assets;
- a vector of starting values for the tangency portfolio weights (provisionally, you can fill it in with "guesses", e.g., you can assign equal weights to all the assets).

At this point, you select a cell where you compute the Sharpe ratio using your vector of guesses for the weights. You also need to prepare a cell with the sum of the weights (this will have to be set equal to 1). At this point you open the Excel Solver from the tab 'Data' and using the appropriate dialog box, set up the following problem:

- in the field "set objective" you select the cell where you computed the SR index;
- you choose that this cell has to be maximized (flag "max");
- you choose the range of cells that you want to change to accomplish the goal of maximizing the objective function, i.e., the vector of weights of the tangency portfolio;
- you set the constraint on the sum of the weights by clicking on "add" and imposing that the relevant cell has to be set equal to one;[7]
- you click "solve" and wait the few seconds (at worst, minutes) that will be required for Excel's algorithms to do their magic.

Basically, the Solver will iteratively change the values of the cells that contain the weights until the value of the Sharpe ratio has been maximized. Appropriate messages will be displayed by the software to warn you in case of problems with the algorithm or the final objective function attained.

---

[7] Additional equality or inequality constraints may be incorporated into the program. Recent versions of Microsoft Excel's Solver® also allow a user to impose non-negativity constraints on the control variables (here, the tangency portfolio weights) by simply ticking an appropriate box. Section 3 expands on this issue.

As discussed, once the tangency portfolio has been identified, the proportion of wealth that each investor will lend or borrow at the risk-free rate will depend on individual risk-preference. A very risk-averse investor will prefer to invest some of her wealth in the riskless asset and therefore she will choose to hold a portfolio somewhere to the left of the market one, while a less risk-averse investor will borrow some money at the riskless rate and so her portfolio will lie somewhere to the right of the market portfolio. Figure 3.9 shows these concepts.

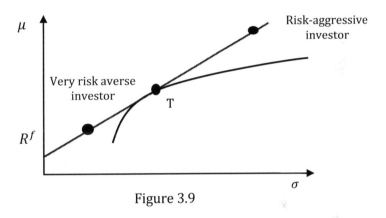

Figure 3.9

The choice of the optimal portfolio among the efficient ones will be discussed again in the next chapter.

Up to this point, we have made the strong assumption that the investor can borrow money at the same riskless rate at which she can lend, which is rarely the case. A more reasonable assumption is that the investor is able to borrow money, but at a higher rate than the one of the risk free (long) investment. In this case, the investor would choose among a number of risky portfolios so that the simple two-fund separation theorem fails. Figure 3.10 shows how the CML is modified when borrowing is only possible at a rate $R^{f'} > R^f$. First of all, there are now two capital transformation lines, both tangent to the efficient frontier. Indeed, any time that the investor chooses to invest part of her wealth in the riskless asset, the return of the portfolio is equal to equation (3.26) above. Nevertheless, when she borrows money to invest in risky assets, the portfolio return becomes

$$\mu_P = R^{f'} + \frac{(\mu_A - R_F)}{\sigma_A} \sigma_P. \tag{3.32}$$

Therefore, there are two tangency points that are relevant for our investor: T, which is the same as before, and Z, which is the point of tangency between the efficient frontier and transformation line in (3.32). In addition, all the points falling on the portion of the efficient frontier delimited by T (below) and Z (above) will still be efficient even though these do not fall on the straight, CML-type line. For instance, the point M is not MV dominated by any other (feasible) point and belongs to the (partially) curved new CML defined by $R^f TMZ$.

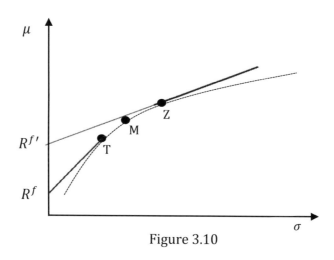

Figure 3.10

In conclusion, when lending and borrowing is only possible at different rates, it is no longer possible to determinate a tangency (hence, market, when the appropriate conditions are present) portfolio. The efficient set would consist of the portfolio T (tangency point between (3.26) and the risky asset efficient frontier), portfolio Z (tangency point between (3.32) and the risky asset efficient frontier), and all the points between T and Z on the risky asset efficient frontier.

3 – The Efficient Frontier under Short-Selling Constraints

While constructing the efficient frontier, we have assumed "equality" constraints (e.g., portfolio weights summing up to one), but no "inequality" constraints (e.g., positive portfolio weights). Indeed, the inclusion of inequality constraints tends to complicate the solution techniques, as it requires the use of quadratic programming with (linear) inequality constraints. However, the frictionless unlimited short-selling assumption is often unrealistic as generally an investor that sells short one asset has to post a (potentially large) part of the proceeds as collateral in appropriately disciplined margin accounts. In addition, once the quadratic programming techniques have been learnt, they can be used to impose virtually any constraint that can be expressed as a linear function of the weights (for instance, concentration limits by which the sum of subsets of the weights cannot exceed some legally mandated or self-imposed thresholds).

When short-selling is not allowed, portfolio weights should be positive, i.e. the constraint $\omega \geq 0$ (to be interpreted in an element-by-element basis, i.e., to mean that each element of ω ought to be non negative) has to be imposed. When ω has to be positive, it is possible that the standard optimization problem that we have set up and solved in section 1 may deliver a solution that is not acceptable, as one or more weights turn out to be negative. In other words, the unconstrained maximum may be at a value of ω that is not feasible. Therefore, it is necessary to impose the Kuhn-Tucker conditions, which include the standard first-order conditions (i.e., setting the set of first derivatives, taken with respect to portfolio weights, to zero) plus complementarity conditions to establish, for each ω_i, when a corresponding *slack variable* should be used in order to avoid unacceptable outcomes.

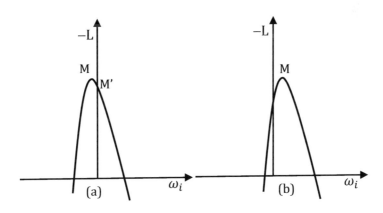

Figure 3.11

To understand how slack variables work in a Kuhn-Tucker program, recall the Lagrangian $L = \frac{1}{2}\omega'\Sigma\omega + \lambda(\bar{\mu} - \omega'\mu) + \gamma(1 - \omega'\iota)$ discussed in section 2 and note that it is just a system of simultaneous equations. Recall that minimize L is always equivalent to maximize $-L$, which explains why in the following we discuss of the maximization of $-L$. Figure 3.11 shows how the

Lagrangian –L for the weight ω_i looks like in two different situations, i.e., when the maximum is not a feasible value (because it occurs at $\omega_i < 0$, panel (a)) and when this is instead feasible, in panel (b). In figure 3.11(a) the maximum (M) value for –L happens at an unfeasible (negative) value of ω_i. It is evident that in figure 3.11(a) the maximum *feasible* value happens at M' and therefore $\left.\frac{\partial L}{\partial \omega_i}\right|_{M'} < 0$ ($\omega_i = 0$), while in figure 3.11(b) $\left.\frac{\partial L}{\partial \omega_i}\right|_{M} = 0$ (in correspondence to $\omega_i > 0$). Therefore, when ω_i is constrained to be positive or equal to zero, we have to solve

$$\frac{\partial L}{\partial \omega_i} \leq 0. \tag{3.33}$$

(3.33) can be transformed into an equality by the use of the variable U_i:

$$\frac{\partial L}{\partial \omega_i} + U_i = 0 \tag{3.34}$$

(3.34) is the first Kuhn-Tucker condition for the maximum. Intuitively, when the optimum occurs at positive values of ω_i, $\frac{\partial L/\partial \omega_i}{} = 0$ and thus $U_i = 0$. Conversely, when the optimum occurs at $\omega_i = 0$, then $\partial L/\partial \omega_i < 0$ and thus $U_i > 0$. This statement describes the second Kuhn-Tucker condition. More compactly, we can write:

$$\frac{\partial L}{\partial \omega_i} + U_i = 0$$
$$\omega_i U_i = 0$$
$$\omega_i \geq 0$$
$$U_i \geq 0 \tag{3.35}$$

When the four conditions in (3.35) are simultaneously satisfied, we have an optimum portfolio. This is intuitive discussion of Kuhn-Tucker conditions applicable to quadratic programs with inequality constraints should be enough for our purposes (for a more detailed discussion see, e.g., Kwan, 2007). Fortunately, Microsoft's Excel Solver® offers the possibility to solve the problem numerically, by-passing the complex analytical details in the equations shown in (3.35).

Example 3.2. (continued) Consider again the three risky security examples that we analyzed already earlier in this chapter. We need the same kind of inputs that we already used before, i.e., the vector of asset mean returns, the variance-covariance matrix and a vector of guessed weights:

$$\mu = \begin{bmatrix} 6.00 \\ 7.50 \\ 9.00 \end{bmatrix} \qquad \Sigma = \begin{bmatrix} 0.005 & 0.004 & -0.002 \\ 0.004 & 0.008 & 0.003 \\ -0.002 & 0.003 & 0.025 \end{bmatrix}$$

For any level of the target mean $\bar{\mu}$, we need to find the weights that minimize the variance. Consider $\bar{\mu} = 9\%$. Therefore, we compute portfolio mean and variance, as already discussed in section 1, using the vector of guessed weights. In this case, we impose constraints. We therefore open the Solver and set up the optimization problem as follows:

- in the field "set objective" you select the cell where you computed the variance;
- you tick the appropriate cell to make sure that the objective is minimized (flag "min");
- you choose the range of cells that you want to change to accomplish the goal of minimizing the objective function, i.e., the vector of weights;
- you set the constraint on the sum of the weights by clicking on "add" and imposing that the relevant cell has to be set equal to one;
- you set the constraint that the mean return should be equal to the target mean $\bar{\mu}$
- you check the box that makes all the unconstrained values positive in order to exclude negative values for weights;
- you click "solve" and wait the few seconds, hopefully.

For instance, for $\bar{\mu} = 9\%$, in the absence of constraints, the solution is

$$\omega_T = \begin{bmatrix} -56.66\% \\ 113.33\% \\ 43.33\% \end{bmatrix}$$

which makes sense because the second asset is characterized by a large Sharpe ratio and hence must be exploited to yield a high mean return by leveraging the first security, which also has an appreciable Sharpe ratio but cannot sufficiently contribute to achieving a relatively high mean portfolio return. However, selling -57% of the first security may represent a major hurdle. Therefore, we impose non-negativity constraints as explained above, to obtain:

$$\boldsymbol{\omega}_T^{constrain} = \begin{bmatrix} 0\% \\ 0\% \\ 100\% \end{bmatrix},$$

which clearly achieves the target of 9%, because the third security does yield exactly a 9% return in expectation. One would then ask: why is the second solution not the obvious one? The answer is quickly discovered:

$$\sqrt{(\boldsymbol{\omega}_T)' \boldsymbol{\Sigma} \boldsymbol{\omega}_T} = 12.40\% \text{ while } \sqrt{\left(\boldsymbol{\omega}_T^{constrain}\right)' \boldsymbol{\Sigma} \boldsymbol{\omega}_T^{constrain}} = 15.81\% \text{ which is}$$

clearly above the level that could be achieved without imposing any constraints. Hence, imposing constraints does have a cost.

References and Further Readings

Cuthbertson, K., and Nitzsche, D. *Quantitative Financial Economics: Stocks, Bonds and Foreign Exchange.* Chichester, Hoboken: John Wiley & Sons, 2005.

DeMiguel, V., Garlappi, L. and Uppal, R. Optimal Versus Naïve Diversification: How Inefficient is the 1/N Portfolio Strategy? *Review of Financial Studies*, 22: 1915-1953, 2009.

Fugazza, C., Guidolin, M., and Nicodano. G. Equally Weighted vs. Long-Run Optimal Portfolios. *European Financial Management*, 21: 742-789, 2015.

Ingersoll, J. E. Theory of Financial Decision Making (Vol. 3). *Rowman & Littlefield*, 1987.

Huang, C.-f., & Litzenberger, R. H. *Foundations for Financial Economics.* Amsterdam: North-Holland, 1988.

Luenberger, D. G. *Investment Science.* New York: Oxford University Press, 1997.

Solnik, B., H. Why not Diversify Internationally Rather Than Domestically? *Financial Analysts Journal*, 51: 89-94, 1995.

Appendix A

Consider the (constrained) minimization problem discussed in section 2, i.e., $\min_{\{\omega,\lambda,\gamma\}} \frac{1}{2}\omega'\Sigma\omega + \lambda(\bar{\mu} - \omega'\mu) + \gamma(1 - \omega'\iota)$. Differentiating with respect to the control variables, we obtain the following first order conditions:

$$\frac{\partial L}{\partial \omega} = \Sigma\omega - \lambda\mu - \gamma\iota = 0 \qquad (A.1a)$$

$$\frac{\partial L}{\partial \lambda} = \bar{\mu} - \omega'\mu = 0 \qquad (A.1b)$$

$$\frac{\partial L}{\partial \gamma} = 1 - \omega'\iota = 0, \qquad (A.1c)$$

where 0 is a Nx1 vector of zeros. Given that Σ is a positive definite matrix, it follows that the first order conditions are necessary and sufficient for the existence of a global optimum. Therefore, the solution is equal to:

$$\omega^* = \lambda\Sigma^{-1}\mu + \gamma\Sigma^{-1}\iota. \qquad (A.2a)$$

In order to obtain λ and γ we can use $(A.1b)$ and $(A.1c)$ from which we know that

$$\bar{\mu} = \omega'\mu \qquad (A.2b)$$

$$1 = \omega'\iota. \qquad (A.2c)$$

If we pre-multiply both sides of equation $(A.2a)$ by μ' and then use $(A.2b)$ we obtain

$$\bar{\mu} = \lambda(\mu'\Sigma^{-1}\mu) + \gamma(\mu'\Sigma^{-1}\iota) \qquad (A.3a)$$

where, for the sake of simplicity, we rename $A \equiv \mu'\Sigma^{-1}\iota$ and $B \equiv \mu'\Sigma^{-1}\mu$. If we pre-multiply both sides of $(A.2a)$ by ι' and the use $(A.2c)$ we obtain

$$1 = \lambda(\iota'\Sigma^{-1}\mu) + \gamma(\iota'\Sigma^{-1}\iota), \qquad (A.3b)$$

where the term $(\iota'\Sigma^{-1}\mu)$ is just equal to $\mu'\Sigma^{-1}\iota$ already denoted with letter A and $C \equiv (\iota'\Sigma^{-1}\iota)$.

Solving $(A.3a)$ and $(A.3b)$ by λ and γ we obtain

$$\lambda = \frac{C\bar{\mu} - A}{D} \qquad (A.4a)$$

$$\gamma = \frac{B - A\bar{\mu}}{D} \qquad (A.4b)$$

where $D \equiv BC - A^2$. Noticeably, due to the fact that the inverse of apposi-tive definite matrix is a positive matrix itself, we know that B and C are positive quantities. In addition, we can also prove that D is a positive quantity too. Indeed, $B(BC - A^2) = (A\mu - B\iota)' \Sigma^{-1}(A\mu - B\iota)$ and since Σ^{-1} is positive definite the right-end of the equation is positive. Consequently, $B(BC - A^2) > 0$ and, given that $B > 0$ also $BC - A^2 > 0$.

Substituting $(A.4a)$ and $(A.4b)$ into equation $(A.2a)$ we find the unique solution ω^* that minimizes portfolio variance given a level of portfolio return $\bar{\mu}$:

$$\omega^* = \mathbf{g} + \mathbf{h}\,\bar{\mu} \tag{A.5}$$

where $\mathbf{g} = \frac{1}{D}[B(\Sigma^{-1}\iota)] - A(\Sigma^{-1}\mu)$ and $\mathbf{h} = \frac{1}{D}[C(\Sigma^{-1}\mu)] - A(\Sigma^{-1}\iota)$.

Appendix B

Consider the following unconstrained optimization problem presented in (3.29):

$$\max_{\{\omega\}} (\tan \vartheta) = \max_{\{\omega\}} \frac{\omega'(\mu - R^f\iota)}{(\omega'\Sigma\omega)^{1/2}}. \tag{B.1}$$

Differentiating the objective function, we can define the FOC:

$$\frac{\partial \tan \vartheta}{\partial \omega} = (\mu - R^f\iota)(\omega'\Sigma\omega)^{-\frac{1}{2}} - \frac{1}{2}\omega'(\mu - R^f\iota)(\omega'\Sigma\omega)^{-\frac{3}{2}}(2\Sigma\omega) = 0. \tag{B.2}$$

If we multiply both the sides of (B.2) by $\sqrt{\omega'\Sigma\omega}$, which is a positive scalar, we obtain:

$$(\mu - R_F\iota) = [\omega'(\mu - R^f\iota)(\omega'\Sigma\omega)^{-1}](\Sigma\omega). \tag{B.3}$$

The term in the square brackets is a scalar and represent the average excess return (risk premium) on a portfolio divided by its variance. This is an (unknown) constant and we shall call it η. Therefore, (B.3) can be rewritten as

$$(\mu - R^f\iota) = \Sigma(\eta\omega) = \Sigma z, \tag{B.4}$$

where $z = \eta\omega$. Therefore, we solve equation (B.4) for z

$$z = \Sigma^{-1}(\mu - R^f\iota) \tag{B.5}$$

and then we normalize (i.e., divide by the sum total to make sure that the resulting weights do cumulate to 100%) to obtain ω_T:

$$\omega_T = \frac{z}{\iota'z} = \frac{\Sigma^{-1}(\mu - R^f{}_F\iota)}{\iota'\Sigma^{-1}(\mu - R^f\iota)} = \frac{\Sigma^{-1}(\mu - R^f\iota)}{\iota'\Sigma^{-1}\mu - R^f\iota'\Sigma^{-1}\iota} = \frac{\Sigma^{-1}(\mu - R^f\iota)}{A - CR^f} \tag{B.6}$$

A Worked-Out Excel Example

One classical, important topic in the theory and practice of portfolio management is the importance of international portfolio diversification, both within asset classes—for instance, how important it may be to broaden a portfolio to include foreign stocks—and across asset classes, for instance the value of including emerging market bonds to internationally risky portfolios. Here "importance" will mean performance enhancement, either ex-ante (in terms of expected utility and/or CER improvement) or ex-post, in back-testing exercises. The expectation is that, because many national markets enjoy modest correlations, the benefits from international diversification might still be massive.

To illustrate this point, and at least make our Reader aware of this important literature, we have performed one exercise in Excel. We have downloaded from Ken French's web site (at http://mba.tuck.dartmouth. edu/pages/faculty/ken.french/data_library.html) monthly stock return data denominated in local currencies for 9 countries (in alphabetical order): Australia, Canada, France, Germany, Italy, Japan, Switzerland, the United Kingdom, and the United States. The sample period is January 1977 – December 2015. Although our main focus is on pure equity diversification problems, we allow riskless borrowing and lending and compute both the tangency portfolio as well as the optimal portfolio subdivision between cash borrowing or lending and the tangency portfolio. We adopt the viewpoint of two different investors, a US investor and an Italian one. However, because the returns are expressed in local currencies, it is as if foreign returns are completely hedged from exchange rate fluctuations affecting the US dollar and the euro, respectively. The riskless (default-free) rate of return is time-varying over the back-testing exercise and corresponds to 1-month T-bill in the case of the US, and 3-month bills in the case of Italy.

We have then performed the following back-testing exercise. Starting from the initial subsample January 1977 – December 1978, the sample mean and the covariance matrix are computed. Combined with some coefficient of risk aversion (κ) and the risk free rate for the period, we use the standard, closed-form tangency portfolio formula in equation (3.31). The Excel apparatus to be employed has been already explained in detail in example 3.2. Because different investors will be characterized by different aversion to risk, the solutions are computed for values of κ that range between 1 and 1000. The optima weights computed with data up to time December 1978 are then used to compute the realized portfolio performance between December 1978 and January 1979.

At this point, the sample is extended to include equity returns data for one additional month, January 1979, to perform estimation afresh and compute again ω_T as well as the optimal share of borrowing or lending. A new realized portfolio performance indicator is then obtained with reference to the period January 1979 – February 1979. This expanding backtesting process is recursively repeated over time up to December 2015 (even though the last performance recorded will concern the month of December 2015). This process yields a total of 26 years of monthly realized performances, for the overall period January 1979 – December 2015. Consistent with the contents of this chapter, two obvious performance indicators are reported as a function of the investor's risk aversion (κ): the mean and the standard deviation of returns. The overall realized performance of the optimized portfolio over this sample is then compared to the performance of three benchmark (risky) portfolios:

1. A 100% US stocks-investment which represents the position of a non-internationally diversified US investor who completely ignores foreign diversification opportunities (such an investor is said to be completely home-biased towards domestic stocks, see Cuthbertson and Nitzsche, 2005, for a discussion of the empirical evidence).
2. A similar 100% Italian stocks-investment.
3. An equally weighted portfolio of all 9 countries that applies the celebrated "1/N" portfolio strategy recently discussed by DeMiguel, Garlappi, and Uppal (2009) as a hard-to-beat benchmark (but see the contrary evidence in Fugazza, Guidolin, and Nicodano, 2015).

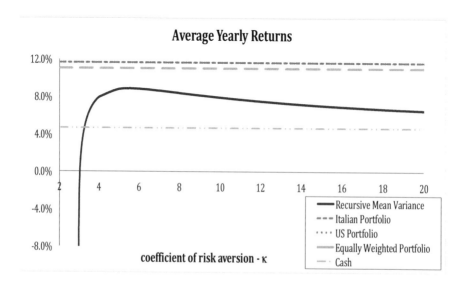

In the following plots, we report average performances over the full sample as a function of κ. For simplicity, we plot the measures in annualized terms, which is simply obtained by multiplying monthly means by 12 and monthly standard deviations by the square root of 12. The first plot compares optimized MV realized means with the benchmark.

The first surprising result is that for investors with extremely high risk tolerance, when κ is below 3, the realized mean goes towards absurdly negative values: when borrowing and short-sales are allowed, an investor would strongly leverage her portfolio. This is ex-ante optimal but this ex-post would end up causing the loss of all or most initial wealth! This is not surprising and in fact well known in the literature: with relatively low κ, MV implies rather extreme and concentrated weights and as such it takes just a few and unforeseen losses in the most heavily invested markets for most or all wealth to be destroyed.

Even as κ grows to exceed 5, in the recursive realized mean return picture we notice that the optimal portfolio performance ranges between 9% for the most aggressive portfolios obtained under κ = 4 to 6, and 6% for the most risk-averse investors. Notably, investing in an internationally diversified portfolio never pays out, however. The Italian, US, and equally weighted markets would have all given mean realized returns between 11 and 12% per year that the optimal MV portfolio cannot even get close to.

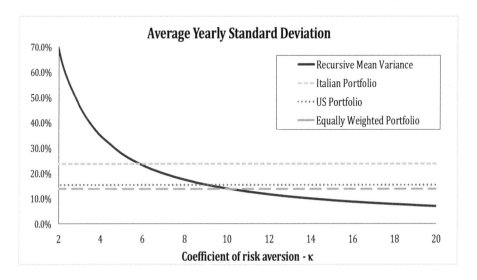

This would seem to be horrible news for international diversification. Yet, such a conclusion would be unwarranted because we are dealing with investors characterized by $\kappa > 0$ that do not only care for realized means, they also want to avoid (ex-ante) variance as a measure of risk. The plot at the bottom shows realized optimal MV portfolio standard deviation. Here the implication is stark: especially for intermediate and high risk-averse individuals, MV optimization applied to an international equity asset menu implies a substantial, ex-post reduction of risk. For κ in excess of 10, international diversification reduces risk even in comparison to a large US stock portfolio and the famous "1/N" equally weighted benchmark. Incidentally, this is the same conclusion reached by Solnik (1995) in a famous paper.

4 Optimal Portfolio Selection: A Few Analytical Results

"When it comes to investing, there is no such thing as a one-size-fits-all portfolio." (B. Barry Ritholtz, in the Washington Post, December 6, 2014)

Summary: – 1. Risk Aversion and the Canonical Portfolio Problem – 2. Aversion to Risk and Optimal Portfolio Selection in the Mean-Variance Framework – 3. Increasing Risk and Stochastic Dominance Criteria.

1 - Risk Aversion and the Canonical Portfolio Problem

In chapter 3, we have discussed how the investor can exclude inefficient portfolios from the analysis. Now we discuss how to find a solution to the allocation problem, according to the preferences of the investor. First, we will take a step back to the general framework of the expected utility theorem and derive some useful analytical results. However, such findings will concern the simplest, starkest set-up, the choice between cash and equity investments. Secondly, we will focus again on MV preferences and tease out from that framework what can be said about optimal portfolio selection, again for a simple canonical portfolio problem. Finally, we shall analyze alternative, more general ways when compared to MV analysis to rule out inefficient portfolios, based on the concepts of stochastic dominance.

Consider a portfolio choice problem of a risk averse individual who strictly prefers more to less (has a strictly increasing and differentiable utility function). If the individual invests a_j euros in the jth risky asset and $(W_0 - \sum_{j=1}^{N} a_j)$ euros in the risk free asset (which yields the sure rate R^f), her uncertain end of period wealth, W, starting from a W_0 initial wealth, is:

$$W = \sum_{j=1}^{N} a_j (1 + R_j) + \left(W_0 - \sum_{j=1}^{N} a_j \right) (1 + R^f)$$

$$= W_0(1 + R^f) + \sum_{j=1}^{N} a_j(R_j - R^f). \tag{4.1}$$

Note here a_j is not a portfolio weight, but the actual amount of wealth invested in an asset. What does it mean to solve an asset allocation problem in this set-up? Because of the EUT and given a VNM utility function, an investor shall simply solve:[1]

$$\max_{\{a_j\}_{j=1}^{N}} E\left[U\left(W_0(1 + R^f) + \sum_{j=1}^{N} a_j(R_j - R^f)\right)\right]. \tag{4.2}$$

This is a static, or one-period, portfolio selection problem: it does not address the issues of (a) revising decisions with the passage of time and taking the possibility of such revisions into account already at the initial time 0, or (b) the possibility that the investor wishes to consume some wealth (or add to wealth by saving non-asset income) before the terminal date. Such limitations should be considered to be the cost paid for the fact that a few interesting results will emerge for problem (4.2).
One first result for this problem may be easily derived. Assume that there exists a solution to the problem. Because $U(\cdot)$ is concave and the investor risk-averse, the first order necessary conditions are also sufficient:[2]

---

[1] The constraints are no longer visible in equations (4.2) because they have been substituted in the system before taking FOCs.

[2] The first order conditions (FOCs) of an unconstrained optimization problem
$$\max_{\{x_j\}_{j=1}^{N}} f(x_1, x_2, \ldots, x_N)$$
are $\partial f(x_1, x_2, \ldots, x_N)/\partial x_j = 0 \ \forall j = 1, 2, \ldots, N$. These are always necessary to an interior optimum (in the domain of the function $f(\cdot): \mathbb{R}^N \to \mathbb{R}$) but also become sufficient when the function is globally concave. The fact that in (4.2), the differentiation can be performed "inside" the expectation operator depends on the ability to exchange the order of integration and differentiation, which is always possible when the utility function is everywhere differentiable. If the investor were a risk lover, there would be no solution at all to the expected utility maximization unless some extra (and perhaps arbitrary) constraints were imposed. Under risk neutrality, there exists no solution to the maximization problem unless the expected return on every asset equals the rate of return on the risk-free asset. In such equilibrium, risk-neutral investors are indifferent about which assets they hold.

$$E\left[U'\left(W_0(1 + R^f) + \sum_{j=1}^{N} a_j(R_j - R^f)\right)(R_j - R^f)\right] = 0 \ j = 1, 2, ..., N \ (4.3)$$

Because $U(\cdot)$ is strictly increasing, equation (4.3) implies that the expectation of the product between a random variable (here MU) that is always positive and the random variable $R_j - R^f$ can be zero if and only if $R_j - R^f < 0$ with some positive probability. In other words, an interior optimum to the asset allocation problem may exist only if any of the risky assets is truly risky, in the sense that their distribution implies positive probability mass on the outcome of a negative *excess return*, $R_j - R^f < 0$.

Mathematically, (4.3) is not an equation, but a system of N equations in N unknowns, $\{a_j\}_{j=1}^{N}$, that needs to be solved to characterize the optimal portfolio investments. However, its solution requires knowledge of the form of the function $U'(\cdot)$ and must be dealt with on a case-by-case basis, often resorting to the computational power provided by computers, through numerical simulations, as shown at the end of this chapter.

1.1 When will risky assets be demanded?

A first remarkable result is that an individual who is risk averse and who strictly prefers more to less will undertake risky investments if and only if the rate return *on at least one risky asset* exceeds the risk-free interest. For the individual to invest nothing or even short sell the risky assets as an optimal choice, it is necessary that the first order conditions evaluated at no risky investments ($a_1 = a_2 = \cdots = a_N = 0$) be non-positive, i.e., for the first-order conditions not to be satisfied in a special way:

$$E[U'(W_0(1 + R^f))(R_j - R^f)] = U'\left(W_0(1 + R^f)\right)E[R_j - R^f] \leq 0 \ \forall j \ (4.4)$$

Because by assumption $U'\left(W_0(1 + R^f)\right) > 0$, (4.4) is equivalent to $E[(R_j - R^f)] = E[R_j] - R^f \leq 0$ for $j = 1, ..., N$. Thus an individual with an increasing and concave utility function will avoid all positive risky investments only if none of the risky assets has a strictly positive risk premium.

Note that nowhere we have said that the positive investment in the risky asset will be limited to the one with a positive risk premium: even though it is sensible that positive weights will be assigned to the positive risk premium assets, also additional assets may be demanded by a rational investor because they play a hedging role. For instance, if stock A were the only stock characterized by a positive risk premium, of course investors would demand it. However, a few additional stocks—say stocks B and C—may also be demanded in spite of their negative or zero risk premia, when B and C provide hedging to the risk that characterizes stock A. It is like ketchup: few of us would eat ketchup alone, but on a juicy grilled burger served on crusty bread, ketchup appears to be in hefty demand! Yet, you need to like either burger meat or bread (or both) for ketchup to become attractive to you. We summarize this rather simple and yet surprising result in:

Result 4.1: An individual who is risk averse and who strictly prefers more to less will undertake risky investments if and only if the rate return *on at least one risky asset* exceeds the risk-free interest rate.

LeRoy and Werner (2000) go on to show that if $R^P \equiv W_0(1 + R^f) + \sum_{j=1}^{N} \hat{a}_j (R_j - R^f)$ is the return on an optimal portfolio of a risk-averse investor and if R^P is riskier than the riskless rate, then it must be $E[R^P] > R^f$. In other words, if there is any demand for risky assets, the resulting optimal risky portfolio will have to yield a positive risk premium. This is far from trivial, because the fact that at least one risky asset commands a positive risk premium does not rule out that other assets (even all but one) may be instead characterized by a non-positive risk premia. Of course, this remains possible when the optimal weights $\{\hat{a}_j\}_{j=1}^{N}$ are tilted in directions that favor the highest expected return assets over the poorest paying ones.

We have already commented that there is no straightforward link between risk premia and the signs of the investments in the individual risky assets. For instance, an optimal portfolio can involve a long position in a security with strictly negative risk premium if the payoff on that security co-varies strongly but negatively (inversely) with the payoff on another security with a strictly positive risk premium. Obviously, when $N = 1$ and there is only one risky asset, $E[R] > R^f$, i.e., a positive risk premium, is necessary and sufficient for an investor to buy any amount of the risky fund. The following example characterizes exactly such an optimal amount invested in the risky asset, $\hat{a}$, when $N = 1$ and preferences are special.

Example 4.1. Assume that Mary is characterized by power utility preferences with $\gamma = 1$, i.e., by log-utility of wealth. For concreteness, let us also
assume that the only risky asset pays out either of two returns (corresponding to a "bull" vs. "bear" stock market, respectively), $R_{bull} > R_{bear}$, with probabilities π and $1 - \pi$, respectively. To avoid that the risk-free asset dominates
the stock market, assume that the riskless rate is such that $R_{bull} > R^f > R_{bear}$.
Moreover, Result 4.1 advises us to also impose that $E[R] = \pi R_{bull} + (1 - \pi)R_{bear} > R^f$, or that the risk premium on the risky asset is positive. Under
this specification, the FOC of the problem becomes

$$E\left[U'\left(W_0(1 + R^f) + \hat{a}(R - R^f)\right)(R - R^f)\right]$$
$$= \frac{\pi(R_{bull} - R^f)}{W_0(1+R^f) + \hat{a}(R_{bull}\text{-}R^f)} + \frac{(1 - \pi)(R_{bear} - R^f)}{W_0(1+R^f) + \hat{a}(R_{bear}\text{-}R^f)} = 0$$

because $U'(x) = 1/x$ when $U(x) = lnx$. At this point,

$$\pi(R_{bull} - R^f)(1+R^f)W_0 + \pi(R_{bull} - R^f)(R_{bear}\text{-}R^f)\hat{a}$$
$$= -(1 - \pi)(R_{bear} - R^f)(1+R^f)W_0 - (1 - \pi)(R_{bear}$$
$$- R^f)(R_{bull}\text{-}R^f)\hat{a}$$
$$\Rightarrow [\pi(R_{bull} - R^f)(R_{bear}\text{-}R^f) + (1 - \pi)(R_{bear} - R^f)(R_{bull}\text{-}R^f)]\hat{a}$$
$$= -(1 - \pi)(R_{bear} - R^f)(1 + R^f)W_0$$
$$- \pi(R_{bull} - R^f)(1 + R^f)W_0$$
$$\Rightarrow (R_{bull} - R^f)(R_{bear} - R^f)\hat{a}$$
$$= [R^f - (1 - \pi)(R_{bear}) - \pi(R_{bull})](1 + R^f)W_0$$
$$= -(E[R] - R^f),$$

which leads to the solution for the optimal weight:

$$\hat{a} = \frac{(E[R]\text{-}R^f)(1+R^f)W_0}{(R_{bull}\text{-}R^f)(R^f\text{-}R_{bear})} \text{ or (as a weight) } \hat{\omega} \equiv \frac{\hat{a}}{W_0} = \frac{(E[R] - R^f)(1+R^f)}{(R_{bull}\text{-}R^f)(R^f\text{-}R_{bear})}$$

The fraction of wealth invested in the risky fund increases with the risk premium paid by the risky asset, and decreases with an increase in the return
dispersion around R^f as measured by $(R_{bull}\text{-}R^f)(R^f\text{-}R_{bear}) > 0$. Although
in a technical sense, this is not variance, the interpretation is very similar, as
we shall see later in section 2. With less risk and unchanged mean returns,
it is not surprising that the proportion invested in the risky asset increases.
We will see, however, that, somewhat surprisingly, this result does not generalize without further assumptions on preferences.
Given $R^f = 1\%$ and $R_{bear} = -10\%$, define $\Delta \equiv R_{bull} - R_{bear} = R_{bull} - 10\%$

a measure of dispersion of asset returns. Note that $E[R] = \pi(-10\% + \Delta) + (1 - \pi)\ F(-10\%) = -10\% + \Delta\pi$. Figure 4.1 plots the optimal portfolio weight obtained using the formula above for Δ that ranges between 16 and 22 percent, and for the probability π that ranges between 0.45 and 0.62. Visibly, a large span of potential optimal portfolio weights is encompassed by this set of parameters. As the dispersion of potential risky asset returns and as the probability of the highest portfolio return increase, the portfolio weight increases.

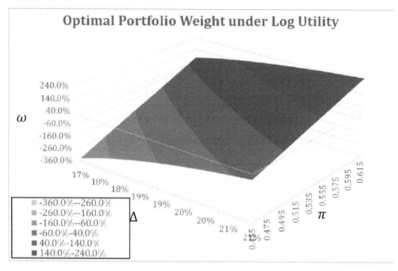

Figure 4.1

It is also possible to characterize the conditions—in the form of a minimum risk premium—that are required to induce a risk-averse, non-satiated individual to invest all of his wealth in the risky assets. This is a practically relevant problem when an investment advisor tries to anticipate a proportionally (in terms of percentage of wealth) "large" demand of the risky fund from an investor. Because the necessary and sufficient condition for positive demand to exist is that at least one asset pays a positive risk premium, to simplify the problem, in the following we consider the case of a single risky asset with return R. For an individual to invest all his wealth in such risky asset it must be that

$$E[U'(W_0(1 + R))(R - R^f)] \geq 0. \qquad (4.5)$$

Taking a first order Taylor series expansion of $U'(W_0(1 + R))$ around $U'(W_0(1 + R^f))$, multiplying both sides by the risk premium $E[R - R^f]$, and taking expectations gives

$$E[U'(W_0(1 + R^f))(R - R^f)] =$$
$$= U'(W_0(1 + R^f))E[R - R^f]$$
$$+ U''(W_0(1 + R^f))E[(R - R^f)^2]W_0 + o(E[(R - R^f)^2]) \quad (4.6)$$

Ignoring the remainder term, the minimum risk premium required to induce full investment in the risky asset may be determined by setting the right-hand side of the above relation to (weakly) exceed zero:

$$U'\left(W_0(1 + R^f)\right)E[R - R^f] + U''\left(W_0(1 + R^f)\right)E[(R - R^f)^2]W_0 \geq 0$$
$$\Rightarrow E[R - R^f] \geq -\frac{U''\left(W_0(1 + R^f)\right)W_0}{U'\left(W_0(1 + R^f)\right)}E[(R - R^f)^2]$$
$$= RRA\left(W_0(1 + R^f)\right)E[(R - R^f)^2]. \quad (4.7)$$

The inequality in (4.7) implies that the higher an individual's relative risk aversion, the higher the minimum risk premium required to induce full investment in the risky asset. If you take the risk premium and the mean square deviations of the risky returns around the riskless rate as objective market parameters, then it takes for an investor a coefficient of relative risk aversion computed in correspondence to the sure wealth level $W_0(1 + R^f)$, less than $E[R - R^f]/E[(R - R^f)^2]$ for her to accept to optimally hold a portfolio composed 100% of the risky asset. For instance, if the investor is characterized by constant relative risk aversion preferences with coefficient γ, it takes $\gamma \leq E[R - R^f]/E[(R - R^f)^2]$ for her to commit all of her wealth to the risky asset.

1.2 A few comparative statics results

From equation (4.3), we know that $E\left[U'\left(W_0(1 + R^f) + \hat{a}(R_j - R^f)\right)(R_j - R^f)\right] = 0$ for the case of a single risky asset, where $\hat{a}$ is the optimal demand of such an asset. Even though the algebra is tedious (see, e.g., Huang and

Litzenberger, 1988, for formal proof), implicit differentiation of this expression makes it possible to prove that when the risk premium on the risky mutual fund is small, then

$$\frac{\hat{a}}{W_0} \cong \frac{E[R - R^f]}{Var[R]ARA(W_0)} \tag{4.8}$$

from which the following result can be proven:

Result 4.2: An individual who is risk averse and who strictly prefers more to less will demand a growing (decreasing/constant) amount of the unique risky asset as her wealth increases, if and only if her absolute risk aversion declines (grows/is constant) as function of initial wealth:

$$\frac{d\hat{a}}{dW_0} \gtreqless 0 \Leftrightarrow \frac{dARA(W_0)}{dW_0} \lesseqgtr 0. \tag{4.9}$$

There is also a related relationship involving the coefficient of absolute risk aversion, that follows directly from Result 2.7 in chapter 2, that $\Pi(W, H) \cong \frac{1}{2}ARA(W, H)Var[H]$. For a given lottery H, clearly

$$\frac{d\Pi(W, H)}{dW_0} \gtreqless 0 \Leftrightarrow \frac{dARA(W_0)}{dW_0} \gtreqless 0, \tag{4.10}$$

i.e., the compensatory risk premium grows/declines/is constant with wealth when the absolute risk aversion coefficient grows/declines/is constant with wealth. When $dARA(W_0)/dW_0 < 0$, we write about decreasing absolute risk aversion (DARA); when $dARA(W_0)/dW_0 = 0$, we write of constant absolute risk aversion (CARA); finally, when $dARA(W_0)/dW_0 > 0$, we have the case of increasing absolute risk aversion (IARA).

Result 4.2 may look like a mathematical curiosity but it has implications for the plausibility of an important type of VNM felicity function, the negative exponential one. As we have seen, under negative exponential utility, $dARA(W_0)/dW_0 = 0$, or the coefficient of absolute risk aversion is constant. However, because of Result 4.2, this is equivalent to $d\hat{a}/dW_0 = 0$, i.e., when an investor's wealth increases, because the optimal weight in the risky asset is defined as $\hat{\omega}(W_0) \equiv \hat{a}(W_0)/W_0$, and assuming this is initially positive, then

$$\frac{d\hat{\omega}(W_0)}{dW_0} = \frac{d(\hat{a}(W_0)/W_0)}{dW_0} = \frac{\dfrac{d\hat{a}(W_0)}{dW_0}W_0 - \hat{a}(W_0)}{W_0^{\,2}} = -\hat{\omega}(W_0)\frac{1}{W_0} < 0, (4.11)$$

i.e., a CARA investor is characterized by weights in the risky asset that oddly decline as the investor becomes wealthier. Correspondingly, the weight invested in cash, $(W_0 - \hat{a}(W_0))/W_0 = 1 - \hat{\omega}(W_0)$, will increase. Thus, the negative exponential utility function implies that the level of the demand for risky assets is unaffected by changes in initial wealth, with riskless borrowing and lending absorbing all changes in initial wealth. Having said this, not many of us—should we find money on the sidewalk—would rush to invest it in pure cash (say, by depositing them in a checking account). In fact, a number of us, after recording a consistent increase in our available wealth, shall engage in activities consisting of starting firms of various types, like buying restaurants and coffee bars. These facts cast a long shadow on the plausibility of the CARA case. Needless to say, IARA utility functions are usually deemed rather implausible too, because they imply that as an individual gets wealthier, she will *sell* risky assets to hoard cash in a more-than-proportional fashion.[3] Only DARA utility functions enjoy adequate plausibility. As we have noted in chapter 2, under power utility we have $ARA(W) = RRA(W)/W = \gamma/W$, which is clearly an inverse function of wealth, and this explains the great popularity that power utility preferences have both with practitioners and academics.

The property of decreasing absolute risk aversion is related to the total, in-currency-denominated demand for the risky asset. One naturally wonders whether the Arrow-Pratt measure of relative risk aversion, $RRA(W_0) = ARA(W_0)W_0$, may also reveal similarly important information when the investor's wealth undergoes any change. Even though the algebra is as tedious as the one mentioned above (see also in this case Huang and Litzenberger, 1988), one can prove that:

---

[3] Because under quadratic utility, $ARA(W) = \kappa/(1 - \kappa W)$, it turns out that this utility function—at least for a wealth below the bliss point, when absolute risk aversion is sensibly defined—will be of IARA type.

Result 4.3: An individual who is risk averse and who strictly prefers more to less will display an *elasticity* of the amount demanded of the risky asset vs. initial wealth that exceeds unity (is one/less than one) if and only if her relative risk aversion declines (grows/is constant) with initial wealth:

$$\hat{\eta}(W_0) \equiv \frac{d\hat{a}(W_0)}{dW_0} \frac{W_0}{\hat{a}(W_0)} \lessgtr 1 \Leftrightarrow \frac{dRRA(W_0)}{dW_0} \gtrless 0. \qquad (4.12)$$

The elasticity of the optimal investment in the risky asset simply measures the percentage change in the optimal demand of the risky asset per unit percentage change in initial wealth. Clearly, when $\hat{\eta} > 1$, the weight of the risky asset increases when wealth increases; when $\hat{\eta} < 1$, the opposite occurs. As we have already shown, under power utility, the investor is characterized by constant relative risk aversion and this means that $dRRA(W_0)/dW_0=0$ and $\hat{\eta} = 1$, i.e., when wealth grows, a power utility investor will keep her percentage holdings of the risky asset constant, and hence increase them at the same proportion as wealth grows.[4] This feature seems plausible and Result 4.3 lies at the heart of one common practice in the asset management industry: to frequently offer identical advice to investors with very different wealth. For instance, how can the same equity strategies inform the trades of mutual funds irrespectively of the number of shares of the funds that an investor may purchase? The answer is that if all investors have power utility, then their starting wealth levels will be irrelevant to asset allocation and fund management strategies.

As noted in chapter 2, a risk neutral investor does not care about risk and ranks investments solely on the basis of their expected returns. As we know, the utility of money function of such an agent is necessarily of the form

---

[4] The fact that under CRRA preferences, risky holdings must grow is partly obvious because from $RRA(W_0) = ARA(W_0)W_0$, we have that

$$\frac{dRRA(W_0)}{dW_0} = \frac{d(ARA(W_0)W_0)}{dW_0} = \frac{dARA(W_0)W_0 + ARA(W_0)dW_0}{dW_0}$$
$$= \frac{dARA(W_0)}{dW_0}W_0 + ARA(W_0) = 0,$$

and this implies that $\frac{dARA(W_0)}{dW_0} < 0$ because $ARA(W_0) > 0$ by construction, given that we are studying a risk-averse investor. Equivalently, CRRA always implies declining absolute risk aversion and characterizes a relatively aggressive investor that buys increasing amounts of the risky asset as her wealth grows.

$U(W) = a + bW$ with $b > 0$. What proportion of her wealth will such a decision maker invest in the risky asset? It is easy to show that provided the premium characterizing the risky fund in excess over the risk free rate is positive, all of her wealth will be invested in the risky asset. This is clearly seen from the following. Consider the portfolio problem when $U(W) = k + bW$:

$$\max_{a} E[k + bW_0(1 + R^f) + ba(R - R^f)] \Leftrightarrow \max_{a} ba\, E[R - R^f]. \quad (4.13)$$

When $E[R - R^f] > 0$, this expression is increasing in a. This means that if the risk neutral investor is unconstrained, she will attempt to borrow as much as possible at R^f and re-invest the proceeds in the risky portfolio. Therefore, she is willing, and without any bounds, to exchange riskless payments for uncertain claims of greater expected value. If we instead specify that the investor is prevented from borrowing, then the maximum will occur at $a = W_0$.

1.3 A second two-fund separation result: Cass-Stiglitz's theorem

The interesting comparative statics results in Section 1.2 depend upon the fact that there are only two assets, one risky and one riskless. In general, when there is more than one risky asset we cannot say, for example, that the wealth elasticity of the demands for risky assets are greater than unity when an individual exhibits decreasing relative risk aversion. When an investor's initial wealth increases, he may want to change his portfolio composition of the risky assets such that the investment in one risky asset increases while the investment in another asset decreases. As we have already commented in Section 1.1, such shifts in demands may also be motivated by hedging purposes, and it is hard to tell on a purely theoretical basis—i.e., without performing any numerical calculations—how asset demands shift when wealth changes.

Obviously, only if an individual always chooses to hold the same portfolio of risky assets and hence simply changes the mix between that portfolio and the riskless asset for differing levels of initial wealth, then the comparative statics for the two-asset case will be valid in a multi-asset world. In such an event, the individual's optimal portfolios for differing levels of initial wealth are always linear combinations of the riskless asset and a risky/uncertain asset mutual fund. This important property of optimal choices in a multi-asset world is commonly called *two fund monetary separation*. Once again, it is not just a curiosity (to some economists, cute mathematical results may also be attractive): the ability to extend a number of results from Section 1.2 to the real, multi-asset world is exactly what we are looking for!

Cass and Stiglitz (1970) have demonstrated that a necessary and sufficient condition on utility functions for two fund monetary separation is that marginal utility satisfies one of two properties:

Result 4.4 (Cass-Stiglitz): An individual who is risk averse and who strictly prefers more to less will exhibit *two-fund separation* if and only if either

$$U'(W) = (A + BW)^C \quad \text{or} \quad U'(W) = A exp(BW), \quad (4.14)$$

where in the former case, $B > 0, C < 0$, and $W \geq \max[0, -(A/B)]$, or $A > 0$, $B < 0$, $C > 0$ and $0 \leq z < -(A/B)$; $A > 0$, $B < 0$ and $W \geq 0$ in the latter case.[5]

The proof can be found in the original article published in 1970 and it is not particularly enlightening. However, it is difficult to understate the importance of this result. Cass-Stiglitz's theorem implies that for a number of standard VNM felicity functions, an investor always holds the same risky portfolio independently of her initial wealth, in the sense that the composition of such a portfolio is constant and that very portfolio may be treated as if it is a large, market portfolio to be demanded. The fact that the utility functions are of standard types comes from realizing that

$$U(W) = const + \int U'(W)dW$$

$$= const + \int (A + BW)^C dW = const + \frac{1}{B}\frac{(A+BW)^{C+1}}{C + 1} \quad (4.15)$$

Clearly, when we set A = 0, B = 1, and C = $-\gamma < 0$ (when $\gamma \neq 1$), the first marginal utility function in Result 4.4 has a CRRA power utility function as its primitive.[6] Alternatively, when A = 1, B = κ, and C = 1, the first type of marginal utility function becomes a simple quadratic utility. Finally,

---

[5] These hardly memorable restrictions on the parameters A, B, and C simply guarantee that the relevant, underlying utility function is strictly concave and increasing.

[6] Moreover, in the case A=0, B = 1, and C = -1, it is possible to check that $U(W) = const + \int (W)^{-1} dW = const + lnW$. In the power utility case, because relative risk aversion is constant, the proportions invested in the riskless asset a and in the risky asset mutual fund $(1 - a)$ are also invariant to different levels of initial wealth.

$$U(W) = \text{const} + \int Aexp(BW)dW = const + \frac{A}{B}exp(BW), \quad (4.16)$$

which delivers a negative exponential utility when the constant is set to 1, B = -θ < 0, and A = θ > 0. As noted earlier, the CARA class of preferences has the property that the total amount invested in risky assets is invariant to the level of wealth. It is not surprising that the proportionate allocation among the available risky assets is similarly invariant as in Result 4.4.

Cass-Stiglitz's result is implicitly at the heart of big portions of the modern financial architecture in which standardized investment products (think of mutual and pension funds, and wealth management services that are tailored not to individual needs but to the inferred targets of clusters of investors) seem to be routinely offered and may imply that:

I.   The composition of the risky portfolio is homogeneous across different investors and the latter differ in a cross-sectional dimension simply because they invest in different proportions in such a risky mutual fund and the riskless asset;

II. identical products, indeed structured as fixed proportion combinations of the risky mutual fund and of cash, are offered to investors with very different wealth levels.

Of course, the latter, stronger characterization requires that Result 4.4 be applied in the presence of a VNM utility of wealth that implies constant relative risk aversion, such as log- or power utility. Such two properties justify the existence of identical equity mutual and pension funds offered as if rather heterogeneous investors (in terms of age and demographic features) may actually desire to buy such standardized products instead of demanding a personalized wealth management. The following example closes this section by exploring in greater depth the implications of Cass-Stiglitz's result.

Example 4.2. Consider John and Mary. John is characterized by negative exponential, CARA utility function of wealth,

$$U_{John}(W) = 1 - e^{-\theta W} \quad \text{with } \theta > 0.$$

Because this is a special case of Cass-Stiglitz's result with A = -B = θ, John enjoys the benefits of two-fund separation: in case his wealth changed, he would keep investing the same proportions in the available risky assets.

However, because he has CARA preferences, when his wealth increases (decreases), John will not change the total amount he invests in a constant-proportion risky mutual fund and will just proceed to scale up (down) his overall cash holdings. Therefore, the case illustrated in the following table is plausible if applied to John.

Initial wealth	Stock A		Stock B		Stock C		Cash		Tot. risky
	Total	% risky	Total	% risky	Total	% risky	Total	% total	
100	30	60	10	20	10	20	50	50	50
50	30	60	10	20	10	20	0	0	50
150	30	60	10	20	10	20	100	66.7	50

Of course, these numbers are just made up and do not reflect any specific calculations. However, they illustrate the fact that the structure of the risky portfolio demanded by John does not depend on his wealth and is always composed of 30% of stock A and 20% of stocks B and C. Moreover, also the overall demand of such a risky portfolio is not affected by wealth and always equals 50 (euros) because John's absolute risk aversion is constant. As a result, the total percentage of wealth invested in cash increases when John's wealth increases, and vice versa.

Mary is instead described by a power utility function of wealth,

$$U_{Mary}(W) = \frac{W^{1-\gamma}}{1-\gamma} \quad \text{with} \quad \gamma > 0.$$

Because this is one more special case of Cass and Stiglitz's result with A = 0, B = 1, and C = - γ, also Mary makes simple two-fund choices: if her wealth changed, she would keep investing the same proportions in the available risky assets. However, because she has CRRA preferences and declining ARA coefficient, when her wealth increases (decreases), Mary will increase (decrease) the total amount she invests in the risky mutual fund to keep the total weight assigned to it constant. Therefore, the numbers seen in John's case can plausibly turn into what follows.

Initial wealth	Stock A		Stock B		Stock C		Cash		Tot. risky
	Total	% risky	Total	% risky	Total	% risky	Total	% total	
100	30	60	10	20	10	20	50	50	50
50	15	60	5	20	5	20	25	50	25
150	45	60	15	20	15	20	75	50	75

The routine usage of asset and country/sector allocation "grids" by all major financial institutions, tailored to the risk profile of different clients, but independent of their wealth levels (and of changes in their wealth), is predicated on the hypothesis that differences in wealth (across clients) and changes in their wealth do not require adjustments in portfolio composition provided risk tolerance is either unchanged or controlled for. Result 4.4 under specific assumptions on the preferences required for it to hold, provide support to such practice.

2 - Aversion to Risk and Optimal Portfolio Selection in the Mean-Variance Framework

2.1 Mean-variance preference representations: pros and cons

In chapter 2, we have already seen that a non-satiated investor with quadratic utility will be equivalently characterized by an expected utility functional with structure:

$$E[U(W)] = E[W] - \frac{1}{2}\kappa E[W^2] = E[W] - \frac{1}{2}\kappa[Var[W] + (E[W])^2]$$
$$= E[W]\left(1 - \frac{1}{2}\kappa E[W]\right) - \frac{1}{2}\kappa Var[W], \qquad (4.17)$$

which explicitly trades off the variance of terminal wealth with its mean. This is the case because $W < 1/\kappa$ implies that $E[W] < 1/\kappa < 2/\kappa$ which is necessary and sufficient for $\left(1 - \frac{1}{2}\kappa E[W]\right) > 0$. Although it is rather special because it is based on one type of utility function that is subject to a number of limitations (e.g., it fails to be monotone increasing and it may imply negative ARA and RRA measures, as we have noted in chapter 2), such a mean-variance analysis objective greatly facilitates the construction of optimal portfolios. More generally, a MV framework is characterized by

$$E[U(W)] = \Gamma(E[W], Var[W]), \qquad (4.18)$$

i.e., by dependence of the VNM functional only on the mean and variance of terminal wealth.

In particular, if the function $U(\cdot)$ is quadratic, we know from (4.17) that the generic function $\Gamma(\cdot)$ will be linear in mean and variance. However, a MV objective can be justified on no other grounds than as the expected value of a quadratic utility function. There are at least three additional ways of justifying a MV objective. First, a quadratic approximation (i.e., a second-order Taylor expansion) to a general utility function can justify mean-variance analysis (see Danthine and Donaldson, 2005, for a formal argument). Second, (4.18) may derive from an application of the EUT when the rates of return are described according to a multivariate Normal distribution.[7] The points to note in obtaining this result are that:

I.   Normal distributions are characterized entirely by their means (expectations), variances, and covariances;

II.   linear combinations of Normal random variables are also Normal (hence, terminal wealth, or the rate of return on a portfolio of assets with Normally distributed returns, is also Normally distributed);

III. therefore, the key properties of terminal wealth may be represented by its mean and variance.

A third way must be noted (and many academics and practitioners seem to subscribe to this view): often a MV objective is directly assumed, on the grounds that such a criterion is plausible, without recourse to more fundamental assumptions, such as those of the EUT. As we are about to argue, such a claim is much less innocent than commonly thought, as it implies a positive statement on the fact that investors actually ignore all features of the distribution of asset returns besides the mean and the variance.

Here it comes natural to ask what other features characterize, or equivalently, what is so special (i.e. restrictive) about, mean-variance analysis? At first sight, mean-variance analysis might appear to provide simply a definite form of the EUT. The problem is that although it may be common to express/report the features of many random variables (for instance, the asymptotic properties of ML estimators, under the central limit theorem, at least) in terms of their means and variances, some key aspects of their probability distributions cannot be simply captured by means and variances. For instance, any *skewness* in the distribution would be ignored. A less obvious feature of probability distributions, not captured by just variance, is the tendency for some random variables to be concentrated either near to, or far

---

[7] While sufficient, Normality is not necessary: a broader class of distributions also implies a mean-variance objective for EU-maximizing investors. Chamberlain (1983) provides an exhaustive characterization of the relevant probability distributions.

from, their means. An index of this tendency is the *kurtosis*.[8] There is abundant evidence that the distributions of many asset prices (for instance, interest rates) and holding period returns display both pervasive asymmetries (e.g., many assets behave like lottery tickets and are right-skewed) and "fat tails", i.e., that extreme values, or outliers, occur more frequently than consistent with Normal random variables. The upshot is that mean-variance analysis is compatible only with a restricted class of random variables. To the extent that asset payoffs (and, hence, rates of return) do not conform with these restrictions, mean-variance analysis is liable to result in misleading conclusions. Importantly, many commonly employed VNM utility functions—for instance, the standard CRRA power utility—fully reflect all these features of the empirical distribution of asset returns. Yet, a MV objective does not and this is problematic.

The problems with MV are not over yet. Even though we may be ready to adopt a single-period framework in which we care for future terminal wealth, W_{t+1}, note that the link between total portfolio returns and terminal wealth is simply $W_{t+1} = (1 + R_{PF,t+1})W_t$ and therefore:

$$E_t[W_{t+1}] = E_t[(1 + R_{PF,t+1})]W_t = (1 + E_t[R_{PF,t+1}])W_t$$
$$Var_t[W_{t+1}] = Var_t[(1 + R_{PF,t+1})]W_t^2 = Var_t[R_{PF,t+1}]W_t^2. \quad (4.19)$$

If you plug these expressions in the conditional MV functional $E_t[U(W_{t+1})]$ $= E[W_{t+1}](1 - 0.5\kappa E[W_{t+1}]) - 0.5\kappa Var_t[W_{t+1}]$, then we obtain

$$E_t[U(W_{t+1})] = (1 + E_t[R_{PF,t+1}])W_t - \frac{1}{2}\kappa Var_t[R_{PF,t+1}]W_t^2$$

$$= \left\{(1 + E_t[R_{PF,t+1}]) - \frac{1}{2}\kappa Var_t[R_{PF,t+1}]W_t\right\}W_t$$

$$\propto E_t[R_{PF,t+1}] - \frac{1}{2}\kappa Var_t[R_{PF,t+1}]W_t, \quad (4.20)$$

---

[8] Skewness is the scaled (by the cube of the standard deviation) third central moment of the probability distribution and reflects the tendency of a random variable to fall systematically either below (left-skewed) or above (right-skewed) its mean. A skewed distribution is non-symmetric. Kurtosis is the scaled (by the square of variance) fourth central moment of a probability distribution. The Normal distribution provides a benchmark and implies a constant zero skewness and a kurtosis of 3. Distributions with more probability than the Normal in the tails are known as *leptokurtic*, and with less probability mass as *platykurtic*.

where we have treated $(1 - 0.5\kappa E[W_{t+1}])$ as a positive constant that can be ignored for the purpose of expected utility maximization. The issue is that in most MV models the objective is written as a function of the expected value and variance of the rate of return to wealth, i.e., the overall portfolio return $R_{PF,t+1}$, rather than the level of wealth, that is

$$E_t[U(W_{t+1})] = E_t[R_{PF,t+1}] - \frac{1}{2}\kappa Var_t[R_{PF,t+1}], \qquad (4.21)$$

Unfortunately, (4.20) and (4.21) are different as the latter ignores the fact that the variance of terminal wealth should depend on initial wealth in a way that cannot be arbitrarily neglected or simplified out. In other words, while the MV objective should be of the type $E[U(W_{t+1})] = \Gamma(E_t[W_{t+1}], Var_t[W_{t+1}])$ the uncritical use of functions of the type $G(E_t[R_{PF,t+1}], Var_t[R_{PF,t+1}]) = G(\mu_{PF}, \sigma_{PF}^2)$ has become widespread but appears to be consistent—even under special assumptions or as a second-order Taylor expansion—with expected utility maximization only if $W_t \cong 1$.[9] In spite of these qualms about its origins and true meaning, in what follows we assume that MV preferences are actually represented by (4.21).

2.2 Indifference curves in mean-variance space

To make sense and represent in a useful way the trade-off between expected returns and risk, assume that—whatever its micro-foundation—the MV objective functional is monotone increasing in the mean, $\partial G(\mu_{PF}, \sigma_{PF}^2)/\partial \mu_{PF} > 0$, and monotone decreasing in risk, $\partial G(\mu_{PF}, \sigma_{PF}^2)/\partial \sigma_{PF}^2 < 0$. Equivalently, expected return is a "good" that gives happiness and risk is a "bad" that hurts an investor's satisfaction. Consider now some small, countervailing changes in μ_{PF} and σ_{PF}^2 that keep the total level of the MV satisfaction index constant at some initial level $\bar{G}$, or $dG(\mu_{PF}, \sigma_{PF}^2) = 0$:

---

[9] Otherwise, it is as if the time-varying W_t is absorbed inside the true risk aversion coefficient κ_t' which must then be varying over time so that $\kappa = \kappa_t' W_t$ be kept constant as assumed. For instance, when W_t grows over time (as one would expect), then the true underlying κ_t' ought to be decreasing over time. This poses further problems: if we identify κ_t' with the ARA coefficient of the investor, we know from chapter 2 that under quadratic utility and second-order approximations of other utility functions, ARA(W_t) should be increasing as W_t increases (this defines the IARA investor type) and not the opposite.

$$0 = dG(\mu_{PF}, \sigma_{PF}^2) = \left.\frac{\partial G(\mu_{PF}, \sigma_{PF}^2)}{\partial \mu_{PF}}\right|_{G=\bar{G}} d\mu_{PF} + \left.\frac{\partial G(\mu_{PF}, \sigma_{PF}^2)}{\partial \sigma_{PF}^2}\right|_{G=\bar{G}} d\sigma_{PF}^2 \quad (4.22)$$

(4.22) is just a total differential function equated to zero in correspondence to some target level $\bar{G}$. This means that the loci of combinations of expected returns and that keep MV unchanged is characterized by the following slope:

$$\alpha(\bar{G}) \equiv \left.\frac{d\mu_{PF}}{d\sigma_{PF}^2}\right|_{G=\bar{G}} = -\frac{\left.\dfrac{\partial G(\mu_{PF}, \sigma_{PF}^2)}{\partial \sigma_{PF}^2}\right|_{G=\bar{G}}}{\left.\dfrac{\partial G(\mu_{PF}, \sigma_{PF}^2)}{\partial \mu_{PF}}\right|_{G=\bar{G}}} > 0. \quad (4.23)$$

The positive sign derives from our earlier assumptions. So such a loci, when drawn in the standard expected return/variance space will have a positive slope: increasing risk must be rewarded by increasing expected return to keep an investor equally satisfied, at an arbitrary level $\bar{G}$. Because for positive σ, σ_{PF}^2 is a monotone increasing function of standard deviation, if the slope of the loci is increasing as σ_{PF}^2 increases, the same must be true of the increase in standard deviation, σ_{PF}. The loci of such combinations of means and standard deviation is also given a very specific name:

MV indifference curve: The loci in the mean-standard deviation of space of the infinite combinations (μ_{PF}, σ_{PF}) that yield some fixed level of identical MV (expected) utility as measured by the function $G(\mu_{PF}, \sigma_{PF}^2) = \bar{G}$ is called a MV indifference curve.

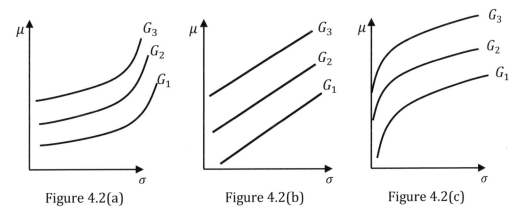

Figure 4.2(a)   Figure 4.2(b)   Figure 4.2(c)

Figure 4.2 shows a few such indifference curves. In the plots, as the index of

G increases, we face increasing levels of satisfaction/utility. Clearly, the issue one faces concerns the type of concavity of the indifference curves, because the earlier definition fails to rule out any case and simply implies that the curves only need to be monotonically increasing. Yet, it is normally assumed that the indifference curves are convex as in figure 4.2(a). The justification for this type of convexity is advanced on several grounds:

I.   Intuitive plausibility, because it seems reasonable that, at higher levels of risk, the greater are the increments to expected return needed to compensate for increments in risk if the decision maker's utility is kept constant; of course this sounds a like the IARA property stated in section 1.

II. As an implication of a quadratic von Neumann–Morgenstern utility function that is increasing in wealth, because as we know, in that case we have

$$E_t[U(W_{t+1})] = \mu_{PF} - \frac{1}{2} \kappa \, \sigma_{PF}^2 \qquad (4.24)$$

and clearly $\partial E_t[U(W_{t+1})]/\partial \mu_{PF} = 1$ while $\partial E_t[U(W_{t+1})]/\partial \sigma_{PF} = -\kappa \, \sigma_{PF} < 0$, so that

$$\left. \frac{d\mu_{PF}}{d\sigma_{PF}} \right|_{G=\bar{G}} = \kappa \, \sigma_{PF} > 0 \qquad \left. \frac{d^2\mu_{PF}}{d(\sigma_{PF})^2} \right|_{G=\bar{G}} = \kappa > 0, \qquad (4.25)$$

i.e., provided the investor is risk-averse, the indifferences curves are also convex.

III. As an implication of a negative exponential von Neumann–Morgenstern utility function, when asset returns are jointly normally distributed (this of course delivers the case knife-edge case of figure 4.2(b)).

IV. Because linear or concave indifference curves would otherwise lead to predictions that are inconsistent with commonly observed behavior, as we are about to show in section 2.3.

2.3 Optimal mean-variance portfolios

At this point, we are ready to assemble all the MV machinery that we have been building in chapter 3 and here. In chapter 3, we traced out the minumvariance frontier and identified the set of efficient portfolios. With agreement about means and variances, the efficient set of portfolios is the same for each investor. There is still scope, however, for different investors to choose different portfolios. The reason is that investors can differ in their preferences, commonly interpreted as reflecting different investors' attitudes towards risk. For instance, assume that the two-fund separation theorem of chapter 3 holds in the presence of a riskless asset and of a unique lending and borrowing rate. The optimal MV portfolio for one investor lies then on the highest indifference curve that is attainable subject to being feasible (i.e., on or below the capital market line, that in this case coincides with the efficient set). For instance, in figure 4.3, the optimum is at point O.

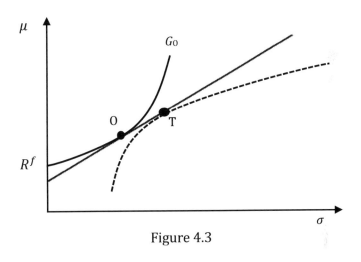

Figure 4.3

Because the trade-off between mean portfolio returns and risk, expressed by the line $R^f OT$ in figure 4.3, can be written as

$$\mu_{PF} = R^f + \frac{\mu_T - R^f}{\sigma_T} \sigma_{PF},\qquad(4.26)$$

where $\mu_{A''} \equiv E[R_T]$ and $\sigma_{A''} \equiv \sqrt{Var[R_T]}$, the tangency condition gives that at the optimum it must be that

$$\alpha(G_O) = \frac{\mu_T - R^f}{\sigma_T} = SR_T,\qquad(4.27)$$

because when two functions are tangent, by elementary differential calculus, we know that they must share the same slope. (4.27) implies that in correspondence to the optimum, the coefficient of risk aversion of the investor—as measured by her trade-off measured by the increase in mean portfolio returns required to compensate any marginal increase in risk, $\alpha(G_o)$—must be identical to the (maximum achievable) Sharpe ratio of the tangency portfolio.

In particular, portfolio O implies less risk than portfolio T. On the CML this can be simply achieved by investing a positive share of wealth in the riskless asset, and the remainder in portfolio T. In this sense, the investor in figure 4.3, is a relatively cautious one. In fact, interestingly there is a direct relationship between the position of portfolio O on the segment connecting R^f to the tangency portfolio T, and the share that is invested in the latter. At least in rough terms, one would estimate that the investor in figure 4.3 leaves 1/3 of her wealth in cash, and invests the remaining 2/3 in the tangency portfolio.

Of course, other optimal portfolios may emerge. In figure 4.4(a), we show the case of an extremely risk-averse, cautious investor who leaves almost all of her wealth in cash, so that her O' optimal portfolio appears to be very close to the vertical axis and the overall risk the investor assumes is almost zero. In figure 4.4(b), we show the case of an aggressive investor who levers her initial wealth by borrowing at the riskless rate in order to be able to invest more than 100% of her wealth in the tangency portfolio, which occurs in correspondence to portfolio O''.

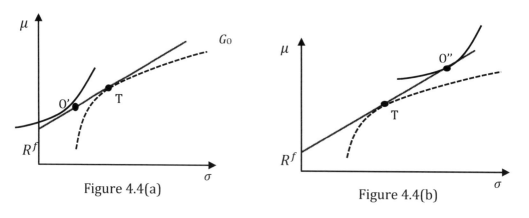

Figure 4.4(a)   Figure 4.4(b)

In the case of either quadratic utility or when expected utility may be accurately approximated by a mean-variance objective, one can also show that the optimal share of the risky portfolio demanded by a risk-averse investor, with convex indifference curves, is simply the solution to:

$$\max_{\omega_t} E[W_{t+1}] - \frac{1}{2}\kappa Var[W_{t+1}]$$
$$s.t. \quad W_{t+1} = (1 + R^f)(1 - \omega_t) + (1 + R_{T,t+1})\omega_t$$
$$= (1 + R^f) + (R_{T,t+1} - R^f)\omega_t, \tag{4.28}$$

where T is the tangency portfolio. Plugging in the budget constraint in the objective function, the problem becomes:

$$\max_{\omega_t}(1 + R^f) + E[(R_{T,t+1} - R^f)\omega_t] - \frac{1}{2}\kappa Var[(R_{T,t+1} - R^f)\omega_t]$$
$$\Leftrightarrow \max_{\omega_t} E[(R_{T,t+1} - R^f)]\omega_t - \frac{1}{2}\kappa\omega_t^2\sigma^2, \tag{4.29}$$

This program is now unconstrained and the objective is quadratic and globally concave. Therefore, the FOC will be necessary but also sufficient:

$$E[(R_{T,t+1} - R^f)] - \kappa\hat{\omega}_t\sigma^2 = 0 \tag{4.30}$$

which can be solved to give:

$$\hat{\omega}_t = \frac{E[(R_{T,t+1} - R^f)]}{\kappa\sigma^2} \tag{4.31}$$

this result:

Result 4.5: Given a quadratic VNM felicity function, or any other case in which the objective function of an investor may be expressed or approximated as $E[U(W_{t+1})] = E[R_{PF,t+1}] - 0.5\kappa Var[R_{PF,t+1}]$, when a riskless asset exists and unrestricted lending and borrowing are possible, then the optimal demand of the investor will be:

$$\hat{\omega}_t = \frac{E[R_{PF,t+1}] - R^f}{\kappa Var[R_{PF,t+1}]} \tag{4.32}$$

confirms the standard intuition that: (a) the greater the excess expected return (risk premium), the larger the holding of the risky portfolio; (b) the riskier the risky portfolio, the lower the holding of the risky asset; and (c) the greater the risk tolerance (i.e. the smaller is κ), the higher the holding of the risky portfolio.

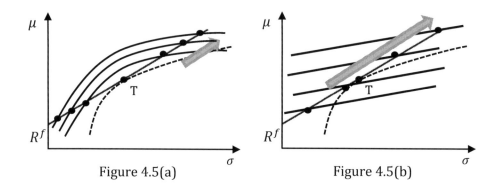

Figure 4.5(a)   Figure 4.5(b)

Finally, one may wonder what would happen to these results if one were not to assume convex indifference curves. Figures 4.5(a)-(b) show such cases. In figure 4.5(a), the indifference curves are concave and as we travel up the map of the indifference curves, new optima can be found as intersections between higher curves and the CML, both to the right and to the left of the tangency portfolio. This means that an investor will have the incentive to borrow an infinite amount of cash at the riskless rate and to invest a share that diverges to infinity in T.[10] In figure 4.5(b), the same occurs with linear indifference curves, but in this case the intersection points only occur to the right of T. Also in this case, the investor has an incentive to borrow an infinite amount of cash at the riskless rate and to invest a share that diverges to infinity in T.[11] Of course, both these solutions to the problem make no sense as nobody will be allowed to either borrow infinite sums or to invest infinite

---

[10] It may appear that in figure 4.5(a), the optimal point of intersection between the CML and the map of indifference curves also travels to the left, in the direction of portfolios which invest more than 100% in cash. However, such portfolios would imply negative risk if we prolong the CML below the point R^f and this makes no sense.

[11] If we had drawn the linear indifferences curves steeper than the CML (as opposed to flatter as in 4.5(b)), then the intersection point would have apparently moved towards the south west, down and to the left. Yet, as explained in the previous footnote, once the point of 100% investment in cash had been received, that would represent the unique optimum. In other words, an investor which is sufficiently averse to risk to possess a set of steep linear indifferences curves, would end up investing all wealth in cash.

(levered) wealth in risky assets (their prices will diverge to infinity). Note that such nonsensical solutions do occur because we fail to find tangency solutions, which remain those that underpin result 4.5.[12]

3 - Increasing Risk and Stochastic Dominance Criteria

Many of the results on canonical portfolio selection in section 1 have been based on the level or properties (increasing or decreasing monotonicity) of the local measures of absolute and relative risk aversion introduced by Arrow and Pratt. However, such measures required that we would know the functional form of the utility of wealth function, at least up to a linear affine monotone increasing transformation. When $ARA(W)$ and $RRA(W)$ could be computed, the allocation to alternative risky assets could be easily characterized. Here we ask a different, harder, and at the same time, deeper question: *Under what conditions can we unambiguously say that an investor will prefer one risky asset to another when the only information we have about this investor is either that he is non-satiable or that he is risk averse (or both)?*
Alternatively, one can think of this goal as an attempt at extending the definition of risk aversion provided in chapter 2, by which an investor is risk averse if she prefers the expectation of her future, random wealth to wealth itself. Equivalently, stochastic wealth is obviously riskier than its expectation, and a risk-averse agent prefers the latter. This definition is however rather simple because it is based on a comparison between random portfolio wealth and a fixed yardstick, the expectation of such wealth. A natural extension of this discussion is to consider a risk-averse investor who *compares two risky assets or portfolios neither of which is deterministic.* In general, without more information about an agent's preferences, two risky assets or gambles cannot be ranked: some risk-averse investors shall prefer one and some the other. In this section we ask whether there is a condition on the distribution of these two assets/gambles such that if the two assets have the same expectation, then all risk-averse agents prefer one to the other. To answer these questions, we will introduce two concepts: first- vs. second-order stochastic dominance. The two notions present well-understood pros and cons. First-order stochastic dominance is useful in comparing the riskiness of assets, a difficult task, but it does not allow us to compare any two

---

[12] Even with convex-from-below indifference curves, investors might still express unrealistically extreme demands for risky assets (depending on the means and variances of returns), but, at least, they are not guaranteed to always do so.

risky assets, because it gives an (highly) incomplete criterion.[13] Second-order stochastic dominance provides more chances to make comparisons but has a more involved and technical nature, as we are about to explain.

3.1 First-order stochastic dominance

We will say that risky asset A dominates risky asset B in the sense of First Order Stochastic Dominance (henceforth FOSD), denoted by A $\succsim^{FOSD}$ B, if all individuals having utility of wealth functions that are increasing and continuous, either prefer A to B or are indifferent between A and B. Intuition suggests that if the probability of asset A's rate of return exceeding any given level is not smaller than that of asset B's rate of return exceeding the same level, then any non-satiable individual will prefer A to B. It turns out that this condition is not only sufficient but also necessary.

In the simple case in which rates of return on A and B lie in the interval [0, 1], let $F_A(\cdot)$ and $F_B(\cdot)$ denote the cumulative distribution functions of the rates of return on A and B respectively.[14] Then a simple result ties together FOSD and the comparative properties of the two cumulative distribution functions (henceforth, CDF):

Result 4.6: A $\succsim^{FOSD}$ B if and only if $F_A(z) \leq F_B(z) \; \forall z \in [0, 1]$.

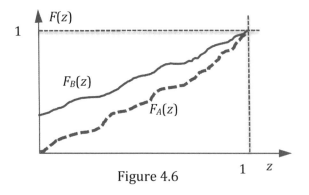

Figure 4.6

---

[13] The Arrow-Pratt measures of risk aversion are too weak to study the comparative statics of an individual's portfolio problem when faced with two risky assets. This means that even though a strong ranking exists over *ARA* or *RRA*, no predictions will be derived as to the reaction of the demand of each of the two risky assets when conditions (for instance, the investor's wealth or their risk premia) change.

[14] Extending these results to the real line or at least to [-1, +∞) is logically straightforward, but entails dealing with some technicalities that add little to our understanding.

Figure 4.6 shows such a FOSD relationship between CDFs. When A $\succsim^{FOSD}$ B, the CDF of gamble/security A is everywhere below the one for security B, and no crossings are possible. Intuitively, for a CDF to give lower values for any given z_0, is "good" because it means that values $z > z_0$ are more likely than under the other, competitive CDF. In this sense, A $\sim F_A(z)$ is better than/preferred to gamble B $\sim F_B(z)$. Putting it differently, the probability that the rate of return on asset A is greater than z is always greater than that for asset B.

Note that result 4.6 does not mean that asset A has a realized rate of return that is always higher than that of asset B in all states. Equivalently A $\succsim^{FOSD}$ B does not imply that A strongly dominates B in the sense of chapter 1. However, quite intuitively, the fact that A dominates B is sufficient for A $\succsim^{FOSD}$ B. Let's use a simple example to illustrate this point.

Example 4.3. Suppose that the rates of return on assets A and B can only take three possible values: 0, 1/2, and 1 with cumulative probabilities described in the table as follows:

z	0	1/2	1	E[z]	Var[z]
$F_A(z)$	1/4	3/4	1	1/2	1/8
$Prob_A(z)$	1/4	1/2	1/4		
$F_B(z)$	1/2	4/5	1	7/20	61/400
$Prob_B(z)$	1/2	3/10	1/5		

Clearly, $F_A(z) \leq F_B(z)$ so that A $\succsim^{FOSD}$ B but ex post, when asset A has a realized rate of return 0, asset B can have a realized rate of return 1 as well. In particular, if the rates of return on A and B were independent, then the probability that the rate of return on A is 0 and the rate of return on B is 1 would be 0.05, which shows that A fails to dominate B. Finally, note that (probably this is trivial but better be said) $F_A(z) \leq F_B(z)$ implies $E_A(z) \geq E_B(z)$ but the opposite does not apply, i.e., the fact that one random variable has an expectation that exceeds that of another random variable does not imply that former variable FOSD the latter.

The following result pins down the exact relationship between FOSD and expected utility maximization that we have alluded to above.

Result 4.7: Let $U(\cdot)$ be any continuous and increasing utility function representing the nonsatiable preferences of an investor and without loss of generality, assume unit initial wealth. Then security A will be preferred to security B for all possible utility of wealth functions $U(\cdot)$ if and only if A $\succsim^{FOSD}$ B, or equivalently, if and only if $F_A(z) \leq F_B(z)$ $\forall z \in [0, 1]$.

In practice, the FOSD property breaks down the dependence between the outcomes of expected utility maximization and the specific utility function one assumes to characterize the investor: if A $\succsim^{FOSD}$ B, no calculations will be required, provided that $U(\cdot)$ is continuous and increasing. Of course, result 4.7 has limited applicability because for any two securities/gambles, the condition $F_A(z) \leq F_B(z)$ $\forall z \in [0, 1]$ is incredibly strong. In this sense, FOSD provides a criterion that is remarkably incomplete, even though it is certainly weaker than the strong dominance criterion stated in chapter 1.[15] Result 4.7 is proven, for instance, in Huang and Litzenberger (1988).
FOSD can also be characterized in an equivalent way that will become useful to contrast with second-order dominance. Such an equivalent characterization is formally stated as follows.

Result 4.8: Let $U(\cdot)$ be any continuous and increasing utility function representing the nonsatiable preferences of an investor. Then security A will be preferred to security B for all possible utility of wealth functions $U(\cdot)$ if and only if $z_A = z_B + \alpha$, where α is a positive random variable, i.e., $\alpha > 0$. Therefore, $z_A = z_B + \alpha$ if and only if A $\succsim^{FOSD}$ B, or equivalently, if and only if $F_A(z) \leq F_B(z)$ $\forall z \in [0, 1]$.

Clearly, this result implies that $E[z_A] = E[z_B] + E[\alpha] > E[z_B]$ because $\alpha > 0$ implies that $E[\alpha] > 0$. But we have seen this already to be the case in example 4.3. Of course, in terms of expected utility maximization this result is far from surprising: $E[U(1 + z_A)] = E[U(1 + z_B + \alpha)] \geq E[U(1 + z_B)]$ derives from the fact that $U(\cdot)$ is monotone increasing and that $\alpha > 0$.
How can we use the FOSD criterion in practice? One idea is to check all possible portfolios to isolate the subset of portfolios/securities that are not dominated by any other portfolio in the sense of FOSD, i.e., to focus our at-

---

[15] In the language of this chapter, strong dominance is obtained when in all possible states, the payoffs in the support of A exceed those in the support of B element-wise, i.e., state by state. Therefore, strong dominance is a very stringent condition directly imposed on the supports of random variables, not on their CDFs.

tention only on securities and portfolios w for which no other security z exists such that $z \succsim^{FOSD} w$. Of course, such a criterion is rather strict but it would offer the advantage that all other portfolios outside the set spanned by w may not be preferred by *at least some non-satiated investors*, i.e., some continuous and increasing utility function of wealth $U(\cdot)$ can be found such that some z will be preferred to the w under examination. However, how to efficiently sort out all such portfolios of type w (non-dominated in a FOSD sense) remains technically challenging and far from trivial.

3.2 Second-order stochastic dominance

Suppose now that the only information we have about an investor is that she is risk averse. Note that risk averse individuals may have utility functions that are not monotonically increasing. For instance, this was the case of quadratic utility. However, the results that follow will remain true if one considers only risk-averse investors with increasing utility functions. We now look for conditions under which we can unambiguously say that one risk-averse investor prefers risky asset A to risky asset B. Such a condition is second-order stochastic dominance (henceforth, SOSD). We shall say that risky asset A dominates risky asset B in the sense of SOSD, denoted by A $\succsim^{SOSD}$ B, if all risk averse individuals having utility functions whose first derivatives are continuous except on a subset of $[1, 2]$ prefer A to B.[16] Although the simplicity of the FOSD characterization is lost, we can still claim the following (see Huang and Litzenberg, 1988, for a proof).

Result 4.9: A $\succsim^{SOSD}$ B if and only if $E[z_A] = E[z_B]$ and the CDF functions of the two securities are such that $\forall y \in [0, 1] \ S(y) \equiv \int_0^y [F_A(z) - F_B(z)] \, dz \leq 0$.

---

[16] We keep focussing on the case in which rates of return lie in the interval $[0, 1]$. If initial wealth equals one, then gross returns will have support $[1, 2]$ as stated in the text.

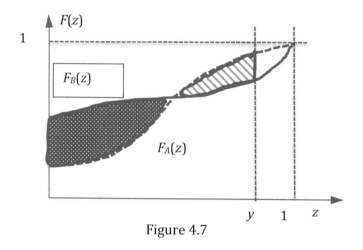

Figure 4.7

Figure 4.7 illustrates the definition of SOSD: A $\succsim^{\text{SOSD}}$ B if and only if the striped area to the right between $F_A(z)$ (on top) and $F_B(z)$ (at the bottom) is inferior to the denser area on the left, between $F_B(z)$ (on top) and $F_A(z)$ (at the bottom), and if and only if this is the case $\forall y \in [0, 1]$. This visibly occurs in the picture. Although this condition is a bit more technical when compared to the definition of FOSD and figure 4.6, the meaning is that—at least in some "weighted terms"— $F_A(z)$ is sufficiently below $F_B(z)$ for all intervals $[0, y]$ in the domain of z. Note that in Figure 4.7, the two CDFs cross and this rules out from scratch any doubt that FOSD may be established between these two gambles/securities. We now formally state the two key properties implied by the definition of SOSD introduced above:

Result 4.10: Let $U(\cdot)$ be any differentiable (with first derivatives that are continuous except on a countable subset of $[1, 2]$) and concave utility function representing the preferences of a risk-averse investor. Then security A will be preferred to security B for all possible utility of wealth functions $U(\cdot)$ if and only if $E[z_A] = E[z_B]$, but $z_B =^D z_A + \varepsilon$, where ε is a conditional zero expectation random variable, i.e., $E[\varepsilon|z_A] = 0$. Therefore, $z_B = z_A + \varepsilon$ if and only if A $\succsim^{\text{SOSD}}$ B, or equivalently, if and only if $\forall y \in [0, 1]$ $S(y) \equiv \int_0^y [F_A(z) - F_B(z)]\, dz \leq 0$.

Some references also add that when A $\succsim^{\text{SOSD}}$ B, then we say that security/gamble B is *more risky* than security/gamble A. When one rules out that ε is a degenerate variable equal to zero, we can also say that security/gamble B is *strictly more risky* than security/gamble A. Furthermore, the condition $E[z_A] = E[z_B]$ may be easily dispensed with by using the definition $(z_B - E[z_B]) =^D (z_A - E[z_A]) + \varepsilon$.

The equivalence between SOSD and *the mean-preserving spread* characterization

$$z_B =^D z_A + \varepsilon \qquad \text{with } E[\varepsilon|z_A] = 0 \qquad (4.33)$$

(note that this statistical relationship implies that $E[z_B] = E[z_A]$ as already stated in result 4.10) is due to Rothschild and Stiglitz (1970). Note that the two gambles are equal in distribution only.[17] The sufficiency part is easy to prove from concavity of $U(\cdot)$:

$$E[U(1+z_B)]=E[U(1+z_A+\varepsilon)] = E\big[E[U(1+z_A+\varepsilon)|z_A]\big] \leq E[U(1+z_A)] \ (3.20)$$

where the second equality follows from the *law of iterative expectations*, and the inequality follows from the conditional Jensen's inequality. The necessity part of the proof is much more difficult, and we refer interested readers to Rothschild and Stiglitz (1970) for details. The following, simple example makes the notion of mean-preserving spread more concrete.

Example 4.4. Let

$$z_A = \begin{cases} 5 & \text{with prob. } 1/2 \\ 2 & \text{with prob. } 1/2 \end{cases}$$

and suppose

$$\varepsilon = \begin{cases} +1 & \text{with prob. } 1/2 \\ -1 & \text{with prob. } 1/2 \end{cases}$$

Then

---

[17] The symbol $=^D$ means that the left-hand side equals the right-hand side in distribution, that is, the left-hand side is a random variable which assumes the same values with the same probabilities as the random variable defined by the right-hand side. Equality in distribution is a much weaker condition than equality: two random variables are equal if they take on the same value in every state, a condition that is sufficient, but not necessary, for equality in distribution. For example, a payoff consisting of 0 in state 1 and 1 in state 2 is equal in distribution to a payoff of 1 in state 1 and 0 in state 2 if the two states are equally probable. Yet these payoffs are not equal since they do not coincide in every state.

$$z_B =^D z_A + \varepsilon = \begin{cases} 6 & \text{with prob. } 1/4 \\ 4 & \text{with prob. } 1/4 \\ 3 & \text{with prob. } 1/4 \\ 1 & \text{with prob. } 1/4 \end{cases}$$

Clearly, $E[z_A] = E[z_B] = 3.5$ and most of us would intuitively agree that z_B is more risky than z_A.

The following example establishes two intriguing facts:

Example 4.5. Let y and z be two securities with independent and identical distributions. First, every strictly risk-averse agent strictly prefers the equally weighted average $(y + z)/2$ to any other weighted average of y and z (and also, therefore, to y and z themselves). Let $ay + (1 - a)z$ denote an arbitrary weighted average of y and z (which equals y when $a = 1$ and z when $a = 0$). We can write

$$ay + (1 - a)z = \frac{y + z}{2} + \left(a - \frac{1}{2}\right)(y - z)$$

Note that $E[y - z|y + z] = E[y|y + z] - E[z|y + z] = 0$ by the linear properties of expectations, while $E[y|y + z] = E[z|y + z]$ because y and z are independent and have identical distributions. Therefore $\left(a - \frac{1}{2}\right)(y - z)$ is such that

$$E\left[\left(a - \frac{1}{2}\right)(y - z)\Big|\frac{y + z}{2}\right] = 0$$

so that $ay + (1 - a)z$ is strictly riskier than $(y + z)/2$. Hence every strictly risk-averse agent strictly prefers the equally weighted average.

Second, for any asset z, $2z$ is strictly riskier than z. To see this, observe first that $U(z + E[z]) > \frac{1}{2}U(2z) + \frac{1}{2}U(2E[z])$ for every strictly concave $U(\cdot)$, from Jensen's inequality, because $z + E[z]$ is an (equally-weighted) average of $2z$ and $2E[z]$. Taking expectations of both sides results in:

$$E[U(z + E[z])] > \frac{1}{2}E[U(2z)] + \frac{1}{2}E[U(2E[z])]$$

Jensen's inequality implies that $U(2E[z]) > E[U(2z)]$, which implies:

$$E[U(z + E[z])] > \frac{1}{2}E[U(2z)] + \frac{1}{2}E[E[U(2z)]] = E[U(2z)]$$

However this inequality holds for any choice of concave functions $U(\cdot)$, and therefore because all risk averse investors prefer $z + E[z]$ over $2z-2z$, it is strictly riskier than $z + E[z]$. Because expectations do not matter, it follows that $2z$ is strictly riskier than z. In fact, generalizing this example, one can prove that z is strictly riskier than λz for every $\lambda > 1$.

What is the connection between FOSD and SOSD? As one may expect, while under appropriate conditions FOSD implies SOSD, the opposite fails and SOSD does not have to imply FOSD. To see this, think that if $U(\cdot)$ is twice differentiable and concave, this is consistent with the utility of wealth being continuous and increasing; moreover, if one defines weak FOSD, security A will be preferred to security B for all possible utility of wealth functions $U(\cdot)$ if and only if $z_A = z_B + \tilde{\alpha}$, where $\tilde{\alpha} \geq 0$ which is equivalent to A $\succsim^{FOSD}$ B weakly. But $\tilde{\alpha} \geq 0$ does not rule out $\breve{\alpha} = 0$ and $z_B =^D z_A + \breve{\alpha}$, where $\breve{\alpha}$ is a conditional zero expectation random variable, i.e., $E[\breve{\alpha}|z_A] = 0$. Therefore, A $\succsim^{SOSD}$ B.

Note that because $E[\varepsilon|z_A] = 0$ implies $Cov[\varepsilon, z_A] = 0$, one direct consequence of result 4.10 is that $Var[z_A] < Var[z_B]$. Therefore, if $E[z_A] = E[z_B]$ (which is assumed to hold by construction), then $Var[z_A] < Var[z_B]$ and security A dominates B in a mean variance sense, but the opposite is not true.

This last remark brings us to discuss the practical value of SOSD. The fact that SOSD implies mean-variance dominance, but not the opposite, is enlightening: it can be interpreted as a refinement of mean-variance dominance that imposes stronger conditions. In practice, while mean-variance dominance requires non-satiation and a preference for higher means over lower means, SOSD does not and also holds for non-monotonic utility functions. Finally, what about distributions (assets) that are not stochastically dominant under either definition and for which also the mean-variance criterion does not give a ranking? In this case we are left to compare distributions by computing their respective expected utilities. That is to say, the ranking between the assets will be preference-dependent: some risk-averse individuals will prefer to invest in one asset, while other risk-averse individuals will prefer the other. This is no reason for concern, but will require carefully performed calculations, often implying numerical optimization algorithms. The worked-out Excel case at the end of this chapter shows exactly that.

References and Further Readings

Cass, D., and Stiglitz, J., E. The Structure of Investor Preferences and Asset Returns and Separability in Portfolio Allocation: A Contribution to the Pure Theory of Mutual Funds. *Journal of Financial Economics*, 2: 122-160, 1970.

Chamberlain, G., A Characterization of the Distributions that Imply Mean-Variance Utility Functions, *Journal of Economic Theory*, 29: 185-201, 1983.

Danthine, J. P., and Donaldson, J. B. *Intermediate Financial Theory*, 2nd Edition, Academic Press, 2005.

Huang, C.-f., and Litzenberger, R., H., *Foundations for Financial Economics*. Amsterdam: North-Holland, 1988.

LeRoy, S. F., and Werner, J., *Principles of Financial Economics*. Cambridge, New York: Cambridge University Press, 2000.

Rothschild, M., and Stiglitz, J. Increasing Risk I: A Definition, *Journal of Economic Theory*, 2: 225-243, 1970.

A Worked-Out Excel Example

One may wonder what the connection between the EUT and practical portfolio management is On the one hand, the link is very simple: given a VNM expected utility functional that represents preferences for risky payoffs and a given time t information set (in case the perceived investment opportunities do vary over time), an investor simply wants to select the share to be allocated to the securities to maximize her expected utility:

$$\max_{\boldsymbol{\omega}} E_t[U(W_{t+1})] \quad subject \ to \ W_{t+1} = \boldsymbol{\omega}' \boldsymbol{R}_{t+1}, \quad \boldsymbol{\omega}' \iota_N = 1,$$

where the symbols have the familiar meanings. On the other hand, solving this problem originates closed-form solutions just under very heroic assumptions. Therefore, we have to resort to numerical methods, in the form of computer software that deploys algorithms to allow us to maximize expected utility by selecting/iteratively adjusting portfolio weights, subject to constraints. Fortunately, Microsoft Excel® does provide a Solver that performs exactly these tasks. In essence, the Solver takes a given objective function (in our case, VNM expected utility) and—starting from given initial values for the control variates (here portfolio weights) proceeds to iteratively search for correct directions of change (i.e., whether and which elements of $\boldsymbol{\omega}$ should be increased/decreased) and step size(s) (i.e., by how much such elements should be changed) in the attempt to increase the objective at each step, when given constraints are imposed.

To illustrate what the solver can do, we perform a set of exercises structured in the following way. For a simple problem consisting of the choice between US stocks and bonds—as represented by value-weighted CRSP index and 10-year government bond returns—we obtain monthly returns data for the period January 1994 – December 2014. We then characterize the joint probability distribution for returns on these two assets in two alternative ways:

I.   Assuming the 2x1 vector R_{t+1} has a bivariate normal distribution with same means, variances, and covariance as the data; the joint distribution can then be "made alive" simply by simulating pseudo-data from such a bivariate normal in an IID fashion; using the *MNormRand* function and inserting as parameters the means of the 2 assets and their covariance matrix, an artificial sample is created.

II. Alternatively, by applying a Montecarlo (also called IID bootstrapping) methods (with replacement) to our sample of 252 observations; in this case no assumption on the nature or shape of the distribution is made so to simply reflect the overall "shape" of the empirical density of the data; however, if the boostrap generates many more resamples than the original 252 observations, by necessity these will repeat themselves a large number of times; the bootstrap is simply generated by extracting from the Dataset worksheet, the asset return in the row corresponding to a random number generated to fall between 1 and 252, i.e., according to a discrete uniform distribution for such an index.

In both cases, we characterize the joint density of the data by simulating/bootstrapping 20,000 resamples. What is such characterization used for? To be able to compute (estimate) for any given choice of the vector of weights ω, expected utility, $E_t[U(W_{t+1})]$ by averaging over the 20,000 values obtained in the ways described above:

$$\hat{E}_t[U(W_{t+1})] \cong \frac{1}{20,000} \sum_{s=1}^{20,000} U(\omega' R_{t+1}^s).$$

Here R_{t+1}^s indicates the sth simulated or bootstrapped vector of asset returns and the constraint $\omega' \iota_N = 1$ is simply and directly imposed by simply setting the first $N - 1$ portfolio weights and then setting the Nth weight in such a way that $\omega' \iota_N = 1$. Note that because $U(\cdot)$ is a nonlinear function,

$$\frac{1}{20,000} \sum_{s=1}^{20,000} U(\omega' R_{t+1}^s) \neq U\left(\omega' \frac{1}{20,000} \sum_{s=1}^{20,000} R_{t+1}^s\right) = U(\omega' \hat{E}_t[R_{t+1}])$$

and because of this reason, one needs to estimate not only the mean of the vector of asset returns, but its entire distribution, as claimed above.

We perform six different exercises. We adopt three alternative utility functions of terminal wealth—negative exponential utility with CARA coefficient θ that ranges between 0.1 and 20, power utility with CRRA coefficient γ that varies between 0.5 and 20 (with the case of log-utility, i.e., $\gamma = 1$ also covered), quadratic utility with risk aversion coefficient κ that varies between 0.1 and 20—and experiment with both the case in which short sales are admitted and the case in which this does not occur and the additional constraint that $\omega_i \in [0,1]$ is imposed for i = 1, 2. For each choice of the utility function and the constraints, the Solver is simply invoked by setting the options in the appropriate dialog window. One example is shown below.

Here we present just a few results to give one example. First, we present how the weights of US stocks and bonds varies with the risk aversion parameters for each of the three utility functions and for the case with (to the left) and without short sale constraints (to the right). We assume joint normality and therefore simulate 20,000 independent draws.

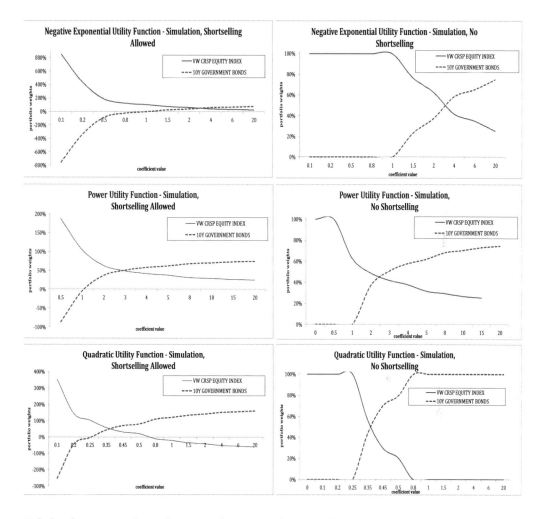

While the general qualitative shape of the two demand functions does not seem to strongly depend on the specific preferences that we have assumed, the scale on the vertical axes do reveal some important differences. Obviously, even though it remains the case that as risk aversion increases, more bonds and less stocks will be demanded, imposing short sale constraints that makes a first-order difference. The following plots propose the same experiment in the case of an IID boostrap, when no distributional assumptions are imposed and, for instance, any skewness and kurtosis are taken into account.

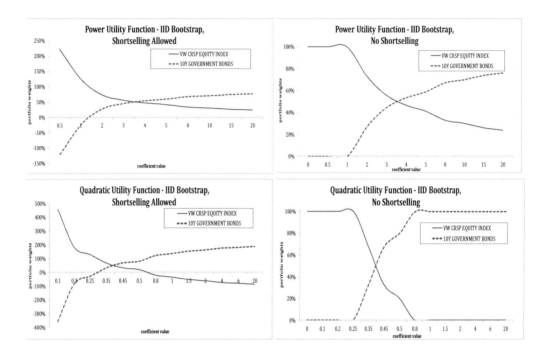

Visibly, both with and without short sale constraints, the general shape of the demand functions are identical to what has been found before.

5 Mean-Variance Theory At Work – Single – and Multi-Index (Factor) Models

"Prediction is very difficult, especially if it's about the future (...)" (quote attributed to Niels Bohr)

Summary: – 1. The Inputs to Mean-Variance Analysis and the Curse of Dimensionality – 2. The Single-Index Model and Its Relationship with the Classical CAPM – 3. Multi-Index Models and their Relationship with the APT.

1 - The Inputs to Mean-Variance Analysis and the Curse of Dimensionality

A considerable portion of the research on portfolio management in the last 50 years—at least since the seminal contributions by Markowitz on MV optimization have appeared (see chapters 3 and 4)—has focused on the best ways to make the general framework directly applicable. There are at least two areas of research that appear to be relevant:

I. Reducing the number and simplifying the types of inputs to be read as number of estimable parameters to be fed into the MV algorithm described in chapter 4.
II. Improving and making increasingly efficient the computational algorithms required to calculate the minimum-variance frontier.

In this chapter, we deal with both these issues, even though we place a special emphasis on the former. In particular, we describe and assess for their practical plausibility and promise, a few asset pricing models that have been proposed as a way to deal with the issues of complexity and parameter proliferation that otherwise plague the MV framework.

From chapters 3 and 4, we know that to define the efficient frontier, we must be able to map the expected returns, the variances, and the covariances of (among) all the $N \geq 2$ securities/assets into the expected return and variance (or better, standard deviation) of all possible portfolios. This means that—for fixed weights assigned to each of the N securities, $\{w_j\}_{j=1}^{N}$—two classical formulas (already presented in chapter 1 and here repeated for convenience) will tie together such inputs,

$$E[R_P] \equiv \sum_{i=1}^{N} w_i E[R_i] \qquad \sigma_P \equiv \sqrt{\sum_{i=1}^{N} w_i^2 \sigma_i^2 + 2\sum_{i=1}^{N}\sum_{\substack{j=1 \\ j>i}}^{N} w_i w_j \sigma_i \sigma_j \rho_{ij}} , \quad (5.1)$$

where the inputs are denoted with identical symbols as in previous chapters. At this point, it is a simple matter of accounting to check that computing the expected portfolio return requires N inputs, represented by N asset-specific expected (predicted) returns, $E[R_1], E[R_2], ..., E[R_N]$; moreover, computing the standard deviation of a portfolio requires knowledge of N variances, one per asset/security, $\sigma_1^2, \sigma_2^2, ..., \sigma_N^2$, and of N(N-1)/2 correlations, one per each possible pair of securities, $\rho_{11}, \rho_{12}, ..., \rho_{1N}, \rho_{23}, ..., \rho_{2N}, ..., \rho_{N-1,N}$. The total number of inputs (in fact, these may be parameters to be estimated using statistical methods) is then $N + N + N(N-1)/2 = 0.5N^2 + 1.5N$.

There are two difficulties with the task of estimating such $0.5N^2 + 1.5N$ inputs. The first is purely quantitative: $0.5N^2 + 1.5N$ represents a lot of parameters for most practically interesting applications of portfolio management. For instance, with a simple asset menu of 25 different portfolios or indices (think of some sectorial equity indices, some commodity and real estate indices, and a selection of the most traded maturities in the government bond markets), one faces as a minimum the task to compute $0.5(25)^2 + 1.5 \times 25 = 350$ inputs.

Let's ask how many observations will be needed for such a task. If we follow common practice to consider acceptable *saturation ratios* (defined as the ratio between the total number of observations across all assets/securities and the number of parameters/inputs) of approximately 20, this creates a need to have 350 x 20 = 7,000 observations. This therefore amounts to 7,000/25 = 280 observations per asset. At a monthly frequency, this implies access to time series that exceed an overall length of 23 years. 23 years of return data are in no way a negligible data requirement for a MV analysis performed on a routine basis. The situation faced by an analyst becomes even more dire when her investment committee has determined to use quarterly and not monthly data, as in our example, quarterly data for as many as 70 years would be required.

Figure 5.1 visualizes the trade-off between the realism of the size of the asset menu (N) and the data requirements to achieve a reliable estimation of MV inputs. In the plot, for N that ranges between 2 and 200 assets, we have computed three quantities:

I.   The number of inputs/parameters required, obtained from the formula $0.5N^2 + 1.5N$, on the right scale. Because this is a quadratic function, Figure 5.1 shows this number increases in a convex fashion; as the realism of the problem and the richness of the asset menu grows, the number of parameters grows in a more-than-proportional way.

II.   The number of observations per series that are required when the saturation ratio is fixed at 20, as per our comments above; clearly this is given by $(20/N)(0.5N^2 + 1.5N) = 10N + 30$, which is clearly a linear function, also on the right scale.

III. The number of years of data per series that are required when the saturation ratio is fixed at 20 and assuming the frequency of the data is annual; clearly this is given by $(5/6)N + (5/2)$, which is another linear function, plotted on the left scale.

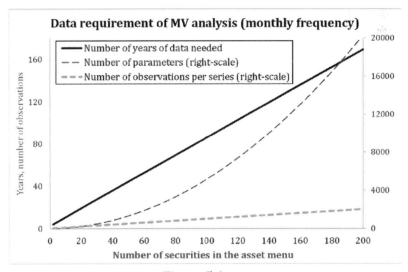

Figure 5.1

The implications of Figure 5.1 for applied portfolio management are devastating. First, an asset menu of 200 assets is still a rather simplistic one (more akin to fund-of-funds management than to mutual or hedge fund management per se); below 20 assets we are probably just considering academic, textbook examples. Most financial institutions follow at least between 150 and 250 stocks. Second, especially if one were to use monthly data, which appears to be typical of both the practice of asset management (where investment committees are summoned on a regular frequency) and of the academic research that investigates it, as we get close to $N = 200$, the number of parameters exceeds 20,000. This implies that one needs more 2,000 observations per series, and this would in principle need 160-year long monthly series, dating back to the middle of the 19th century!

In short, this issue of parameter proliferation needs to be addressed, already in purely numerical, accounting terms: few analysts and realistic asset allocation problems may truly count on the availability of one century-long time series. Of course, it is occasionally possible to resort to higher frequency time series. For instance, and imposing again a saturation ratio of 20, because there are 52 weeks in a year, the number of years of weekly observations required to provide adequate inputs to a MV problem is $(5/26)N + (15/26) \cong 0.5 + 0.2\ N$. If one takes as 5 years the typical length of the times series used in applied finance, then

$$\frac{1}{2} + \frac{1}{5}N = \frac{5 + 2N}{10} \leq 5 \Longrightarrow N \leq 22.5, \tag{5.2}$$

which means that even with weekly data and standard 5-year long time series, the largest asset menu that can be handled is a rather simplistic 22-23 wide asset menu. This is of course inadequate. Even using 20-year long weekly time series—and assuming that such series can be found—it is easy to verify that the largest admissible asset menu includes only 87-88 different assets. Finally, the use of daily data (these would solve most problems in the sense that with 5-year long series asset menus of several hundred assets could then be managed) appears to be uncommon in asset management. Moreover, daily return data tend to imply rapidly growing complexity in the selection and estimation of adequate models to forecast variances and covariances.

There is also a second difficulty with plain estimation and forecasting of MV inputs. The principal job of a security analyst is to estimate the future performance of the stocks (or other assets) she follows. At a minimum, this means producing estimates of the expected returns; because the risk dimension of portfolio management has received an increased attention over time, analysts have also started providing estimates of risk as well. However, correlations are an entirely different matter. Portfolio analysis calls for estimates of the pairwise correlations between all assets that are candidates for inclusion in a portfolio, $\rho_{11}, \rho_{12}, \ldots, \rho_{1N}, \rho_{23}, \ldots, \rho_{2N}, \ldots, \rho_{N-1,N}$. Yet, research departments and analysts within financial institutions organize themselves along traditional industry (in the case of stocks) and asset class lines. For instance, one analyst may specialize in automotive stocks and another analyst in banks. While they may be both extremely skilled in yielding precise forecasts of mean and variance of the returns on the stocks they cover, to them producing forecasts of correlations between pairs of such stocks represents a harder challenge because it requires an understanding of how stocks interact with each other, globally and within the sectors they belong to. Such a task becomes daunting when analysts are called to produce correlation forecasts involving pairs of stocks where they do not follow both. If John covers stock A, and Mary covers stock B (from a different sector from A), who will then be supposed to forecast the correlation between A and B? Will John or Mary be able to exchange enough information to make this possible? If so, will then John become able to also provide coverage of Mary's stocks and vice versa? They may both resent that.

Needless to say, the complexity of the task grows when analysts have to deal with correlations across different asset classes, because the logic and language of the task may become heterogeneous. To our knowledge, there is no non-overlapping organizational structure that allows such estimates to be directly produced. In any event, it seems unlikely that analysts will be able to directly estimate as many as $0.5N^2 + 1.5N$ model inputs.

1.1 Asset pricing models as a way to recover mean-variance inputs

The issues discussed above have spurred a stream of research concerning best practice modelling of either no-arbitrage or equilibrium asset returns, a field of investigation commonly called *asset pricing* (see Danthine and Donaldson, 2005, for an introduction). A model is defined as being of a no-arbitrage type, when the relationships pinning down the dynamics of asset returns can be simply derived by imposing that no prices can cause the existence of arbitrage opportunities, i.e., configurations in which riskless, zero net investment strategies may be set up to yield sure profits. A model is defined as of an equilibrium type, when asset prices are directly or indirectly derived from equating the supply of assets to their demand. Of course, when demand equals supply, no arbitrage strategies will be possible. However, the absence of arbitrage strategies does not imply that asset prices are expression of markets being in equilibrium (i.e., markets in dis-equilibrium may still be arbitrage-free).

Fortunately, the randomness displayed by the returns of risky assets often can be traced back to a smaller number of underlying sources of risk (often called *factors*) that influence individual returns. A factor model that repre-sents this connection between factors and returns leads to a simplified structure for the covariance matrix, and also may provide important in-sights into the relationships among assets. In this chapter, we shall discuss how asset pricing models can be used to compute estimates/forecasts of means, variance, and especially covariances. As emphasized above, while alternative sources of smart estimates of means and variances can be found, correlations tend to be problematic and this is where asset pricing models become handy. In some generality, we can express the general structure of an asset pricing model in the following way:

$$R_{i,t+1} = f\left(I_{1,t+1-l}, I_{2,t+1-l}, \dots, I_{K,t+1-l}; \theta_{i,1}, \theta_{i,2}, \dots, \theta_{i,M}\right) + \epsilon_{i,t+1}, \quad (5.3)$$

where $f(\cdot)$ is a generic return generating function that maps K factors (also called *indices*) into estimates/forecasts of asset returns (i = 1, 2, ..., N). When l = 0, the model describes a contemporaneous relationship and simply describes the behavior of asset returns; when $l \geq 1$, the model ac-quires a predictive nature. The $\epsilon_{i,t+1}$ variables are additive shocks, innova-tions to returns that are assumed to be orthogonal to the component cap-tured by $f(I_{1,t+1-l}, I_{2,t+1-l}, \dots, I_{K,t+1-l}; \theta_1, \theta_2, \dots, \theta_M)$ so that $E[\epsilon_{i,t+1} | f(I_{1,t+1-l} \dots, I_{K,t+1-l}; \theta_{i,1}, \dots, \theta_{i,M}] = 0$ and

$$E[R_{i,t+1}] = f\left(I_{1,t+1-l}, I_{2,t+1-l}, \dots, I_{K,t+1-l}; \theta_{i,1}, \theta_{i,2}, \dots, \theta_{i,M}\right). \quad (5.4)$$

In practice, $\epsilon_{i,t+1}$ captures any deviation of returns from what the model predicts. In finance this is commonly attributed to forces that drive prices and that are not captured by the common factors $I_{1,t+1-l}, I_{2,t+1-l}, \dots, I_{K,t+1-l}$.

The fact that $E[\epsilon_{i,t+1} | f(I_{1,t+1-l}, \dots, I_{K,t+1-l}; \theta_{i,1}, \dots, \theta_{i,M})] = 0$ for all possible values assumed by the common factors also implies that $E[\epsilon_{i,t+1}] = 0$, for i = 1, 2, ..., N. This means that such (often called *idiosyncratic*) influences not imputable to common factors do tend to average out over time. Note that if $f(\cdot)$ were to contain a constant index, then any $E[\epsilon_{i,t+1}] \to 0$ might be easily absorbed inside the constant of the model.

Many asset pricing models are formulated like equation (5.4), i.e., they impose restrictions on expected asset returns, although this is not a necessity. Note that not only $Var[\epsilon_{i,t+1}] = \sigma_i^2 > 0$, but also that at least in principle $Cov[\epsilon_{i,t+1}, \epsilon_{j,t+1}] = \sigma_{ij} \neq 0 \; \forall i \neq j$. Some asset pricing models impose that these covariances be zero, but this not always the case. When the zero covariance restrictions are imposed, we speak of a *strict factor model*. Finally, the coefficients $\theta_{i,1}, \theta_{i,2}, ..., \theta_{i,M}$ are M asset-specific parameters typically inferred (estimated) from the data.

What is the benefit of switching from the initial $0.5N^2 + 1.5N$ input set up to the asset pricing models in equations (5.3)-(5.4)? Assuming that $Cov[\epsilon_{i,t+1}, \epsilon_{j,t+1}] = 0 \; \forall i \neq j$, the answer is a purely quantitative one: the shift will be advantageous when $MN + N << 0.5N^2 + 1.5N$, i.e., *when the models imply the estimation of many less parameters than the inputs that would otherwise be required by a straight implementation of the MV framework.*[1] Note that the number of estimable parameters implied by (5.3)-(5.4) is not simply M: because each equation contains M parameters and this in general may be different across different assets, the total is at least MN. Moreover, to these MN parameters, one needs to add the N variance parameters $\sigma_1^2, \sigma_2^2, ..., \sigma_N^2$. Interestingly, the restrictions $Cov[\epsilon_{i,t+1}, \epsilon_{j,t+1}] = 0 \; \forall i \neq j$ need to be imposed or the very covariance matrix of the errors $\epsilon_{1,t+1}, \epsilon_{2,t+1}, ... \epsilon_{N,t+1}$, would require, once more, the estimation of $N(N + 1)/2$ parameters, once more a quantity that turns out to grow with the square of N.

To make the comparisons of the models reviewed in sections 2 and 3 that follow as stark as possible, let's list here the several features that may distinguish any given model from others:[2]

---

[1] In principle at least, the total number of parameters characterizing each stochastic equation in model (5.3) may also depend on the specific asset $i = 1, 2, ..., N$: $R_{i,t+1} = f(I_{1,t+1-l}, I_{2,t+1-l}, ..., I_{K,t+1-l}; \theta_{i,1}, \theta_{i,2}, ..., \theta_{i,M_i}) + \epsilon_{i,t+1}$, where M_i depends on the specific asset. In this case, the condition stated in text should read as $\sum_{i=1}^{N} M_i + N << 0.5N^2 + 1.5N$. However, in practice it is extremely unlikely that the number of parameters be made to depend on the specific asset or portfolio to which an asset pricing model is applied. Hence, in what follows, we shall explicitly or implicitly assume that $\sum_{i=1}^{N} M_i = MN$ for some fixed M. The appearance of a strong inequality (<<) in the condition $MN + N << 0.5N^2 + 1.5N$ is also due to the fact that the left-hand side ignores the potential need to also forecast/estimate parameters (or moments) related to the K indices that appear on the right-hand side of the asset pricing model.

[2] At least in theory, some rather convoluted asset pricing models may imply a need to build and estimate multivariate systems of stochastic equations to be jointly estimat-

I.   The choice of the functional form specification of $f(\cdot)$ that links the K factors to asset returns; $f(\cdot)$ can be linear—this occurs in sections 2 and 3 to follow and appears to be the dominant case in the literature, also because of its simplicity—or nonlinear; one important example of nonlinear, two-parameter $f(\cdot)$ is the consumption capital asset pricing model (CCAPM), when under the assumption of CRRA preferences and constant subjective discount rate N, asset returns are implicitly defined by the *Euler equation*:

$$E\left[(1 + R_{i,t+1})\left(\frac{C_{t+1}}{C_t}\right)^{-\gamma}\right] = 1 + \delta, \qquad (5.5)$$

where C_t is time t real consumption.

II.   Even though the choice of $f(\cdot)$ often makes it clear which and how many parameters the model will entail, in principle the number of parameters M may also be subject to choice.

III. The selection of the number of factors (K) to be included in the model; here the key choice is whether $K > 1$ ought to be entertained, instead of resorting to simpler, single-factor models.

IV.   For a given K, the identification of which specific factors should be included in the model.

V.   Whether or not the model should have a predictive nature, i.e., whether $l = 0$ or $l > 0$.

In sections 2 and 3, we shall explain what kind of choices of the function $f(\cdot)$ and the number of indices K appear to be typical of the literature and in practice. Moreover, we investigate how equations (5.3)-(5.4)—which are written as asset-specific stochastic equations—may be used to produce forecasts of pairwise correlations, because these represent the vast majority of the inputs that need to be fed into a MV framework.

2 - The Single-Index Model and Its Relationship with the Classical CAPM

Casual observation of the price behavior of risky assets reveals that when the overall market goes up (say, as measured by any of the widely available stock market indices), most (not all, clearly, but at least the majority, in value-weighted terms) assets tend to increase in price, and when the mar-

---

ed, i.e., when the model concerns directly the random *vector* of N returns $\mathbf{R}_{t+1}$, $\mathbf{R}_{t+1} = f(I_{1,t+1-l}, I_{2,t+1-l}, \dots, I_{K,t+1-l}; \boldsymbol{\theta}) + \boldsymbol{\epsilon}_{t+1}$. However, this does not seem to be an important driver of choices in applied portfolio management and we shall disregard.

ket goes down, most assets tend to decrease in price. This suggests that one reason security returns might be correlated is because of a common response to market changes, and a useful measure of this correlation may be obtained by relating risky returns to the return on a stock market index. This is the basic intuition that underlies *single-index models*:[3]

$$R_{i,t+1} = \alpha_i + \beta_i I_{1,t+1} + \epsilon_{i,t+1} = \alpha_i + \beta_i R_{m,t+1} + \epsilon_{i,t+1}, \qquad (5.6)$$

(i = 1, 2, ..., N) where the single index $I_{1,t+1}$ corresponds to the return on the market portfolio, here denoted as $R_{m,t+1}$, β_i measures the loading of returns on the specific asset i on market portfolio returns, i.e., what is the reaction of $R_{i,t+1}$ to a unit change in $R_{m,t+1}$, and α_i is the component of asset i's return that is independent of the market's performance. In this case, M = 2 and the two parameters are α_i and β_i in each of the asset-specific equations. Moreover, the function $f(\cdot)$ in this case is linear affine, i.e., of the simplest possible type, and K = 1. Finally, the single-index model is often presented in contemporaneous terms, i.e., after setting l = 0, which means that the model will simply yield an unconditional, constant estimate $E[R_{i,t+1}]$ as a function of the unconditional, constant estimate of $E[R_{m,t+1}]$.

When we can safely assume (and empirically get support for) the restriction $Cov[\epsilon_{i,t+1}, \epsilon_{j,t+1}] = 0 \; \forall i \neq j$, then we call $\epsilon_{j,t+1}$ *idiosyncratic risk*. This assumption implies that the only reason risky assets vary together, systematically, is because of a common co-movement with the market. There are no effects beyond the market (e.g., industry effects) that account for co-movement between assets. This assumption may seem very restrictive, but it represents the core of the single-index model, in the sense that the models performance will depend, in part, on how good (or bad) this approximation is.

We also assume that $E[\epsilon_{i,t+1}| I_{1,t+1}; \theta_{i,1}, \theta_{i,2}] = E[\epsilon_{i,t+1}|(R_{m,t+1} - E[R_{m,t+1}]); \alpha_i, \beta_i] = 0$ which means that idiosyncratic risk conveys no information on market risk: if it were the case, then idiosyncratic risk would not be such, as it would also reflect a portion of market risk. Note that $E[\epsilon_{i,t+1}|(R_{m,t+1} - E[R_{m,t+1}])] = 0$ implies $Cov[\epsilon_{i,t+1}, R_{m,t+1}] = 0$. This assumption, also called *orthogonality condition*, also facilitates the least

---

[3] Sometimes single-index models are called *market models*. However, Elton et al. (2009) discuss a subtle difference between single-index and market models, whereby the latter would not impose zero cross-sectional correlations on the residuals.

squares estimation of (5.6) to pin down sample-based values for $\hat{\alpha}_i, \hat{\beta}_i$, and $\hat{\sigma}_i^2$ in regressions of asset returns on market portfolio returns.[4] In practice, there is evidence that historical betas provide useful information about future betas. Furthermore, some interesting forecasting techniques have been developed to increase the information that can be extracted from historical data, see Elton et al. (2009) for a review.

Using the linear properties of the expectation operator and the fact that $Cov[aX, bY] = abCov[X, Y]$ and $Cov[X, X] = Var[X]$, the following results are easy to prove for all $i \neq j = 1, 2, \dots, N$:

$$E[R_{i,t+1}] = \alpha_i + \beta_i E[R_{m,t+1}] \tag{5.7}$$

$$\begin{aligned} Var[R_{i,t+1}] &= \beta_i^2 Var[R_{m,t+1}] + 2\beta_i Cov[\epsilon_{i,t+1}, R_{m,t+1}] + Var[\epsilon_{i,t+1}] \\ &= \beta_i^2 Var[R_{m,t+1}] + \sigma_i^2 \end{aligned} \tag{5.8}$$

$$\begin{aligned} Cov[R_{i,t+1}, R_{j,t+1}] &= \beta_i \beta_j Var[R_{m,t+1}] + Cov[\epsilon_{i,t+1}, \epsilon_{j,t+1}] \\ &= \beta_i \beta_j Var[R_{m,t+1}]. \end{aligned} \tag{5.9}$$

While the predicted expectations and variances do not only depend on market risk, but also display an asset-specific component (α_i and σ_i^2, respectively), the covariance between a pair of assets only depends on market risk. This reflects the fact that assets are assumed to move together as a common response to market movements. As a result:

$$\begin{aligned} \rho_{ij} &= \frac{Cov[R_{i,t+1}, R_{j,t+1}]}{\sqrt{Var[R_{i,t+1}]Var[R_{j,t+1}]}} \\ &= \frac{\beta_i \beta_j Var[R_{m,t+1}]}{\sqrt{(\beta_i^2 Var[R_{m,t+1}] + \sigma_i^2)(\beta_j^2 Var[R_{m,t+1}] + \sigma_j^2)}}. \end{aligned} \tag{5.10}$$

Note that the (absolute value of the) expression in (5.10) degenerates to 1 when $\sigma_i^2 = \sigma_j^2 = 0$.[5] The expressions for the model-implied moments in

---

[4] In practice, the market portfolio is usually proxied by a broad-based market-weighted index, such as the S&P 500 or the New York Stock Exchange index in the case of the US, or the CAC 40, the DAX, or the FTSE MIB indices in Europe.

[5] One of the most striking results in the literature is that, at least for the US data, the historical correlation matrix that contains $N(N-1)/2$ inputs tends to be the poorest of

(5.7)-(5.9) can now be plugged into the expressions for portfolio mean and variance in equation (5.1) to yield:[6]

$$E[R_P] \equiv \sum_{i=1}^{N} w_i E[R_{i,t+1}] = \sum_{i=1}^{N} w_i(\alpha_i + \beta_i E[R_{m,t+1}])$$

$$= \sum_{i=1}^{N} w_i \alpha_i + \left(\sum_{i=1}^{N} w_i \beta_i \right) E[R_{m,t+1}] = \alpha_P + \beta_P E[R_{m,t+1}] \quad (5.11)$$

$$\sigma_P^2 \equiv \sum_{i=1}^{N} w_i^2 \left(\beta_i^2 Var[R_{m,t+1}] + \sigma_i^2 \right) + 2 \sum_{i=1}^{N} \sum_{\substack{j=1 \\ j>i}}^{N} w_i w_j \beta_i \beta_j Var[R_{m,t+1}]$$

$$= \sum_{i=1}^{N} w_i^2 \sigma_i^2 + \left(\sum_{i=1}^{N} w_i^2 \beta_i^2 \right) Var[R_{m,t+1}]$$

$$+ 2 \left(\sum_{i=1}^{N} \sum_{\substack{j=1 \\ j>i}}^{N} w_i w_j \beta_i \beta_j \right) Var[R_{m,t+1}], \quad (5.12)$$

where α_P is the weighted average of the individual security "intercepts", and β_P is the weighted average of the individual "betas", the exposures to the market risk factor. (5.11) and (5.12) now only depend on $3N + 2$ parameters: N intercept coefficients, $\alpha_1, \alpha_2, ..., \alpha_N$; N betas vs. the market portfolio, $\beta_1, \beta_2, ..., \beta_N$; N measures of idiosyncratic variance/risk, $\sigma_1^2, \sigma_2^2, ...,$ σ_N^2; finally, $E[R_{m,t+1}]$ and $Var[R_{m,t+1}]$, for a total of $3N + 2$ inputs. Note that by the associative property of sums and from $\sum_{i=1}^{N} w_i \beta_i =$

---

all techniques in forecast future correlations. In most cases, it is outperformed by single-index beta techniques and the difference is often statistically significant. This indicates that a large part of the observed correlation structure between securities, not captured by the single–index model represents random noise. Interestingly then, the single-index model—developed to simplify the inputs to portfolio analysis and thought to imply a loss information—ends up improving the overall forecasting power.

[6] Equation (5.7) implies that $E[R_{m,t+1}] = \alpha_m + \beta_m E[R_{m,t+1}]$, which is a sensible expression if and only if $\alpha_m = 0$ and $\beta_m = 1$, i.e., the market portfolio is characterized by unit beta. Hence assets with betas that exceed one are considered to be "aggressive" because they magnify movements in the market factor; securities/assets with beta below one (or even negative, as in the case of some commodities such as gold) are considered to be "defensive" because they tame market movements. Additionally, $\alpha_m = \sum_{i=1}^{N} w_i^m \alpha_i = 0$, i.e., on average the market is characterized by zero intercepts.

$\sum_{j=1}^{N} w_j \beta_j = \beta_P$, equation (5.12) can also be written as:

$$
\begin{aligned}
\sigma_P^2 &= \sum_{i=1}^{N} w_i^2 \sigma_i^2 + \sum_{i=1}^{N}\sum_{j=1}^{N} w_i w_j \beta_i \beta_j Var[R_{m,t+1}] \\
&= \sum_{i=1}^{N} w_i^2 \sigma_i^2 + \left(\sum_{i=1}^{N} w_i \beta_i\right)\left(\sum_{j=1}^{N} w_j \beta_j\right) Var[R_{m,t+1}] \\
&= \sum_{i=1}^{N} w_i^2 \sigma_i^2 + \beta_P^2 Var[R_{m,t+1}],
\end{aligned}
\tag{5.13}
$$

which is a portfolio beta-driven expression augmented by a weighted sum of idiosyncratic risk measures. To gain insight on the implications of this result, assume for a moment that an investor forms a portfolio by placing equal amounts into each of N stocks. The risk of this portfolio can be written as $\sigma_P^2 = \left(\frac{1}{N}\right)\sum_{i=1}^{N} \sigma_i^2 + \beta_P^2 Var[R_{m,t+1}]$. When $Cov[\epsilon_{i,t+1}, \epsilon_{j,t+1}] = 0\ \forall i \neq j$, as the number of stocks in the portfolio increases, the importance of the average residual risk diminishes drastically. The risk that is not eliminated as we hold larger and larger portfolios is the risk associated with the term $\beta_P^2 Var[R_{m,t+1}]$. If we assume that residual risk approaches zero, the risk of the portfolio approaches exactly this quantity, or $\sigma_P \rightarrow \beta_P \sigma_m$, where σ_m is the market portfolio standard deviation. Because σ_m is the same regardless of which asset we consider, the measure of the contribution of an asset to the risk of a large portfolio is indeed β_i (or $w_i \beta_i$, in weighted terms).

In general, because the effect of idiosyncratic risk can be made to approach zero as the portfolio gets larger, it is common to refer to $\sum_{i=1}^{N} w_i^2 \sigma_i^2$ as *diversifiable risk*. On the contrary, the effect of $\beta_P^2 Var[R_{m,t+1}]$ on portfolio risk does not diminish as the N gets larger and because $Var[R_{m,t+1}]$ is independent of the securities, it represents the measure of a security's *non-diversifiable risk*. Since diversifiable risk can be eliminated by holding a large enough portfolio, β_i is often used as the measure of the *systematic risk exposure* of an asset i.

The factor (3N + 2) grows linearly with N, differently from 0.5N² + 1.5N which grows at a quadratic rate. In fact, it is simple to calculate for which minimal value of N it becomes advantageous to use a single-factor model over no model, which means estimating directly N means, N variances, and N(N-1)/2 covariances:

$$3N + 2 < \frac{N^2 + 3N}{2} \Longrightarrow \frac{N^2 - 3N - 4}{2} > 0 \Longrightarrow N^2 - 3N > 4, \quad (5.14)$$

which is satisfied (for positive N) when $N = 5$. This means that for asset menus of five securities and larger, using the single-factor model allows us to economize on the number of inputs. Of course, for large N the simplification obtained becomes massive. For instance, when $N = 100$, the one-factor model implies a need to estimate 302 parameters, while the standard approach that separately calibrates means, variances, and co-variances, implies that 5,150 different inputs need to be provided, i.e., 17 times as many!

At a qualitative level, it is a fact that with increasing frequency, analysts that specialize in specific stocks or asset classes tend to supply not only estimates of expected return and predicted risk, but also betas vs. general market movements. Alternatively, betas can be purchased through subscriptions to data services (like the famous Merrill Lynch's Beta Book) and can be often obtained for free from the finance pages of famous internet search engines. Of course, when historical data on asset returns and the market portfolio returns are easily accessible, standard regression techniques easily implementable in (for instance) Excel will deliver N intercept estimates, $\hat{a}_1, \hat{a}_2, ..., \hat{a}_N$; N asset beta estimates, $\hat{\beta}_1, \hat{\beta}_2, ..., \hat{\beta}_N$; N estimates of the idiosyncratic variances, $\hat{\sigma}_1^2, \hat{\sigma}_2^2, ..., \hat{\sigma}_N^2$, and standard sample estimates (i.e., the sample mean and the sample variance, easily computed using most statistical software) for market returns, $\hat{E}[R_{m,t+1}]$ and $\widehat{Var}[R_{m,t+1}]$. A regression model simply minimizes the sum of squares residual (SSR) objective

$$SSR(\alpha_i, \beta_i) \equiv \sum_{t=1}^{T} \epsilon_{i,t}^2 = \sum_{t=1}^{T} (R_{i,t} - \alpha_i - \beta_i R_{m,t})^2 \quad (5.15)$$

by selecting the best possible parameters $\hat{a}_i$ and $\hat{\beta}_i$. These are called (ordinary) least squares (OLS) coefficients. Idiosyncratic variance is estimated in a subsequent step as:

$$\hat{\sigma}_i^2 = \frac{1}{T} \sum_{t=1}^{T} \hat{\epsilon}_{i,t}^2 = \frac{1}{T} \sum_{t=1}^{T} (R_{i,t} - \hat{a}_i - \hat{\beta}_i R_{m,t})^2, \quad (5.16)$$

which obviously shows that $\hat{\sigma}_i^2$ is simply the minimized value of the SSR function divided by T. It is also well known that the solutions to the SSR minimization problem are available in closed form as

$$\hat{\beta}_i = \frac{\sum_{t=1}^{T}(R_{i,t} - \bar{R}_{i,t})(R_{m,t} - \bar{R}_{m,t})}{\sum_{t=1}^{T}(R_{m,t} - \bar{R}_{m,t})^2} \qquad \hat{\alpha}_i = \bar{R}_{i,t} - \hat{\beta}_i\bar{R}_{m,t}, \qquad (5.17)$$

where $\bar{R}_{x,t} \equiv T^{-1}\sum_{t=1}^{T} R_{x,t}$, the sample mean of a generic variable, x. The expression for $\hat{\beta}_i$ in (5.17) is the sample covariance of the returns on asset i with the market portfolio's divided by the variance of market returns. The following example shows how this estimation process could play out with actual financial data.

Example 5.1. Consider a portfolio choice problem with 6 assets: three major European equity indices (the French CAC 40, the German DAX, and the Italian FTSE MIB, in all cases returns include dividends and are adjusted for cash distributions and stock splits) and the three (closest to-) 10-year government bond portfolios (the French OAT, the German Bund, and the Italian BTP). Note that also in the case of bonds, we compute ex-post realized returns inclusive of their cash coupons. We collect data for a March 1994 – December 2015 sample, a length which may be realistic in many applications. We manually build a European aggregate wealth/market portfolio by simply taking an equally weighted average of the six return series.
Note that although possibly unusual, it is actually appropriate to build the market portfolio by including all assets in the problem and not only equities (if any, one may object that more assets need to be considered, such as real estate). Equal weighting can of course just provide a rough approximation to the true market portfolio. The following plots show the seven series under consideration.

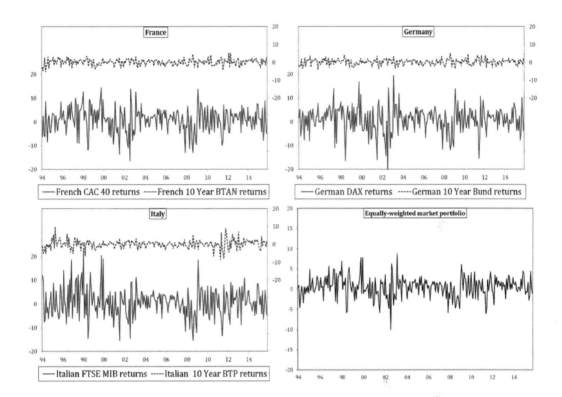

Clearly, stock returns are much more volatile than bond returns are. Visibly, the stock return series tend to be correlated, in the sense that their spikes tend to be synchronized over time, while in all series the subsample 2003-2007 tends to be stable. Because it is a diversified portfolio that also includes bonds, the equally-weighted market proxy is considerably less volatile than stock index returns are.

The results of estimating by simple OLS the market model for these six asset portfolios can be visualized with simple scatter plots in which we have also drawn the regression line. As we may expect, stocks are characterized by large betas in excess of one, in fact rather close to 2, which implies a remarkable systematic risk; government bonds are instead characterized by small betas, between 1/10 and 1/20 of stock betas. The truth is simply that a single-index model explains much less of the variation of bond vs. stock returns, as the pictures show. In fact, while the (unreported) R-square of bond regressions is in the order of a puny 1-2%, in the case of the stock indices the coefficient of determination is between 70 and 80%.

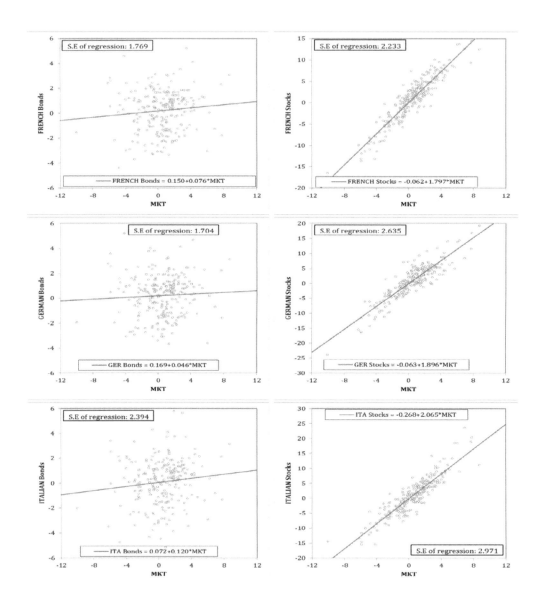

At this point, we use the model estimate to plug the parameters in the equations (5.11) and (5.12), to obtain:

$$E[R_P] = 0.150w_{bonds}^{France} - 0.062w_{stocks}^{France} + 0.169w_{bonds}^{Ger} - 0.063w_{stocks}^{Ger}$$
$$+ 0.072w_{bonds}^{Italy}$$
$$- 0.268\left(1 - w_{bonds}^{France} - w_{stocks}^{France} - w_{bonds}^{Ger} - w_{stocks}^{Ger}\right.$$
$$\left. - w_{bonds}^{Italy}\right) + [0.076w_{bonds}^{France} + 1.797w_{stocks}^{France}$$
$$+ 0.046w_{bonds}^{Ger}$$

$$+1.896w_{stocks}^{Ger} + 0.120w_{bonds}^{Italy}$$
$$+ 2.065\big(1-w_{bonds}^{France}-w_{stocks}^{France}-w_{bonds}^{Ger}-w_{stocks}^{Ger}-w_{bonds}^{Italy}\big)\big] \times 0.459$$

$$\sigma_P^2 = (1.769)^2(w_{bonds}^{France})^2 + (2.233)^2(w_{stocks}^{France})^2$$
$$+ (1.704)^2(w_{bonds}^{Ger})^2 + (2.635)^2(w_{stocks}^{Ger})^2$$
$$+ (2.394)^2(w_{bonds}^{Italy})^2 + (2.971)^2(1 - w_{bonds}^{France} - w_{stocks}^{France}$$
$$- w_{bonds}^{Ger} - w_{stocks}^{Ger} - w_{bonds}^{Italy})^2 + [0.076w_{bonds}^{France}$$
$$+ 1.797w_{stocks}^{France} + 0.046w_{bonds}^{Ger} + 1.896w_{stocks}^{Ger}$$
$$+ 0.120w_{bonds}^{Italy}$$
$$+ 2.065\big(1 - w_{bonds}^{France} - w_{stocks}^{France} - w_{bonds}^{Ger} - w_{stocks}^{Ger}$$
$$- w_{bonds}^{Italy}\big)]^2 \times (2.626)^2$$

Exploiting these formulas and assuming a zero riskless rate and a coefficient of risk aversion equal to 0.20, it is then easy to apply the methods presented in chapter 3 to find that the tangency portfolio will be:

$$\widehat{\omega} \equiv \begin{bmatrix} \widehat{w}_{bonds}^{France} \\ \widehat{w}_{stocks}^{France} \\ \widehat{w}_{bonds}^{Ger} \\ \widehat{w}_{stocks}^{Ger} \\ \widehat{w}_{bonds}^{Italy} \\ \widehat{w}_{stocks}^{Italy} \end{bmatrix} = \frac{1}{0.2}(\widehat{Var}[R_t])^{-1}\widehat{E}[R_t]$$

$$= 5\begin{bmatrix} 3.169 & 0.942 & 0.024 & 0.994 & 0.063 & 1.557 \\ 0.942 & 27.711 & 0.570 & 23.495 & 1.487 & 25.589 \\ 0.024 & 0.570 & 2.918 & 0.601 & 0.038 & 0.655 \\ 0.994 & 23.495 & 0.601 & 31.733 & 1.569 & 26.999 \\ 0.063 & 1.487 & 0.038 & 1.569 & 5.831 & 1.709 \\ 1.557 & 25.589 & 0.655 & 26.999 & 1.709 & 38.232 \end{bmatrix}^{-1}\begin{bmatrix} 0.185 \\ 0.763 \\ 0.190 \\ 0.807 \\ 0.127 \\ 0.680 \end{bmatrix}$$

$$= \begin{bmatrix} 0.260 \\ 0.099 \\ 0.298 \\ 0.083 \\ 0.073 \\ -0.055 \end{bmatrix}$$

The optimal MV portfolio will overweight French and German securities over Italian ones, and especially bonds (63%) over stocks (13% with a small negative position in Italian stocks); 24% of the portfolio is invested in the riskless asset. Obviously, the data implies a rather cautious portfolio.

2.1 Relationship with the CAPM

When does the asset pricing model in equation (5.6) turn in the famous CAPM? Assuming the simplest and more standard case in which a riskless asset with constant rate of return R^f may be defined, this occurs when:

$$R_{i,t+1} = R^f + \beta_i(R_{m,t+1} - R^f) + \epsilon_{i,t+1}, \tag{5.18}$$

and $E[\epsilon_{i,t+1}] = Cov[\epsilon_{i,t+1}, R_{m,t+1}] = Cov[\epsilon_{i,t+1}, \epsilon_{j,t+1}] = 0 \ \forall i \neq j$. In essence, this is a single-index model in which for all assets their intercepts are restricted to equal the riskless rate and such that $E[R_{i,t+1} - R^f] = \beta_i E[R_{m,t+1} - R^f]$, i.e., the (unconditional) risk premium on all assets is proportional to the market risk premium. Interestingly, the CAPM is an equilibrium model, in the sense that (5.18) emerges from a mathematical development when the demand for all traded assets equals their fixed (at least in the short-term) supply.[7] Importantly, as emphasized by Markowitz (1984), while equation (5.6) is assumed, in the CAPM, the model in (5.18) is a result; (5.18) is consistent with (5.6) but does not require it. For instance, the CAPM is compatible with a multi-index model provided all factors depend linearly on the market portfolio. Hence, although denoted with the same Greek letter, the two betas in these equations need to receive very different interpretations. The resulting modifications to equations (5.7)-(5.13) are straightforward and do not need to be detailed.[8]

The risk premium in the CAPM is a reward for how an asset pays off in bad times. Bad times are defined in terms of the factor, which is the market portfolio, so bad times correspond to low (or negative) market returns. If the asset yields losses when the market has losses, the asset has a high be-

---

[7] However, (5.18) does not imply the existence of an equilibrium in the sense that the same statistical relationship may emerge from other models. For instance, (5.18) may also be interpreted as a single-factor case of the no-arbitrage pricing model presented later in this chapter.

[8] It must be recognized that CAPM is well known to be a spectacular empirical failure. It predicts that asset risk premia depend only on the asset beta and there is only one factor, the market portfolio. Both of these predictions have been disproved in thousands of published empirical studies. See Ang (2014) for a readable discussion.

ta. When the market records gains, the high beta asset also gains in value. Investors are, on average, risk averse so that the gains during good times do not cancel out the losses during bad times. Thus, high beta assets are risky and require high expected returns to be held in equilibrium by investors. Conversely, if the asset pays off when the market records losses, the asset has a low beta; this asset is attractive and as the expected return on the asset can be low, investors do not need much compensation.

The CAPM derives the market risk premium in terms of underlying agent preferences,

$$E[R_{m,t+1} - R^f] = \gamma Var[R_{m,t+1}] \qquad (5.19)$$

i.e., γ is the average (relative) risk aversion across all investors, where the average is taken weighting each individual's degree of risk aversion in proportion to the wealth of that agent). According to the CAPM, as the market becomes more volatile, the expected return of the market increases and equity prices contemporaneously fall, all else being equal. As a result,

$$E[R_{i,t+1} - R^f] = \beta_i \gamma Var[R_{m,t+1}], \qquad (5.20)$$

which expresses asset risk premia as a linear function of market variance. At this juncture, it is useful to briefly discuss one portfolio choice implication of the CAPM. Under its strong (in some respects, heroic) assumptions, the model states that one factor exists and that factor is the market portfolio, where each stock is held in proportion to its market capitalization. The factor can be optimally constructed by holding many assets so that non-factor, or idiosyncratic risk, is diversified away. However, in equilibrium the model also implies that investors are better off holding the factor—the market portfolio—than individual stocks according to some optimal weighting scheme. Individual stocks are exposed to the market factor, which carries the risk premium, but also have idiosyncratic risk, which is not rewarded by a risk premium. Investors can diversify away the idiosyncratic part and increase their returns by holding the market factor portfolio, rather than any other combination of individual stocks. As investors diversify more and more, they will end up holding the most diversified portfolio possible—the market portfolio.

Of course, there is one inherent contradiction between using the CAPM to forecast the inputs of MV portfolio selection and the CAPM itself, because under the latter model, optimal asset allocation cannot concern the composition of the risky portfolio. Such a composition is simply settled by exactly replicating the structure of the market portfolio, which normally represents the core business of (domestic and international) index mutual funds and exchange traded funds that passively replicate wide market indices.[9] However, in practice, we understand that the CAPM is derived under extreme assumptions and that empirically the model has been bitterly rejected by a variety of tests implemented on a range of data sets.[10]

Many investors do attach importance to the CAPM (which may be considered a result of studying too hard in their graduate courses) but are not completely satisfied with the CAPM prescription that they should simply invest in the market portfolio, i.e., in passive index or exchange traded funds. Therefore they adopt a mixed approach by solving the Markowitz MV portfolio problem but working on improving the quality (forecast accuracy) of its inputs over and above using historical data (i.e., econometrics) alone. In particular, better estimates of the expected returns in a MV model may be obtained if there is information regarding the future prospects of the security-issuing company or institution to supplement the information contained in the historical record. For instance, such information may come from detailed fundamental analyses of firms, including an analysis of their future projects, its management, its financial condition, its competitors, and the projected market of its products or services. Often, portfolio managers resort to sell-side analysts forecasts and recommendations. However, an investor sometimes feels uncomfortable departing significantly from the CAPM's recommendation to select the market portfolio A compromise described by Luenberger (1997) which uses both the CAPM view and additional information. In a first step, a user would employ the

---

[9] A different issue is the fact that under the CAPM, each investor will express her own optimal exposure (hence, weight) to the single market factor and a riskless investment, what we have called the two-fund separation theorem. In other words, it is not the need to perform asset allocation that disappears altogether, but only the usefulness of active asset management and the selection of risky assets that become modest at best. Chapter 7 presents this limited view of the role of (strategic) asset allocation.

[10] The CAPM is derived using very strong assumptions: investors have only financial wealth and one abstracts from the role of human capital, work incomes, and the leisure/work decision; investors are characterized by simple mean-variance utility and hold a single-period investment horizon (but continuous time extensions exist in which the CAPM holds dynamically, in each single period); investors have homogeneous expectations; there are no taxes or transactions costs; investors are price takers and never access any private information because information is costless and public.

CAPM to back out the vector of expected asset returns which, when used as the rates in a MV problem, would lead to the market portfolio being the optimum. Given these expected returns, all other information will be incorporated to impress tilts in expected values that reflect historical, fundamental, etc. information. The overall degree of departure, or tilt, from the market portfolio will depend on the degree of confidence the investor has in them. For instance, Bayesian methods such as those in Guidolin, Ravazzolo, and Tortora (2013) may be useful to this end.

2.2 Practical implementation: conditional vs. unconditional inputs

So far, we have limited ourselves to predicate the use of single-index models because they help reducing the dimensionality and complexity of mean-variance portfolio calculations, simply by reducing the number of inputs. Therefore our objects of choice were represented by unconditional moments, such as $E[R_P], \sigma_P^2, E[R_{i,t+1}], E[R_{m,t+1}], Var[R_{i,t+1}], Var[R_{m,t+1}]$, etc. Correspondingly, we have not drawn very careful distinctions between estimates of parameters and forecasts of moments. This is justified because given an estimate of $\hat{E}[R_{i,t+1}] = \hat{\alpha}_i + \hat{\beta}_i \hat{E}[R_{m,t+1}]$, or $\widehat{Var}[R_{i,t+1}] = \hat{\beta}_i^2 \widehat{Var}[R_{m,t+1}]$, the assumption is that the future, time $t + 1$ efficient set will be characterized by $\hat{E}[R_{i,t+1}], \widehat{Var}[R_{i,t+1}]$, etc. for $i = 1, 2, ..., N$. This makes completely sense when the (marginal and bivariate, when it comes to covariances) distributions of all involved asset returns are *homogeneous over time*, i.e., $\hat{E}_t[R_{i,t+1}] = \hat{E}_{t-l}[R_{i,t+1}] = \hat{E}[R_{i,t+1}], \widehat{Var}_t[R_{i,t+1}] = \widehat{Var}_{t-l}[R_{i,t+1}] = \widehat{Var}[R_{i,t+1}]$ for $l > 1$, i.e., changing the information set on the basis of which the conditional moments are computed, does not affect them. In practice, it is typical to find that conditional expectations, variances, and also covariances (i.e., $\widehat{Cov}_t[R_{i,t+1}, R_{j,t+1}]$ for $i \neq j$) change over time as new information arrives (see Christoffersen, 2012, for an introduction to the stylized facts and key modelling approaches).

When the distribution of asset returns does change over time, *a conditional MV approach* to asset allocation is warranted. In general, the focus becomes:

$$\hat{E}_{t-l}[R_{P,t+1}] = \sum_{i=1}^{N} w_{i,t-l} \hat{\alpha}_{i,t-l} + \left(\sum_{i=1}^{N} w_{i,t-l} \hat{\beta}_{i,t-l}\right) \hat{E}_{t-l}[R_{m,t+1}] \quad (5.21)$$

$$\hat{\sigma}_{P,t-l}^2 = \sum_{i=1}^{N} w_{i,t-l}^2 \hat{\sigma}_{i,t-l}^2 + \left(\sum_{i=1}^{N} w_{i,t-l}^2 \hat{\beta}_{i,t-l}^2 \right) \widehat{Var}_{t-l}[R_{m,t+1}]$$

$$+ 2 \left(\sum_{i=1}^{N} \sum_{\substack{j=1 \\ j>i}}^{N} w_{i,t-l} w_{j,t-l} \hat{\beta}_{i,t-l} \hat{\beta}_{j,t-l} \right) \widehat{Var}_{t-l}[R_{m,t+1}], \qquad (5.22)$$

where the estimates (e.g., $\hat{E}_{t-l}[R_{P,t+1}], \hat{\alpha}_{i,t-l}, \hat{\beta}_{i,t-l}, \ldots$) indexed $t - l \le t$ represent conditional moments (hence forecasts), obtained using information up to time $t - l$, and the weights $w_{i,t-l}$ indicate weights obtained conditional on time $t - l$ information. The models from which such forecasts may be derived are numerous. For instance, one may simply obtain conditional time $t - l$ estimates using data up to time $t - l$: $\hat{E}_{t-l}[R_{m,t+1}]$ and $\widehat{Var}_{t-l}[R_{m,t+1}]$ are then sample estimates using an expanding or rolling window of data $R_{m,1}, R_{m,2}, \ldots, R_{m,t-l}$; $\hat{\alpha}_{i,t-l}, \hat{\beta}_{i,t-l}$, and $\hat{\sigma}_{i,t-l}^2$ will come from regressions that are estimated using the same expanding or rolling window of data,

$$\hat{\beta}_{i,t-l} = \frac{\sum_{\tau=1}^{t-l} (R_{i,\tau} - \bar{R}_{i,\tau})(R_{m,\tau} - \bar{R}_{m,\tau})}{\sum_{\tau=1}^{t-l} (R_{m,\tau} - \bar{R}_{m,\tau})^2} \qquad (5.23)$$

$$\hat{\alpha}_{i,t-l} = (t-l)^{-1} \sum_{\tau=1}^{t-l} R_{i,t} - \hat{\beta}_{i,t-l} \left[(t-l)^{-1} \sum_{\tau=1}^{t-l} R_{m,t} \right] \quad (5.24)$$

$$\hat{\sigma}_{i,t-l}^2 = (t-l)^{-1} \sum_{\tau=1}^{t-l} (R_{i,\tau} - \hat{\alpha}_{i,t-l} - \hat{\beta}_i R_{m,\tau})^2. \qquad (5.25)$$

Alternatively, one can estimate GARCH (Generalized Autoregressive Conditional Heteroskedastic, see Christoffersen, 2012, for an introduction to such models) models for dynamic variances and covariances (between asset returns and the market portfolio), to find forecasts for time $t + 1$ as

$$\hat{\beta}_{i,t-l}^{GARCH} = \frac{\widehat{Cov}_{t-l}^{GARCH}[R_{i,t+1}, R_{m,t+1}]}{\widehat{Var}_{t-l}^{GARCH}[R_{m,t+1}]}, \qquad (5.26)$$

$\hat{\alpha}_{t-l}^{GARCH} = \hat{E}_{t-l}[R_{i,t+1}] - \hat{\beta}_{i,t-l}^{GARCH} \hat{E}_{t-l}[R_{m,t+1}]$ (here any method of forecasting of the samples means involved will do), and $\hat{\sigma}^2_{i,t-l} = \widehat{Var}^{GARCH}_{t-l}[R_{i,t+1}] - (\hat{\beta}^{GARCH}_{i,t-l})^2 \widehat{Var}^{GARCH}_{t-l}[R_{m,t+1}]$.

There is an intermediate approach to conditioning that preserves some of the spirit of the complete, information conditioning described above and the unconditional MV approach that was described as a default at the beginning of this section. This corresponds to using unconditional, full-sample estimates of asset-specific intercepts and betas, but letting at least conditional means and variances of market portfolio returns vary over time:

$$\hat{E}_{t-l}[R_P] = \check{\alpha}_P + \check{\beta}_P \hat{E}_{t-l}[R_{m,t+1}] \tag{5.27}$$

$$\sigma^2_{P,t-l} = \sum_{i=1}^{N} w^2_{i,t-l} \check{\sigma}^2_i + \left(\sum_{i=1}^{N} w^2_{i,t-l} \check{\beta}^2_i \right) \hat{E}_{t-l}[R_{m,t+1}]$$
$$+ 2 \left(\sum_{i=1}^{N} \sum_{\substack{j=1 \\ j>i}}^{N} w_{i,t-l} w_{j,t-l} \check{\beta}_i \check{\beta}_j \right) \widehat{Var}_{t-l}[R_{m,t+1}], \tag{5.28}$$

where $\check{\alpha}_P$, $\check{\beta}_P$, $\check{\beta}_i$, and $\check{\sigma}^2_i$ ($i = 1, 2, ..., N$) are full-sample estimates of intercepts and betas. In this case, for instance, one may posit:

$$R_{m,t+1} = \hat{\delta}_0 + \hat{\delta}_1 dy_{t-l} + \hat{\delta}_2 tspread_{t-l} + \hat{\delta}_3 dfspread_{t-l} + \hat{\eta}_{t+1} \tag{5.29}$$

$$\widehat{Var}_{t-l}[R_{m,t+1}] = \hat{\zeta}_0 + \hat{\zeta}_1 \hat{\eta}^2_{t-l} + \hat{\zeta}_2 \widehat{Var}_{t-l-1}[R_{m,t}], \tag{5.30}$$

where equation (5.29) represents a linear predictive regression in which past (log-) dividend yields, term spreads (the difference between long- and short-term riskless rates), and default spreads (the difference between long-term speculative grade and long-term investment grade corporate bond rates) forecast future market portfolio returns. The model in (5.30) is instead a GARCH(l, l) model that makes the predicted variance of market returns time-varying and persistent (when the estimated coefficients are restricted to be $0 < \hat{\zeta}_1 + \hat{\zeta}_2 < 1$, see Christoffersen, 2012, for additional details on specification and estimation).

2.3 Summary of the model

We find it useful to summarize the features of the single-index model by appealing to the list of characterizations reported above:

I.   The functional form specification $f(\cdot)$ is linear affine.
II. The number of parameters M equals three per asset/security (two when the CAPM is imposed); this number must be augmented by the expectation and variance of market (excess, in the case of the CAPM) returns.
III.-IV. $K = 1$ and the single factor is the market, aggregate risk factor.
V. $l = 0$.

2.4 Determining the MV frontier under the single-index model

The adoption of the single-index model is beneficial not only in terms of reducing the number of parameters to be estimated, but also because the development of a system for computing the composition of optimum portfolios is so simple it can often be performed without the use of a computer. Moreover, these very methods of portfolio selection make it clear why a stock does or does not enter into an optimal portfolio; additionally, if a stock enters an optimal portfolio, any higher ranked stock must also enter the optimal portfolio; similarly, if a stock does not enter an optimal portfolio, any lower ranked stock will not enter the optimal portfolio.

The calculation of optimal portfolios can be simplified if there were a single number that measured the desirability of including a stock in the optimal portfolio. If one is willing to accept the standard form of single-index model as describing the co-movement between securities, such a number exists. In this case, the desirability of any asset $i = 1, 2., ..., N$ is directly related to its risk premium (average excess return)-to-beta ratio:

$$\frac{E[R_i] - R^f}{\beta_i}, \tag{5.31}$$

also called *Treynor ratio*. Assume $\beta_i \neq 0$. The ratio in (5.31) is the average additional return on a security (in excess of the riskless rate) per unit of non-diversifiable risk. Under the single-index model, if assets are ranked by the Treynor ratio (from highest to lowest), the ranking represents the desirability of any stock's inclusion in a portfolio. In other words, if an asset is included in an optimal portfolio, all stocks with a higher ratio will also be included. Conversely, all stocks with lower ratios than a stock excluded from an optimal portfolio will be also excluded (or if short selling is allowed, sold short). Finally, how many stocks are selected depends on a unique cut-off rate—call it *Cut-off*—such that all stocks with higher ratios will be included and all stocks with lower ratios excluded.

Such a cut-off rate corresponds to a special choice of the index j in the (rather messy) expression

$$C_j \equiv \frac{Var[R_{m,t+1}]\sum_{i=1}^{j}\dfrac{(E[R_{i,t+1}]-R^f)\beta_i}{Var[\epsilon_{i,t+1}]}}{1+Var[R_{m,t+1}]\sum_{i=1}^{j}\dfrac{\beta_i^2}{Var[\epsilon_{j,t+1}]}}, \tag{5.32}$$

that satisfies some special conditions. In particular, we proceed to calculate progressively C_j starting from $j = 1$ (i.e., as if the first security is the only one to be included in the optimal portfolio), 2, ... We know we have found the optimum $C_j^* = Cut\text{-}off$ when all the first j securities used in the calculation of C_j^* have risk premium-to-beta ratio above C_j^* and all securities not used to calculate C_j^* have excess returns to beta below C_j^*. In other words, C_j^* is the only C_j that, when used as a cut-off rate, selects only the assets used to construct it. There will always be only one cut-off rate with this property and it is C_j^*. It can be shown that using such an algorithm applied to Treynor ratio-sorted assets, is equivalent to stating that stock j will be added to the optimal portfolio when it pays a risk premium that exceeds the one that is justified by their beta with the portfolio that includes all securities up to the $(j-1)th$.

Although the algebra that proves this claim is tedious (see Elton et al., 2009), the algorithm is completed by a formula that expresses the optimal weights for each of the j assets that are selected in the previous step:

$$\widehat{w}_i = \frac{\dfrac{\beta_i}{Var[\epsilon_{i,t+1}]}\left(\dfrac{E[R_{i,t+1}]-R^f}{\beta_i}-C_j^*\right)}{\sum_{i=1}^{j}\dfrac{\beta_i}{Var[\epsilon_{i,t+1}]}\left(\dfrac{E[R_{i,t+1}]-R^f}{\beta_i}-C_j^*\right)}. \tag{5.33}$$

The denominator simply scales the weights to sum to one. Let us stress that this is identical to the result that would be achieved had the problem been solved using the established quadratic programming methods mentioned in chapters 3 and 4. When short sales are not allowed, the assets indexed as $j + 1, j + 2, ..., N$ will not enter the optimal portfolio because these do not belong to mean-variance frontier. The following, simple example, illustrates these points.[11]

Example 5.2. Consider the monthly percentage statistics for the following five securities and assume the riskless rate is 0.1% per month:

	$E[R_{i,t+1}]$	$E[R_{i,t+1}] - R^f$	Beta	$Var[\epsilon_{i,t+1}]$	Treynor ratio
Security A	1.2	1.1	0.8	22	1.38
Security B	0.3	0.2	0.6	8	0.33
Security C	2.4	2.3	2.0	20	1.15
Security D	-0.3	-0.4	0.1	11	-4.00
Security E	0.8	0.7	1.1	14	0.64

Assuming now that $Var[R_{m,t+1}] = 12$, we proceed to compute the C_j for $j = 1, 2, ..., 5$ and therefore C_j^* in the absence of short sales.

	Treynor	$\frac{(E[R_{i,t+1}]-R^f)\beta_i}{\sigma_{\epsilon_i}^2}$	$\frac{\beta_i^2}{\sigma_{\epsilon_i}^2}$	$\sum_{i=1}^{j} \frac{(E[R_{i,t+1}]-R^f)\beta_i}{Var[\epsilon_{i,t+1}]}$	$\sum_{i=1}^{j} \frac{\beta_i^2}{\sigma_{\epsilon_i}^2}$	C_j
Security A	1.38	0.040	0.029	0.040	0.029	0.356
Security C	1.15	0.230	0.200	0.270	0.229	**0.864**
Security E	0.64	0.055	0.086	0.325	0.315	0.816
Security B	0.33	0.015	0.045	0.340	0.360	0.767
Security D	-4.00	-0.036	0.001	0.304	0.361	0.684

---

[11] Elton et al. (2009) present a few readable and instructive proofs of the foundations of these portfolio algorithms and in particular of the origins of the formulas in (5.32) and (5.33). Of particular interest is also their proof that—when investors can replicate the market index (which is the case thanks to index funds and ETFs) and short sales are allowed—the expression for the optimal weight is simply:

$$\widehat{w}_i = \frac{\alpha_i}{Var[\epsilon_{i,t+1}]} = \frac{E[R_{i,t+1}] - R^f - \beta_i(E[R_{m,t+1}] - R^f)}{Var[\epsilon_{i,t+1}]}$$

Where $\alpha_i \equiv E[R_{i,t+1}] - R^f - \beta_i(E[R_{m,t+1}] - R^f)$ is the classical CAPM/Jensen's alpha, see chapter 7.

This shows that the optimal MV portfolio ought to include only the securities A and C so that $C_2^* = 0.864$. Additionally:

$$\frac{\beta_A}{Var[\epsilon_{A,t+1}]}\left(\frac{E[R_{A,t+1}] - R^f}{\beta_A} - 0.864\right) = \frac{0.8}{22}(1.38 - 0.864) = 0.0188$$

$$\frac{\beta_C}{Var[\epsilon_{C,t+1}]}\left(\frac{E[R_{C,t+1}] - R^f}{\beta_C} - 0.864\right) = \frac{2}{20}(1.15 - 0.864) = 0.0286$$

so that

$$\widehat{w}_A = \frac{0.0188}{0.0188 + 0.0286} = 0.397 \qquad \widehat{w}_C = \frac{0.0286}{0.0188 + 0.0286} = 0.603,$$

while $\widehat{w}_C = \widehat{w}_D = \widehat{w}_E = 0$. Of course, security E yields a local cut-off of $C_3 = 0.816$ which is just 0.048 below $C_2^* = 0.864$. A slightly different estimate of the risk premium on this security would be sufficient for us to start also investing in this security, albeit probably on a modest scale. At this point, the portfolio manager will have to assess whether she feels absolutely confident of her estimates, or whether taking into account of some estimation uncertainty may advise some positive weight onto security E as well. One of the advantages of these simple portfolio rules is that money managers who are uncertain about some estimates can easily manipulate them to determine if reasonable changes may lead to radical shifts in portfolio structures.

When short sales are instead admitted, all the securities will be traded. However, while securities A and C are held long, assets B, C, and D are to be shorted. The weights can be computed as:

$$\frac{\beta_A}{Var[\epsilon_{A,t+1}]}\left(\frac{E[R_{A,t+1}] - R^f}{\beta_A} - 0.864\right) = \frac{0.8}{22}(1.38 - 0.864) = 0.0188$$

$$\frac{\beta_C}{Var[\epsilon_{C,t+1}]}\left(\frac{E[R_{C,t+1}] - R^f}{\beta_C} - 0.864\right) = \frac{2}{20}(1.15 - 0.864) = 0.0286$$

$$\frac{\beta_E}{Var[\epsilon_{E,t+1}]}\left(\frac{E[R_{E,t+1}] - R^f}{\beta_E} - 0.864\right) = \frac{1.1}{14}(0.640 - 0.864) = -0.0176$$

$$\frac{\beta_B}{Var[\epsilon_{E,t+1}]}\left(\frac{E[R_{E,t+1}] - R^f}{\beta_E} - 0.864\right) = \frac{0.6}{8}(0.330 - 0.864) = -0.0400$$

$$\frac{\beta_D}{Var[\epsilon_{D,t+1}]}\left(\frac{E[R_{D,t+1}] - R^f}{\beta_D} - 0.864\right) = \frac{0.1}{11}(-4 - 0.864) = -0.0442$$

so that the denominator of the weight expressions is $0.088+0.0286 -$

$0.0176 - 0.0400 - 0.0442 = -0.054$ and $\widehat{w}_A = -34.55$, $\widehat{w}_C = -52.57$, $\widehat{w}_E = 32.35$, $\widehat{w}_B = 73.52$, and $\widehat{w}_D = 81.25$. Of course, these weights are rather extreme but this can hardly be attributed to the algorithm used in the calculations.

The last part of the example shows that the procedures used to calculate the optimal portfolio when short sales are allowed are closely related to the procedures in the no short sales case. As a first step, all stocks are ranked by their Treynor ratio, but the cut-off point is still derived from (5.32) when the numerator and denominator of this equation are summed over all assets. Assets that have a Treynor ratio above C_N^* are held long (as before), but assets with a Treynor ratio C_N^* are now sold short.

These techniques can be generalized to the multi-index factor models presented in section 3, see Elton et al. (2009) and references therein. However, the cut-off rate for multi-index models is different from the cut-off rate for single-index models. For example, assume a multi-index model where securities are related to a general market index and an industry index. In this model, the cutoff rate is different for each industry but depends on the members of all industries.

3 - Multi-Index Models and Their Relationship with the APT

There is of course no reason to restrict the general framework in equation (5.3) to include one single factor. On the one hand, when such a single index corresponds to returns on the aggregate market portfolio and this brings around natural ties with the celebrated CAPM, it is easy to detect well-understood advantages from such a selection. On the other hand, it is well known (see Danthine and Donaldson, 2005 for an overview of the relevant empirical tests) that the CAPM is rejected by most data on a variety of asset classes (not only the cross-section of US stock returns, in fact). This casts a long shadow on single-factor models in portfolio management and paves the way to multi-index extensions. Moreover, if one interprets multi-index models as extensions of single-factor ones, in the sense that they are expected to include the market portfolio returns and in addition encompass $K - 1 \geq 1$ additional indices, then factor models can be seen as an attempt to capture some of the non market influences —(macro)economic factors or structural groups (industries)—that move securities together. Of course, the cost of introducing additional indices is the chance that they are picking up random noise rather than real influences. Additionally, as K grows, the parsimony advantage offered by index models over the need to estimate the many inputs of MV analysis, declines.

The use of multi-index models (equilibrium versions included, such as the APT, see section 3.2) in the management and evaluation of portfolios is growing rapidly. Many brokerage firms, financial institutions, and consulting firms have developed their own multi-index models to aid in the investment process (e.g., Ang, 2014, describes in detail a few such examples, in the form of readable case studies). These models have become increasingly popular because they allow risk to be more tightly controlled and allow an investor to protect from or to place bets on specific types of risk to which she may be particularly sensitive, as we shall discuss in section 3.3. Let's start by introducing the structure of a general K-factor model:

$$R_{i,t+1} = \beta_i^0 + \beta_i^1 I_{1,t+1} + \beta_i^2 I_{2,t+1} + \cdots + \beta_i^K I_{K,t+1} + \epsilon_{i,t+1}$$

$$= \sum_{k=0}^{K} \beta_i^k I_{k,t+1} + \epsilon_{i,t+1} \tag{5.34}$$

(i = 1, 2, ..., N; k = 1, 2, ..., K) where the first index $I_{1,t+1}$ often corresponds (although it does not have to) to the return on the market portfolio, β_i^k measures the loading of returns on asset i on the index k, i.e., what is the reaction of $R_{i,t+1}$ to a unit change in $I_{k,t+1}$, and β_i^0 is the component of asset i's return that is independent of the market's performance. For example, stocks of cyclical firms (say, producers of TV plasma screens) will have larger betas to the "growth in GDP" factor than noncyclical firms will, such as grocery store chains. Likewise, you will hear discussions about interest-sensitive stocks. All stocks are affected by changes in interest rates; however, some experience larger impacts, for instance real estate development companies. In this case, $M = K + 1$ and the parameters are $\beta_i^0, \beta_i^1, ..., \beta_i^K$ and β_i in each of the asset-specific equations.

With reference to equation (5.3), also in this case the generic function $f(\cdot)$ is linear affine, i.e., of the simplest type. Also the multi-index model is often presented in contemporaneous terms, i.e., after setting $l = 0$, which means that the model will yield an unconditional, constant estimate $E[R_{i,t+1}]$ as a function of the unconditional, constant estimate of the index expectations, $E[I_{k,t+1}]$. Typical examples of indices used in the construction of multi-factor models are macroeconomic variables such as the (surprises in, i.e., the unanticipated shocks to the) rate of growth of industrial production, the level or change of the unemployment rate, the level or change in the consumer or production price inflation, the riskless term spread implied by the government bond yield curve, the default spread implied by corporate bond yields (i.e., the spread between junk and investment grade ex-ante yields), etc. It is not infrequent to find that the RHS of (5.34) also includes industry or sector dummies that represent clusters of non-market effects that stem from corporate securities (stocks but also corporate bonds) belonging to the same sector.[12]

There is also a mathematical technique—called *principal component analysis* (henceforth PCA)—that allows a set of indices to be constructed from a given set of returns (these may also coincide with the test assets of the exercise). PCA uses an eigenvalue-eigenvector decomposition of the sample (historical) covariance matrix of asset returns to extract a first index (that weighs individual returns) that best explains (reproduces) the variance of the original data. This index is called the first principal component. PCA then proceeds to extract the index that explains as much as possible of the variance of the original data unexplained by the first principal component, given that this second index is constrained to be uncorrelated with the first index. PCA proceeds then to sequentially form additional indices, ensuring that each index formed explains as much as possible of the variation in the data that has not been explained by previous indices, given that each index extracted is uncorrelated with each index previously estimated. In principle at least, this technique can be used until the number of indices extracted equals the number of stocks whose variance-covariance matrix is being examined. At this point the principal components can exactly reproduce the sample covariance matrix. However, since the first principal component explains the historical covariance matrix as much as possible, the second explains the remaining variance as much as possible, and so on, we would expect the last few principal components to have almost no explana-

---

[12] There is a tradition of building multi-index models that start with the basic single-index model and add indices to capture industry effects. For example, in such a model two different automotive stocks may display positive correlation even after the effects of the market have been removed, and this is caused by industry effects that are constrained by being uncorrelated with the market and uncorrelated with each other. Of course, such effects are more useful in stock markets-dominated (at least in value-weighted terms) by companies that specialize in particular industries. When large conglomerates are prevalent, forcing companies within industry classifications may introduce more random noise into the process than the information they supply.

tory power. In fact, to the extent that there is any actual underlying structure to the data, most of the correlation matrix should be explained by the first few principal components (see Zhou and Fabozzi, 2011, for details and one example). Most of the literature (see, e.g., Connor and Korajczyk, 1986) has found that between three and five principal components can explain a significant portion of the variance of stock returns. Roll and Ross (1984) point out that the number of factors is a secondary issue compared to how well the model explains expected security returns in comparison to alternative models. Also, one would expect the number of factors to increase with the sample size because more potential relationships would arise (e.g., you would introduce industry effects). However, PCA in portfolio choice has been criticized because it is common to find that in many cases, the principal components lack a clear economic interpretation.

Although this is not compulsory, in applied work it is also common to use as explanatory factors in the RHS of equation (5.34) not the shocks to macroeconomic and sector variables, but the returns on portfolios of securities (especially stocks) that are first sorted on the basis of their correlation with each given factor, and then turned into (long-short) spreads. Unfortunately, asset prices do not move one-for-one with macro factors, and in fact, many of their movements are perverse or at least unintuitive. Equities, for example, are a claim on real profits NS yet a poor choice for tracking inflation. Such special portfolios are called *factor-mimicking portfolios*. For instance, consider the role played by employment as an explanatory variable for asset returns. One option is simply to pick some variable, say $I_{emp,t+1}$, to measure the rate of growth (say) of non-farm payroll employment over two consecutive periods, like months. However, this choice would cause a problem: given a portfolio beta $\beta_{PF}^{Emp} > 0$, suppose we would like to increase the expected return of the portfolio by 0.5% per month simply by tilting it to be more exposed to the employment factor. In principle this is trivial: just "buy" $\Delta I_{emp,t+1} = 0.5/\beta_{PF}^{Emp} > 0$ more of the employment factor and increase the return of the portfolio. Yet, it is obscure how one would buy such a factor because it is not traded in financial markets, at least directly (there is no derivative product or exchange-traded fund that tracks any employment indicators). One factor-mimicking portfolio may then be constructed as follows: collect data on a large set of traded securities, let's say stocks, that can be cheaply and freely purchased and shorted.[13] For all stocks, a sample correlation between their returns and the employment factor should be estimated and stocks sorted in percentiles (e.g., deciles), on the basis of such correlations. At this point a portfolio is formed that goes long in the stocks that belong to the top, highest decile, and that sells short the bottom decile by correlation sorting. Such sorting may be revised at some regular frequency. The goal of building long-short dynamic strategies is to make them market-neutral, i.e., to reduce to zero their beta to the market portfolio. However, this requires shorting a large number of assets, which may difficult but this aspect is often ignored.[14] Such a portfolio ought to be value-weighted in a way that makes the initial cost of the long leg exactly identical to the short leg. This way, the resulting portfolio will give on average high returns when employment grows and low, presumably negative returns, when employment declines. At this point, the employment factor has been turned into a tradable portfolio of stocks, comparable to a market-based *index of performance of the true employment factor.*

After the mimicking portfolio has been built, buying $R_{emp,t+1} = 0.5/\beta_{PF}^{R_{Emp}} > 0$ more of the employment index portfolio makes sense, where $R_{emp,t+1}$ is the rate of return of the factor-mimicking index.[15] Of course, such a portfolio will not have a statistical correlation of +1 with the employment series, but thanks to decile-sorting and the fact that one goes both long in high correlation stocks (with employment) and short in negative, possibly negatively correlated stocks (with employment), the resulting portfolio performance ought to be attractive in the perspective that we have discussed.

---

[13] Shorting a stock implies that it is borrowed and sold without ownership, with the understanding that the same stock shall be purchased back and returned to the lender at a given maturity.

[14] Even if shorting is not possible, factor strategies still work: Israel and Moskowitz (2013) show that there are still significant value and momentum factor premiums available even if an investor cannot short, but the profitability of the strategies is reduced by 50% to 60%.

[15] In practice, the time series dynamics of the factor-mimicking index is given and what a portfolio manager ought to do, in order to increase her portfolio's expected return by 0.5% per periods consists of increasing β_{PF}^{Emp} by exactly $0.05/E[R_{emp,t+1}]$. Recalling that within all linear factor frameworks, the beta of a portfolio is simply the weighted average of the beta of the assets included in the portfolio, this can be simply accomplished by over-weighting assets that present a high beta relative to employment-mimicking returns and under-weighting those that show a low or negative beta.

Example 5.3. Consider the Italian FTSE MIB index and suppose that a simple correlation analysis with ISTAT's (the Italian national statistical agency) employment growth series has revealed the existence of five quintiles of stocks with the following properties (expressed at a monthly basis).

Quintile	Mean Return	Std. Dev.	Correlation w/Employment growth	Quintile 1 – Quintile 5
1	0.904	6.949	0.459	Mean:
2	1.084	6.049	0.248	1.852
3	0.334	4.958	0.134	
4	0.485	4.646	0.043	St. Dev.
5	-0.948	7.394	-0.149	6.439

Therefore, while the macroeconomic factor "employment growth rate" is hard to directly relate to asset returns, the factor-mimicking portfolio is characterized by a sample mean return of 1.85% and a standard deviation of 6.44%. Given everything else, if a portfolio manager wanted to tilt her portfolio to gain more exposure to this risk factor to increase her average monthly portfolio return by as much as 0.5%, then her portfolio beta with respect to this factor-mimicking index ($\beta_{PF}^{R_{Emp}}$) should be increased by 0.5 x 1.852 = 0.926, which may be achieved by buying stocks from the top 2-3 deciles and selling short stocks from the bottom 2-3 deciles.

It is also interesting to ask whether it will be easy to achieve such an increase by more than 0.9 in $\beta_{PF}^{R_{Emp}}$. Recalling that $\beta_{PF}^{R_{Emp}} = Cov[R_{PF,t}, R_{emp,t}]/ Var[R_{emp,t}] = Corr[R_{PF,t}, R_{emp,t}]SD[R_{PF,t}] SD[R_{emp,t}]/ (SD[R_{emp,t}])^2 = \rho[R_{PF,t}, R_{emp,t}] SD[R_{PF,t}]/SD[R_{emp,t}]$ and noting that $SD[R_{emp,t}] = 6.44$, such an increase may be obtained only in two ways. First, by a substantial increase in $\rho[R_{PF,t}, R_{emp,t}]$ when $SD[R_{PF,t}] \lesssim SD[R_{emp,t}]$. However, given the type of beta increase that one needs to achieve, this will imply that the investor's portfolio will have to acquire a structure similar to the factor-mimicking employment portfolio or even represent a leveraged version of the same. The requirement that the portfolio acquires such a structure may easily violate the "Given everything else" clause that we have imposed at the outset. Second, with some possibly modest increase in $\rho[R_{PF,t}, R_{emp,t}]$ when $SD[R_{PF,t}] \gg SD[R_{emp,t}]$ so that the factor $SD[R_{PF,t}]/SD[R_{emp,t}]$ acts as a multiplier; but this requires that the portfolio under consideration is already rather risky to start with, certainly riskier than the factor-mimicking portfolio.

Zero-investment, factor-mimicking portfolios can also be created by considering many factors simultaneously. This approach is more rigorous than the unidimensional approach examined in Example 5.3, because we can examine the joint significance of factors. Construction of the zero-investment portfolio proceeds almost in the same way as before. The portfolio manager ranks all stocks by each of the K factors of interest. Then each stock will be assigned K rankings. Based on these rankings, the investor can group stocks into a number of joint quintiles or deciles. If the portfolio manager wants to create 5 quintiles of each factor, then there will be 5^K groups eventually, which are intersections of these quintile portfolios. For instance, if we "double sort" on the basis of book-to-market ratio and size, we can form 25 intersection portfolios from 5 deciles in each dimension. By taking differences of extreme portfolios located at convenient extremes, then a variety of zero-investment portfolios may be constructed.

The $\epsilon_{i,t+1}$ terms in (5.34) represent idiosyncratic pricing errors. When we can safely assume (and empirically get support for this restriction) that $Cov[\epsilon_{i,t+1}, \epsilon_{j,t+1}] = 0 \ \forall i \neq j$, i.e., what is commonly called a *strict* multifactor model, then we call $\epsilon_{j,t+1}$ *idiosyncratic risk*. This assumption implies that the only reason risky assets vary together is because of common co-movements with one or more of the factors that appear in (5.34). The performance of the model will be determined by how good this approximation is. This, in turn, will be determined by how well the indices that we have chosen to represent co-movement really capture the pattern of joint fluctuations of securities. We also assume that $E[\epsilon_{i,t+1}|I_{1,t+1},] I_{2,t+1},$ $\ldots, I_{K,t+1}] = 0$ which also implies that idiosyncratic risk conveys no information on the modelled risk factors, $Cov[\epsilon_{i,t+1}, I_{k,t+1}] = 0$ for k=1, 2, ..., K: if it were the case, then idiosyncratic risk would not be such, as it would also contain a portion of systematic risks. Interestingly, because of this property and assuming that indices have been de-meaned and are represented by $\tilde{I}_{k,t+1} \equiv I_{k,t+1} - E[I_{k,t+1}]$ so that $E[\tilde{I}_{k,t+1}] = 0$, we have that

$$E[R_{i,t+1}] = \beta_i^0 + E\left(\sum_{k=1}^{K} \beta_i^k (\tilde{I}_{k,t+1} + E[I_{k,t+1}])\right) + E[\epsilon_{i,t+1}]$$

$$= \left(\beta_i^0 + \sum_{k=1}^{K} \beta_i^k E[I_{k,t+1}]\right) + \sum_{k=1}^{K} \beta_i^k E[\tilde{I}_{k,t+1}]$$

$$= \beta_i^0 + \sum_{k=1}^{K} \beta_i^k E[I_{k,t+1}]. \tag{5.35}$$

While a multi-index model of this type can be employed directly, the model has very convenient mathematical properties when the indices are uncorrelated (orthogonal). This allows us to simplify both the computation of risk and of the correlations of optimal portfolios. Fortunately, this presents no theoretical problems because it is always possible to take any set of correlated indices and convert them into a set of uncorrelated indices, as we shall see in section 3.1. At this point, the basic linear properties of any asset or pair of assets, can be characterized from (5.34) and the assumed orthogonality of the factors, to be:[16]

$$E[R_{i,t+1}] = \beta_i^0 + \sum_{k=1}^{K} \beta_i^k E[I_{k,t+1}] \tag{5.36}$$

$$Var[R_{i,t+1}] = \sum_{k=1}^{K} (\beta_i^k)^2 Var[\tilde{I}_{k,t+1}] + 2\sum_{k=1}^{K} \beta_i^k Cov[\tilde{I}_{k,t+1}, \epsilon_{i,t+1}] + Var[\epsilon_{i,t+1}]$$

$$= \sum_{k=1}^{K} (\beta_i^k)^2 Var[I_{k,t+1}] + \sigma_i^2 \tag{5.37}$$

$$Cov[R_{i,t+1}, R_{j,t+1}] = \sum_{k=1}^{K} \beta_i^k \beta_j^k Var[I_{k,t+1}], \tag{5.38}$$

because $\tilde{I}_{k,t+1} \equiv I_{k,t+1} - E[I_{k,t+1}]$ implies that $Var[\tilde{I}_{k,t+1}] = Var[I_{k,t+1}]$. While the predicted expectations and variances not only depend on the assumed risk factors, but also display an asset-specific component (β_i^0 and σ_i^2, respectively), the covariance between a pair of assets

---

[16] The detailed derivation of these formulas can be found in many textbooks, for instance Elton et al. (2009). It is just tedious but not difficult and as such omitted.

only depends on the risk factors, their variances, and asset exposures to them. Similarly to section 2, we have:

$$\rho_{ij} = \frac{Cov[R_{i,t+1}, R_{j,t+1}]}{\sqrt{Var[R_{i,t+1}]Var[R_{j,t+1}]}}$$

$$= \frac{\sum_{k=1}^{K} \beta_i^k \beta_j^k Var[I_{k,t+1}]}{\sqrt{(\sum_{k=1}^{K}(\beta_i^k)^2 Var[I_{k,t+1}] + \sigma_i^2)(\sum_{k=1}^{K}(\beta_j^k)^2 Var[I_{k,t+1}] + \sigma_j^2)}}. \qquad (5.39)$$

The expressions for model-implied moments in (5.36)-(5.39) can now plugged into the expressions for portfolio mean and variance in equation (5.1) to yield:

$$E[R_P] \equiv \sum_{i=1}^{N} w_i E[R_{i,t+1}] = \sum_{i=1}^{N} w_i \left(\beta_i^0 + \sum_{k=1}^{K} \beta_i^k E[I_{k,t+1}] \right)$$

$$= \sum_{i=1}^{N} w_i \beta_i^0 + \left(\sum_{i=1}^{N} w_i \sum_{k=1}^{K} \beta_i^k \right) E[I_{k,t+1}]$$

$$= \sum_{i=1}^{N} w_i \beta_i^0 + \left(\sum_{k=1}^{K} \sum_{i=1}^{N} w_i \beta_i^k \right) E[I_{k,t+1}]$$

$$= \beta_P^0 + \sum_{k=1}^{K} \beta_P^k E[I_{k,t+1}] \qquad (5.40)$$

(where the portfolio beta on index k is defined as $\beta_P^k \equiv \sum_{i=1}^{N} w_i \beta_i^k$ for $k = 1, 2, ..., K$)

$$\sigma_P^2 \equiv \sum_{i=1}^{N} w_i^2 \left(\sum_{k=1}^{K} (\beta_i^k)^2 Var[I_{k,t+1}] + \sigma_i^2 \right)$$

$$+ 2 \sum_{i=1}^{N} \sum_{\substack{j=1 \\ j>i}}^{N} w_i w_j \left(\sum_{k=1}^{K} \beta_i^k \beta_j^k Var[I_{k,t+1}] \right)$$

$$= \sum_{i=1}^{N} w_i^2 \sigma_i^2 + \sum_{k=1}^{K} \left(\sum_{i=1}^{N} w_i^2 (\beta_i^k)^2 \right) Var[I_{k,t+1}]$$

$$+ 2 \sum_{k=1}^{K} \left(\sum_{i=1}^{N} \sum_{\substack{j=1 \\ j>i}}^{N} w_i w_j \beta_i^k \beta_j^k \right) Var[I_{k,t+1}], \qquad (5.41)$$

(5.40) and (5.41) depend on $(K+2)N + 2K = (2 + N)K + 2N$ parameters: N intercept coefficients, $\beta_1^0, \beta_2^0, ..., \beta_N^0$; NK asset betas measuring the exposure to each of the K factors in the model, $\beta_1^1, \beta_1^2, ..., \beta_1^K, \beta_2^1, ..., \beta_2^K, ..., \beta_N^K$; N measures of idiosyncratic variance/risk, $\sigma_1^2, \sigma_2^2, ..., \sigma_N^2$; finally, $E[I_{k,t+1}]$ and $Var[I_{k,t+1}]$ for $k =1, 2, ..., K$. Similarly to (5.13), by the associative property of sums and from $\sum_{i=1}^{N} w_i \beta_i^k = \beta_P^k$, equation (5.41) can also be written as:

$$\sigma_P^2 = \sum_{i=1}^{N} w_i^2 \sigma_i^2 + \sum_{k=1}^{K} \left(\sum_{i=1}^{N} \sum_{j=1}^{N} w_i w_j \beta_i^k \beta_j^k \right) Var[I_{k,t+1}]$$

$$= \sum_{i=1}^{N} w_i^2 \sigma_i^2 + \sum_{k=1}^{K} \left(\sum_{i=1}^{N} w_i \beta_i^k \right) \left(\sum_{j=1}^{N} w_j \beta_j^k \right) Var[I_{k,t+1}]$$

$$= \sum_{i=1}^{N} w_i^2 \sigma_i^2 + \sum_{k=1}^{K} (\beta_P^k)^2 Var[I_{k,t+1}]. \tag{5.42}$$

Similarly to what was shown in section 2, if we assume that an investor forms a portfolio by placing equal amounts of money into each of N stocks, the risk of this portfolio can be written as $\sigma_P^2 = (1/N) \sum_{i=1}^{N} \sigma_i^2 + \sum_{k=1}^{K} (\beta_P^k)^2 Var[I_{k,t+1}]$. When $Cov[\epsilon_{i,t+1}, \epsilon_{j,t+1}] = 0 \, \forall i \neq j$, as the number of stocks in the portfolio increases, the importance of the average residual risk diminishes drastically. The risk that is not eliminated as we hold larger and larger portfolios is the risk associated with the term $\sum_{k=1}^{K} (\beta_P^k)^2 Var[I_{k,t+1}]$ so that the risk of the portfolio approaches exactly this quantity, or $\sigma_P \longrightarrow \sqrt{\sum_{k=1}^{K} (\beta_P^k)^2 Var[I_{k,t+1}]}$. Because this quantity does not diminish as N gets larger and because the inputs $Var[I_{1,t+1}]$, $Var[I_{2,t+1}], ... , Var[I_{K,t+1}]$ are constant across to all securities, it is the measure of a security's non-diversifiable risk.

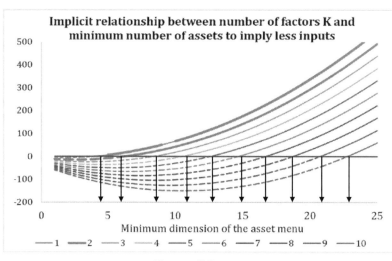

Figure 5.2

Similarly to the single-index case, the quantity $(2 + N)K + 2N$ grows linearly in N, differently from $0.5N^2 + 1.5N$ which grows at a quadratic rate. Also in this case, given a selection for the number of factors K, we can compute for which minimal value of N it becomes advantageous to use a K-factor model over no model, which means estimating directly N means, N variances, and $N(N-1)/2$ covariances:

$$2K + NK + 2N < \frac{N^2 + 3N}{2} \implies \frac{N^2 - N(2K + 1) - 4K}{2} > 0$$
$$\implies N^2 - N(2K + 1) - 4K > 0, \tag{5.43}$$

which is quadratic inequality that can be solved (for positive N) treating the number of factors K as a parameter. Figure 5.2 plots the function $N^2 - N(2K+1) - 4K$ for K that varies between 1 and 10 (these are the 10 lines in the plot). Visibly, the function is a convex parabola that crosses the axis in correspondence to an integer N that grows as K grows. For instance, in a four-factor model, it takes an asset menu of a minimum $N = 11$ assets for the number of inputs implied, $2 \times 4 + 11 \times 4 + 2 \times 11 = 74$ to be inferior to the standard inputs in a MV framework, $0.5N^2 + 1.5N = 0.5(11^2) + 1.5 \times 11 = 77$. Obviously, for a four-factor model, as the number of assets grows, the advantage increases. For example, with $N = 100$, $2 \times 4 + 100 \times 4 + 2 \times 100 = 608$ is much less than $0.5(100^2) + 1.5 \times 100 = 5,150$ parameters.

3.1 Can macroeconomic factors help in mean-variance analysis?

As mentioned earlier, a number of multi-index models have recently been developed relating security returns to macroeconomic variables. The classic paper is Chen, Roll, and Ross (1986), who followed fundamental finance theory in assuming that the value of a share of stock is equal to the present value of the future cash flows to the equity holder. Thus any factors that affect either the size of the cash flows or the function (discount rates) used to value cash flows, will affect prices and hence returns. Moreover, once a set of candidate variables able to affect stock prices has been identified, Chen et al. also emphasize that because current beliefs about these variables are incorporated in current stock prices, it is only innovations or unexpected changes in these variables that can affect returns.

In particular, using monthly US stock returns data, a rich literature has reported that only five variables are sufficient to describe security returns. Researchers typically employ two variables that are related to the discount rate used to find the present value of cash flows—the unexpected difference in return between 20-year government and 20-year corporate bonds and the return on long-term government bonds minus the return on one-month Treasury bill one month in the future. A third variable is related both to the size of the cash flows and to discount rates, a measure of unexpected consumer price deflation: to the extent that investors are concerned with real cash flows (cash flows after adjusting for inflation) or adjust discount rates to real values, the rate of deflation should affect stock prices. Expected inflation is found by time series modelling (e.g., ARMA) of past inflation series. The fourth variable is related only to cash flows: the unexpected change in the growth rate in real final sales as a proxy for the unexpected changes in long-term profits of the economy. To the extent that these four influences do not capture all of the macroeconomic (and psychological) factors affecting stock returns, there may be an impact of the market itself. Therefore, one additional factor captures the impact of the market not incorporated in the first four variables, e.g., the excess return on the S&P 500 index, which is uncorrelated with any of the four indices already discussed, as explained in section 3.2 to follow.

A large literature has found that for large cross-sections of stock returns, most of the NK beta coefficients estimated within the multi-index model tend to be statistically significant, explaining on average between 30% and 50% in the variation of the returns investigated. When this multi-index model is implemented with reference to portfolios of securities in similar industries, the resulting coefficients turn out to be sensible and of intuitive interpretation. For instance, financial stocks have the largest loading on the slope of the riskless yield curve and the default spread, because the transformations of maturities and credit risks they usually perform.

3.2 How does one orthogonalize factor series?

We have claimed that given an initial set of K factors, it is easy to obtain an equivalent set of orthogonal factors that do simplify the calculations/estimation required by a need to obtain the inputs of MV analysis.[17] To make matters concrete, we illustrate the procedure with a two-index model in which the first factor is represented by the returns on the market portfolio:

$$R_{i,t+1} = \beta_i^0 + \beta_i^1 R_{m,t+1} + \beta_i^2 \check{I}_{2,t+1} + \epsilon_{i,t+1}, \tag{5.44}$$

where $\check{I}_{2,t+1}$ may for instance be the rate of growth of industrial production (IP, or the rate of return of a IP growth factor-mimicking portfolio). In addition to all the assumptions that we have introduced above, assume that $Cov[R_{m,t+1}, \check{I}_{2,t+1}] \neq 0$, which is normally expected to be the case, as most aggregate macroeconomic indices will correlate with financial (stock) market conditions. The apex on top of $\check{I}_{2,t+1}$ emphasizes that this is the raw index, before any correlation is removed. In particular, it is easy to remove from the IP growth index, the impact of aggregate stock market forces by simply estimating (say, by simple OLS) the regression:

$$\check{I}_{2,t+1} = \hat{\zeta}_0 + \hat{\zeta}_1 R_{m,t+1} + \hat{I}_{t+1}. \tag{5.45}$$

By construction, the least squares estimates of the coefficients $\hat{\zeta}_0$ and $\hat{\zeta}_1$ imply that $Cov[R_{m,t+1}, \hat{I}_{t+1}] = 0$, i.e., $\hat{I}_{t+1}$ can be interpreted as an inferred residual IP growth series that nets out the effects of market movements. Therefore, $\hat{I}_{t+1}$ is a new aggregate index that is uncorrelated with the market and the two-factor model

$$\begin{aligned}
R_{i,t+1} &= \beta_i^0 + \beta_i^1 R_{m,t+1} + \beta_i^2 \check{I}_{2,t+1} + \epsilon_{i,t+1} \\
&= \beta_i^0 + \beta_i^1 R_{m,t+1} + \beta_i^2 (\check{I}_{2,t+1} - \hat{\zeta}_0 - \hat{\zeta}_1 R_{m,t+1}) + \epsilon_{i,t+1} \\
&= (\beta_i^0 - \beta_i^2 \hat{\zeta}_0) + (\beta_i^1 - \beta_i^2 \hat{\zeta}_1) R_{m,t+1} + \beta_i^2 \check{I}_{2,t+1} + \epsilon_{i,t+1} \\
&= \delta_i^0 + \delta_i^1 R_{m,t+1} + \delta_i^2 \check{I}_{2,t+1} + \epsilon_{i,t+1}, \tag{5.46}
\end{aligned}$$

---

[17] Note that PCA always obtains factors that are orthogonal by construction.

involves now orthogonalized factors only. In fact, the very last equation shows that the process of orthogonalization may also be re-interpreted as an adjustment performed to the coefficients of the multi-index model that takes into account the estimates of the partial model relating the factors to each other in (5.45). However, a Reader should now use caution in interpreting and describing her multi-index empirical results: while δ_i^1 can be interpreted as a standard CAPM-style beta factor, δ_i^2 now captures the loading of the returns on an asset $i = 1, 2, ..., N$, on the IP growth factor after this index has been netted out of the influence of market portfolio returns, i.e., pure IP growth variations or surprises that are not explained by general financial market conditions.

This sequential procedure is easy to generalize to any number K of factors. If the model contained a third index, for example, a surprise deflation index, then this index could be made orthogonal to the other two indices by estimating a regression of this factor on the two defined above and using the estimated residuals of this new regression to replace the surprise deflation index in the multi-factor model. By construction, these regression residuals will be uncorrelated with the already existing two orthogonal factors in the regression. A concrete demonstration of the concepts illustrated in sections 3.1-3.2 appears in the following example.

Example 5.4. Consider the same portfolio choice problem as in example 5.1, with 6 assets: three major European equity indices and three (closest to-) 10-year government bond portfolios for France, Germany, and Italy. The data refer to a sample from February 1996 – December 2015 (the shorter sample is due to availability of macroeconomic data sourced by Eurostat) and we use the same European aggregate wealth/market portfolio constructed as the equally weighted arithmetic average of the six series. Differently from example 5.1, in this case we adopt an orthogonal three-factor approach. The three factors are represented by (manufacturing volume production) growth surprises in the Euro area, inflation surprises in the Euro area orthogonal to growth surprises, and market portfolio returns orthogonal to the two previous factor series.[18]

As a first step, we fit to all series a flexible ARMA(2,2) model and treat the

---

[18] The source for both macroeconomic series is Eurostat, the "Prodcom" industrial production volume statistics and the Harmonized Index of Consumer Prices, All Items. Both statistics refer to a definition of the Euro area based on 19 countries and are not seasonally adjusted. We performed seasonal adjusting using simple moving average methods. Results are robust to the type of seasonal adjustment performed.

residuals of the model as the surprises that were perceived in real time by the investors. ARMA(2,2) just represents a filter that captures the expectations that an investor may reasonably form about the future of a series based on its past. Of course, other time series (or even economic) models might be applied in the attempt to extract surprises from the raw (seasonally adjusted) monthly series for industrial production and consumer price inflation. The two resulting series of surprises are plotted below.

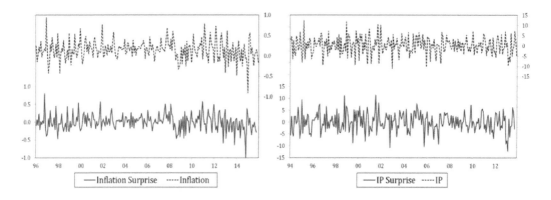

However, these two series are not yet orthogonal to each other and to the market portfolio. In fact, at this point, the sample correlation matrix of the three proposed factors (in the order *growth, inflation, market*), is:

$$\widehat{Corr} = \begin{bmatrix} 1 & 0.049 & 0.170 \\ 0.049 & 1 & -0.038 \\ 0.170 & -0.038 & 1 \end{bmatrix}.$$

In particular, as we should probably expect, growth surprises positively correlate with market portfolio returns. In order to make the three factors orthogonal, we then fix growth surprises as the base factor and proceed in the following way. Note that the order in which the following two steps are performed matters. First, we regress inflation surprises on growth surprises, obtaining that:

$$inflation_{surprise,t} = 2.47 \times 10^{-5} + 0.0031 ip_{surprise,t} + \hat{u}_t^{inflation}.$$

The link is of course weak, as the sample correlation matrix made us suspect. In any event, we use $\hat{u}_t^{inflation}$ as our factor which, by construction, is now orthogonal to $ip_{surprise,t}$. Next, we regress equally weighted market portfolio returns on growth surprises and orthogonalized inflation surprises, obtaining:

$$R_t^{mkt} = 0.4953 + 0.0106ip_{surprise,t} - 0.7196\hat{u}_t^{inflation} + \hat{u}_t^{mkt}.$$

We treat $\hat{u}_t^{mkt}$ as our third factor. We have implicitly considered the returns to the market portfolio to be surprises. The two new factors ($ip_{surprise,t}$ has been plotted already), $\hat{u}_t^{inflation}$ and $\hat{u}_t^{mkt}$ are plotted below, also in comparison to the original series, $inflation_{surprise,t}$ and R_t^{mkt}.

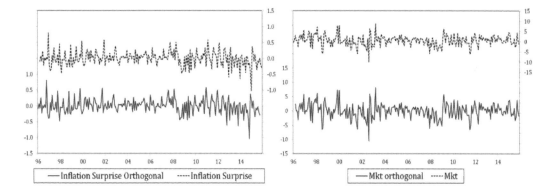

Visibly, the orthogonalized series are almost identical to the original series. We have checked that the three surprise, orthogonalized factors are now uncorrelated in pairs, which does simplify considerably the calculations that follow. The following table reports the OLS estimates of the factor exposures for each of the six portfolios under investigation (p-values are in parentheses and coefficients significant at a confidence level of 90% or higher have been boldfaced):

Portfolio	$\hat{\beta}_i^0$	$\hat{\beta}_i^{IP}$	$\hat{\beta}_i^{infl}$	$\hat{\beta}_i^{mkt}$	$\hat{\sigma}_i$	R-square (%)
French 10Y BTAN	**0.203** (0.066)	0.027 (0.327)	-0.481 (0.315)	0.061 (0.140)	1.689	1.760
French CAC 40	**0.845** (0.000)	0.014 (0.664)	**-1.237** (0.031)	**1.826** (0.000)	2.014	85.74
German 10Y Bund	**0.212** (0.052)	0.008 (0.778)	-0.289 (0.540)	0.032 (0.428)	1.669	0.464
German DAX	**0.814** (0.000)	0.037 (0.382)	-0.564 (0.449)	**1.919** (0.000)	2.628	79.55
Italian 10Y BTP	0.127 (0.393)	0.041 (0.268)	-0.986 (0.128)	0.076 (0.173)	2.280	2.281
Italian FTSE MIB	**0.771** (0.000)	-0.064 (0.147)	-0.764 (0.318)	**2.087** (0.000)	2.700	81.36

Unfortunately, switching to multi-index model further improves the fit to stock returns data, but does little to increase by much the R square for the government bond return series. These appear not to respond to growth surprises and to imprecisely respond (i.e., the estimate coefficients are systematically negative as one expects but with large standard errors) to inflation surprises. A positive inflation surprise—in this case, independent of growth news—hurts bond returns because it presumably triggers a central bank reaction consisting in tighter credit conditions and higher short-term rates that usually are transmitted to lower long-term bond prices. Interestingly, surprises to industrial production hardly produce any effects on either stock or bond returns. Stock returns seem to respond to general financial market conditions but not the real side of the economy, as measured here. As for bond returns, it would probably be important to incorporate monetary factors over and beyond inflation surprises.

At this point, we use the model estimates to plug the parameters in the equations (5.37), (5.38), and (5.40), to obtain the following estimates of the model implied vector of means and covariance matrix (we use tildas over estimated sample quantities to stress that they are different from those obtained from the single-index model in example 5.1):

$$\tilde{E}[R_t] = \begin{bmatrix} 0.203 \\ 0.845 \\ 0.212 \\ 0.814 \\ 0.127 \\ 0.771 \end{bmatrix} \quad \widetilde{Var}[R_t] = \begin{bmatrix} 2.905 & 0.839 & 0.025 & 0.872 & 0.076 & 0.907 \\ 0.839 & 28.123 & 0.063 & 25.249 & 1.072 & 27.446 \\ 0.025 & 0.063 & 2.798 & 0.455 & 0.038 & 0.484 \\ 0.872 & 25.249 & 0.455 & 33.433 & 1.103 & 28.791 \\ 0.076 & 1.072 & 0.038 & 1.103 & 5.319 & 1.139 \\ 0.907 & 27.446 & 0.484 & 28.791 & 1.139 & 38.715 \end{bmatrix}$$

which are (never dramatically) different from those in example 5.1. However, such small differences may eventually amount to important heterogeneity when it comes to optimal weight calculations. Exploiting the standard tangency, MV formula and assuming a zero riskless rate and a coefficient of risk aversion equal to 0.2, the tangency portfolio is:

$$\hat{\omega} \equiv \begin{bmatrix} \hat{w}_{bonds}^{France} \\ \hat{w}_{stocks}^{France} \\ \hat{w}_{bonds}^{Ger} \\ \hat{w}_{stocks}^{Ger} \\ \hat{w}_{bonds}^{Italy} \\ \hat{w}_{stocks}^{Italy} \end{bmatrix} = \frac{1}{0.2} (\widetilde{Var}[R_t])^{-1} \tilde{E}[R_t] = \begin{bmatrix} 0.305 \\ 0.160 \\ 0.375 \\ 0.026 \\ 0.085 \\ -0.048 \end{bmatrix}$$

The optimal MV portfolio will overweight French and German securities even more than in example 5.1, and especially bonds (76%) over stocks

(14% with a small negative position in Italian stocks); 10% of the portfolio is invested in the riskless assets. This is due to the fact that the multi-index model reveals implied correlations that tend to be structurally lower than under a single-index model: hence a risk-averse investor can keep the same (modest) amount invested in stocks (14% vs. 13% in example 5.1) but use risky long-term government bonds to hedge risk instead of resorting to cash positions that give no risk premium.

3.3 Relationship with the Arbitrage Pricing Theory (APT)

The model in equation (5.34) bears close links to another key asset pricing framework that represents a cornerstone of modern theory of finance, the APT (Arbitrage Pricing Theory) developed by Ross (1976). The APT is a no-arbitrage model that restricts *asset risk premia* to prevent the possibility of arbitrage strategies. The (unconditional) risk premium on an asset is simply the mean excess return on the same, i.e., $E[R_{i,t} - R^f]$. Of course, because ruling out arbitrage is weaker than imposing a fully-fledged equilibrium, the fact that the APT holds does not rule out the CAPM.[19] When interpreted as an empirical implementation of the APT, the model in (5.34) carries the intuition that assets pay risk premia, not because the assets themselves earn risk premia, but because assets are instead *bundles of factor risks*, and it is the exposures to the underlying factor risks that earn risk premia.[20] Therefore, factors matter, not assets and rational investing re-

---

[19] The APT obtains under weaker assumptions than the CAPM: for instance, no restrictions are imposed on preferences. As argued by Elton et al. (2009), it is possible for the CAPM to hold for each of the individual (tradable) factors that appear in the APT and hence for all securities or assets, even though a multi-index representation exists and fails to be rejected by the data.

[20] As discussed by Ang (2014), some asset classes can be considered factors themselves—like equities and government bonds, which are indeed static, buy-and-hold factors—while other assets contain many different factors. For instance, corporate bonds, hedge funds, and private equity contain different amounts of equity risk, volatility risk, interest rate risk, and default risk. The boundary separating static and dynamic factors is fuzzy. Asset-class excess returns over the riskless rate—for example, from holding a value-weighted stock market index—are the prototypical static factor premia, yet even these portfolios require some asset turnover due to, for example, new issuance and new entries to an index. Momentum strategy profits are at the other extreme, the prototypical dynamic factor premia with more than 100% annual turnover. The 2007-2009 financial crisis demonstrated that asset class labels can be highly misleading, lulling investors into the belief that they are safely diversified when in fact they are not, see e.g., Ilmanen and Kizer (2012).

quires looking through asset class labels to understand their factor "content". The model can be represented as:

$$R_{i,t+1} = \left(R^f + \sum_{k=1}^{K} \beta_i^k E[I_{k,t+1}]\right) + \sum_{k=1}^{K} \beta_i^k \tilde{I}_{k,t+1} + \epsilon_{i,t+1} \qquad (5.47)$$

and, under no arbitrage, it must be $E[R_{i,t+1}] - R^f = \sum_{k=1}^{K} \beta_i^k E[I_{k,t+1}]$. When factor-mimicking portfolios may be formed, then

$$R_{i,t+1} = R^f + \sum_{k=1}^{K} \beta_i^k E[FMR_{k,t+1}\text{-}R^f] + \sum_{k=1}^{K} \beta_i^k (FMR_{k,t+1} + R^f) + \epsilon_{i,t+1}, (5.48)$$

where $FMR_{k,t+1}$ is the return on the kth factor-mimicking portfolio and $E[FMR_{k,t+1}\text{-}R^f]$ is the risk premium on such a portfolio. Although this is not the subject of this book, it is also possible to use multi-step, sequential estimation procedures (e.g., the famous Fama-MacBeth's approach) to obtain the risk premia parameters $\lambda_1, \lambda_2, ..., \lambda_K$ as estimates in the no-arbitrage mean representation $E[R_{i,t+1}] - R^f = \sum_{k=1}^{K} \beta_i^k \lambda_k$.

3.4 Which factors among many?

Some famous factors that have received a clear interpretation—either behavioral, i.e., not necessarily based on the standard theory of efficient and maximizing investors, or rational—in an APT perspective are: the inflation rate, the rate of growth of the economy (e.g., as captured by industrial production, aggregate sales, employment numbers or the unemployment rate change), volatility (e.g., as captured by the option-implied VIX index), real productivity risk (e.g., as measured by total factor productivity), demographic risk (i.e., shocks to a birth rate index), the market portfolio, the size, value, and momentum factors.[21] The market, size, value, and momentum factors are often defined to be *investment style* factors and reflect the seminal strand of literature started by Fama and French (1993);[22] infla-

---

[21] The VIX index is a measure of option volatilities on the S&P 500 maintained by the Chicago Board Options Exchange.

[22] These factors are also called "smart beta" and "alternative beta," mostly by practitioners, or dynamic factors because the associated mimicking portfolios require highly

tion, growth, volatility, productivity, etc. are considered to be *macroeco-nomic* factors. The two types of factors are of course linked, and macro fac-tors are often embedded in the performance of investment factors and cor-related with them.[23] Macro factors are often responsible for a lot of the variation in expected returns, at least in the US. All these factors need to have a pervasive influence on the returns of all (at least, most) asset clas-ses to be considered as APT indices and to be unpredictable, i.e., to repre-sent true risk, see e.g., Berry, Burmeister, and McElroy (1988). [24] This means that predictable variables (especially when close to contain a unit root, e.g., real GDP, real consumption, the realized inflation rate, etc.) and firm-specific events and variables cannot represent legitimate APT factors. The level of a factor often does not matter as much as a shock to a factor. Many macro factors are persistent: for instance, when inflation or a risk-less yield is low today, we know that it will very likely be low next month. The fact that it is then low at the end of the month is no surprise. What is surprising are any movements in macro factors not anticipated at the be-ginning of the period. As we have already mentioned, multi-factor models often use shocks to factors and not their level or growth rate.

The investment style factors are generally tradable, either directly (think of the exchange traded funds that easily and cheaply allow us to trade the market portfolio), or indirectly. The macro factors are usually not tradable instead and in this case one may need to form/structure appropriate and tradable factor-mimicking portfolios, see example 5.2.

Volatility is a special and rather novel factor because it is characterized by a negative price of risk. To collect a volatility premium requires selling vol-

---

dynamic trading strategies. An important feature of dynamic factors is that they re-move market exposure because they have a long-short structure.

[23] Ilmanen, Maloney, and Ross (2014) present empirical evidence, based on US data, on the sensitivity of investment (traditional long-only asset class premia and alterna-tive long/short style premia) to macroeconomic risk factors (such as economic growth and inflation). They find that investment style factors are less sensitive than asset-class premia to macroeconomic environments.

[24] A famous, alternative set of risk factors is represented by MSCI Barra's, that at one point in time featured the following factors: Market variance, "Success" (similar to standard momentum), Size, Trading Activity, Growth Orientation (a measure designed to predict subsequent growth in earnings per share), Book to Price, Earnings to Price, Earnings Variability, Financial Leverage, Foreign Income (the proportion of earnings derived from foreign sources), Labor Intensity (the ratio between labor and capital costs), and the Dividend Yield. Barra's model is continuously updated of course; a re-cent academic presentation can be found in Fabozzi, Vardharaj, and Jones (2011).

atility protection, especially selling out-of-the-money put options.[25] Selling volatility is not a free lunch: it produces high and steady payoffs during stable times. Then, rather episodically, a huge crash occurs that causes sellers of volatility to experience large, negative payoffs. Selling volatility is like selling insurance. During normal times, you collect a premium for withstanding the inevitable large losses that occur every decade or so. The losses endured when volatility spikes represent insurance payouts to investors who purchased volatility protection. Only investors who can tolerate periods of very high volatility—which tend to coincide with negative returns on most risky assets—should be selling volatility protection through derivatives markets.

The *size factor* captures the tendency of small cap stocks to yield a higher average excess returns than large caps. It is indeed mimicked by dynamic strategies that pocket the spread in returns between the top deciles stocks (i.e., going long in them) and bottom deciles stocks (i.e., shorting them) when ranked by their total market capitalization (also after adjusting for CAPM beta exposure).[26] The corresponding dynamic strategy is also called SMB, from "small-minus-large". The rational background to this premium is that small-cap stocks receive less analyst coverage or less attention in general, so it takes longer for information about them to diffuse. Ambiguity aversion may also explain why investors require a risk premium on small-cap companies, which tend not to be well-known to most.

The *value factor* captures the tendency of high book-to-market stocks to yield a higher average excess return than growth-oriented, low book-to-market stocks. However, many portfolio managers derive qualitatively similar signals from the price-earnings, price-to-cash flows, and price-dividend ratios. Value is indeed mimicked by dynamic strategies that pocket the spread in returns between the top deciles stocks (i.e., going long

---

[25] The VIX index trades, on average, above the volatilities observed in actual stocks: VIX implied volatilities are approximately 2% to 3%, on average, higher than realized volatilities. Options are thus expensive, on average, and investors can collect the volatility premium by short volatility strategies. This 2-3% difference represents a proxy of the (negative) volatility risk premium.

[26] Ang (2014) describes the progressive weakening of the size premium (i.e., the average return of the SMB dynamic strategy) over time. For instance, Fama and French (2012) find no size premia in an extensive international data set in recent periods. It has been suggested that size would no longer deserve to be a systematic factor and should be removed from the Fama-French model. However, there is also evidence of structure in the time-variation of the mean, variance, Sharpe ratio, and more generally in the statistical features of the SMB strategy, see Guidolin and Timmermann (2008).

in them) and bottom deciles stocks (i.e., shorting them) when ranked by book-to-market ratio (also after adjusting for CAPM beta exposure). The corresponding dynamic strategy is also called HML, from "high-minus-low" (book-to market ratio). Basically, a value strategy consists of buying stocks that have low prices (normalized by book value, sales, earnings, or dividends, etc.) and selling stocks that have high prices (again appropriately normalized). Value in essence buys assets with high yields (or low prices) and sells assets with low yields (or high prices). While in equities the strategy is called value-growth investing, the same strategy of buying high-yielding assets and selling low-yielding assets works in all asset classes but goes by different names. In fixed income, the value strategy is called "riding the yield curve" that pays out a duration premium; in commodities, it is called the "roll return" strategy, and the sign of the return is related to whether the future curve is upward- or downward-sloping; in foreign exchange markets, the strategy is called carry (long currencies with high interest rates and short currencies with low interest rates).[27]

Momentum is the strategy of buying stocks that have gone up over the past six (or so) months (winners), and shorting stocks with the lowest returns over the same period (losers), see Carhart (1997). The momentum effect refers to the phenomenon that winner stocks continue to win and losers continue to lose. We call the momentum-mimicking factor WML, for past winners minus past losers. Momentum is also observed in many asset classes besides stocks, such as international equities, commodities, government bonds, corporate bonds, industries and sectors, and real estate. In one sense, momentum is the opposite of value. Value is a negative feedback strategy, where stocks with declining prices eventually fall far enough that they become value stocks. Then value investors buy them when they have fallen enough to have attractive expected returns. Value investing is inherently stabilizing. Momentum is a positive feedback strategy. Stocks with high past returns are attractive, momentum investors continue buying them, and they continue to go up.

---

[27] The value factor in the APT has been often adjusted to reflect factor-mimicking returns from these special asset markets. For example, Lustig, Roussanov, and Verdelhan (2011) capture the carry returns of a foreign currency by using a carry factor HMLFX, which is formed by going long currencies with high interest rates minus currencies with low interest rates.

3.5 Getting a top-down handle on factor exposures

Recent academic literature (see, e.g., Ang, 2014) and practical strategic as-set management have emphasized the usefulness of controlling not the op-timal weights assigned to different assets or asset classes, but instead the need to go from optimizing factor exposures to optimal portfolio selection. On the one hand, factor investing seems to be a good idea. Contrary to Ellis' (1975) adage—active management is "loser's game" by construction be-cause for every winner there is a loser and after transactions costs, there are only losers—on average, factor investing can turn all traders into win-ners. While for every person on one side of a factor trade, there is a person on the other side, both investors are happy because they improve their risk–return profiles by offsetting factor positions. For example, certain in-vestors are happy to forego the premium for selling volatility to avoid pe-riodic crashes. Instead, they purchase protection that pays off when volatil-ity spikes. This makes everyone better off.

How investors' preferences may affect portfolio choices through the opti-mal selection of beta exposures is best seen in the case of a special index (say, q) that commands a zero risk premium, i.e., $E\left[FMR_{q,t+1}\text{-}R^f\right] = 0$. This means that while index q movements (as mimicked by the qth portfolio) almost surely affect returns on some assets (think of the importance of in-terest rate spreads just in industries where firms engage in the transfor-mation of the maturities of assets and liabilities, but not elsewhere), index q is not a pervasive enough influence to be priced by the market. At first glance, one might think that the sensitivity of an optimal portfolio to index q should be set to zero. After all, why take on a risk (increased variability in returns) with no commensurate increase in expected returns? For the av-erage investor this is correct. However, think of an investor whose cash outflows increase with increases in index q. Such an investor would want to hold a portfolio that has a positive sensitivity to index q.[28] The fact that an investor desires a position different from the aggregate allows the in-vestor to improve his or her portfolio with no decrease in expected return, although there will be some increase in total risk.

On the other hand, factor investing poses some important problems. We can best understand how such a top-down approach could work by a step-by-step description. Let's start with the market factor. The average inves-tor holds the market portfolio, a passive, long-only collection of all availa-ble securities held with market capitalization weights. Thus the average

---

[28] Of course, if everybody wanted to hold portfolios that exhibited increased return with increases in index q, then the corresponding risk premium would be positive.

investor collects no dynamic factor risk premiums, because in the process, she will also outperform a majority of active managers! Moreover, we know that under the classical CAPM, this is all the portfolio advice that you either need or can give others. But if a money manager deals with a customer (type) that is different from the average, she will optimally tilt away from the market depending on the assessed investor-specific characteristics, whether horizon, background risk (nature of labor or entrepreneurial income), aversion to volatility, etc..

However, this process also presents important limitations. For instance, one would tend to ask questions such as "What losses during bad times can I bear?", which is tantamount to estimating *one's risk aversion with respect to each factor*. Here the difficulties begin: while financial economics has given us a very sensible as well as mathematically rigorous definition of what risk aversion means, the notion of "risk aversion with respect to any special risk factor" is rather hard to pin down even though—on some subjective and intuitive level—many of us may even be able to provide rough quantitative estimates.[29] For instance, factor allocation usually produces returns that are highly left-skewed. That is, they can occasionally produce some very large losses. Viewing the potential of these losses as a function of the size of the factor exposures allows investors to calibrate their desired holdings to the factor risks. However, how such asymmetries in the distribution of portfolio returns might be traded-off vs. the potential increase in Sharpe ratios that factor models make possible, remains obscure. The following example emphasizes exactly these limitations of a factor-exposure based approach to portfolio selection.

Example 5.5. Consider a model with only two risk factors, inflation and growth (surprises, i.e., realizations of the factors diverging from their expectations). Assume that the APT holds. The risk free rate is 0.1% in

---

[29] Quoting Andrew Ang's (2014) excellent book, "This approach is very different from slamming a value-growth factor into a mean-variance optimizer. We start with the needs and characteristics of the asset owner (his utility function, in the language of an economist). (...) This requires an economic understanding, not just a statistical optimization procedure (...). The appropriateness of a factor strategy depends on whether the investor can tolerate the factor's bad times more readily than the average investor, or how he differs in behavior from the average investor." Our claim is however that the very language of economists lacks a sufficiently precise way to compare and "sum up" how one investor may tolerate the numerous, factor-specific bad times. Hence, resorting to a MV optimizer suffers from obvious limitations, but gives us much needed quantitative guidance on optimal factor exposures.

monthly terms. The two factors carry—as measured through their factor-mimicking portfolios—monthly risk premia of 0.3% and 0.5%, respectively. Their monthly standard deviations are 1.5% and 1%. There are three (hypothetical) large asset classes with the following beta exposures to the two factors:

Asset Class	Inflation beta	Growth beta
Stocks	0.5	3
Real estate	2	2
Corporate bonds	1.5	-1

First, note that even though

$$E[R_P] = 0.1 + [0.5w_{stock} + 2w_{RE} + 1.5(1 - w_{stock} - w_{RE})]0.3$$
$$+ [3w_{stock} + 2w_{RE} - (1 - w_{stock} - w_{RE})]0.5$$
$$= 0.05 + 1.7w_{stock} + 1.65w_{RE}$$

$$\sigma_P^2 = w_{stock}^2\sigma_{stock}^2 + w_{RE}^2\sigma_{RE}^2 + (1 - w_{stock} - w_{RE})^2\sigma_{corp}^2$$
$$+ [w_{stock}^2(0.5)^2 + 2w_{stock}w_{RE}(0.5 \times 2)$$
$$+ 2w_{stock}(1 - w_{stock} - w_{RE})(0.5 \times 1.5) + w_{RE}^2(2)^2$$
$$+ 2w_{RE}(1 - w_{stock} - w_{RE})(2 \times 1.5)$$
$$+ (1 - w_{stock} - w_{RE})^2(1.5)^2](1.5)^2$$
$$+ [w_{stock}^2(3)^2 + 2w_{stock}w_{RE}(3 \times 2)$$
$$+ 2w_{stock}(1 - w_{stock} - w_{RE})(3 \times -1) + w_{RE}^2(2)^2$$
$$+ 2w_{RE}(1 - w_{stock} - w_{RE})(2 \times -1)$$
$$+ (1 - w_{stock} - w_{RE})^2(-1)^2](1)^2$$
$$= 6.0625 + w_{stock}^2\sigma_{stock}^2 + w_{RE}^2\sigma_{RE}^2$$
$$+ (1 - w_{stock} - w_{RE})^2\sigma_{corp}^2 + 18.25w_{stock}^2 + 9.5625w_{RE}^2$$
$$+ 21.75w_{stock}w_{RE} - 14.75w_{stock} - 2.625w_{RE},$$

i.e., the mean and the variance of any portfolios can be characterized as a function of portfolio weights, variance is also affected by the idiosyncratic variances $\sigma_{stock}^2, \sigma_{RE}^2$, and σ_{corp}^2. Therefore, in the perspective of solving a MV problem, simply adjusting for the factor exposures will not suffice. In fact, the APT (or any multi-index model) will just impose restrictions on factor risk premia and beta exposures, not on idiosyncratic variances.

To make progress in this example, we therefore assume $\sigma_{stock}^2 = \sigma_{RE}^2 = \sigma_{Corp}^2 = 0$. Hence, given a target portfolio mean $\bar{\mu}$, we can write

$$\bar{\mu} = 0.05 + 1.7w_{stock} + 1.65w_{RE}$$

$$\Rightarrow w_{stock} = \frac{\bar{\mu} - 0.05 - 1.65w_{RE}}{1.7} = \frac{10}{17}\bar{\mu} - \frac{5}{170} - \frac{165}{170}w_{RE}$$
$$= 0.588\bar{\mu} - 0.029 - 0.971w_{RE}$$

so that

$$\sigma_P^2 = 6.0625 + 18.25(0.588\bar{\mu} - 0.029 - 0.971w_{RE})^2$$
$$+ 9.5625w_{RE}^2 + 21.75(0.588\bar{\mu} - 0.029 - 0.971w_{RE})w_{RE}$$
$$- 14.75(0.588\bar{\mu} - 0.029 - 0.971w_{RE}) - 2.625w_{RE}$$
$$= 6.0625$$
$$+ 18.25(0.346\bar{\mu}^2 + 0.000865 - 0.942w_{RE}^2 - 0.034\bar{\mu}$$
$$- 1.1419\bar{\mu}w_{RE} + 0.057w_{RE}) + 9.5625w_{RE}^2 + 12.794\bar{\mu}w_{RE}$$
$$- 21.1103w_{RE}^2 - 8.676\bar{\mu} + 0.4338 + 13.676w_{RE} - 2.625w_{RE}$$
$$= 6.3150\ \bar{\mu}^2 - 9.308\bar{\mu} + 6.5121 + 5.6445w_{RE}^2$$
$$- 8.0451\bar{\mu}w_{RE} + 12.093w_{RE}$$

It is easy now to compute

$$\frac{d\sigma_P^2}{dw_{RE}} = 11.2888w_{RE} + (12.094 - 8.0449\bar{\mu}).$$

Setting this derivative to zero and solving for $\hat{w}_{RE}$, yields the first-order condition of the problem:

$$\frac{d\sigma_P^2}{dw_{RE}} = 11.2888w_{RE} + (12.094 - 8.0449\bar{\mu}) = 0$$

$$\Rightarrow \hat{w}_{RE} = 0.7126\bar{\mu} - 1.071$$

Note that because $\frac{d^2\sigma_P^2}{dw_{RE}^2} = 11.2888 > 0$, the FOC is also sufficient in this case, as portfolio variance turns out to be convex everywhere in the RE portfolio weight. Interestingly, the optimal weight in real estate is increasing in the target mean $\bar{\mu}$. However, because $\bar{\mu}$ is a target monthly mean, for low $\bar{\mu}$ such a weight may as well be negative. This can be best understood when we supplement the original data with a calculation of implied expected asset returns and variances under the APT:

Asset Class	Inflation beta	Growth beta	Expected return	Volatility	Sharpe ratio
Stocks	0.5	3	0.44	3.09	0.11
Real estate	2	2	1.70	3.61	0.44
Corporate bonds	1.5	-1	0.55	1.50	0.30

Clearly, the only way to achieve a high target mean is by placing a higher weight on w_{RE}. Correspondingly:

$$\Rightarrow \widehat{w}_{stock} = 0.588\bar{\mu} - 0.029 - 0.971\widehat{w}_{RE}$$
$$= 0.588\bar{\mu} - 0.029 - 0.971(0.7126\bar{\mu} - 1.071)$$
$$= -0.1035\bar{\mu} + 1.0103$$

$$\widehat{w}_{corp} = 1 - \widehat{w}_{stock} - \widehat{w}_{RE} = 1 + 0.1035\bar{\mu} - 1.0103 - 0.7126\bar{\mu} + 1.071$$
$$= 1.0609 - 0.6092\bar{\mu}$$

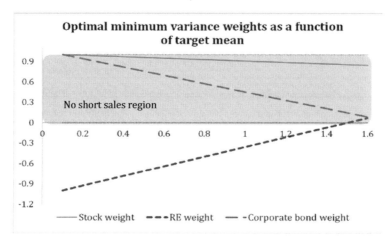

While also the weight in stocks slowly decreases with the target mean (even though more slowly than the corporate bond weight does), clearly the corporate bond share must decline. The plot shows these optimal minimum variance weights (note that these are MV for a given target mean only). It is counterintuitive that $\widehat{w}_{corp}$ declines (to negative weights for means that approach 20% a year) as $\bar{\mu}$ increases from a minimum of 0.1% per month (here the global minimum variance portfolio, because there is a riskless asset) because the expected returns and Sharpe ratios of corporate bonds both grossly exceed those of stocks. However, this simple logic does not apply when there are more than three assets in the menu of choice. One may think as follows: as $\bar{\mu}$ increases, an investor will want to expand the weight to real estate and this rather easily takes care of the desired increase in the target mean. However, real estate is extremely exposed to both risk factors and as such as $\bar{\mu}$ rises up, variance also quickly increases; at this point, also increasing the weight in stocks provides a source of diversification because stocks are less exposed to the inflation index than real estate is; in this perspective, stocks represent a better hedge of an important source of risk than corporate bonds are. This explains why the weight in corporate bonds declines as $\bar{\mu}$ increases even though in isolation their Sharpe ratio is higher than equities.

However, even though the factor exposures and risk premia are key inputs to the MV optimization, as in chapters 3 and 4, we went—from a given target expected return—from such inputs to the optimal portfolios and did not reason directly on the factor exposures by introducing some sort of mapping between the mean-variance (say, quadratic?) preferences of investors and such factor exposures. For instance, consider the case of $\bar{\mu} = 0.8\%$ per month, i.e., 9.6% a year. It is easy to check that for such a rather moderate target mean, $\hat{w}_{stock} = 0.93$, $\hat{w}_{RE} = -0.50$, and $\hat{w}_{Corp} = 0.57$, which is a rather well-diversified portfolio with a tilt towards stocks. Such a choice makes sense because with such a conservative target mean, a rational investor will not be inclined to take on the largest risks implied by real estate investments. In correspondence to such weight, we have:

$$\sigma_P^2 = 6.31488(0.8)^2 - 9.3079(0.8) + 6.5121 + 5.6444(-0.50)^2$$
$$- 8.0449(0.8)(-0.50) + 12.094(-0.50)$$
$$= 1.69 \text{ (hence volatility is 5.85\% per year)}$$

$$\beta_{opt\ ptf}^{inf} = \hat{w}_{stock}\beta_{stock}^{inf} + \hat{w}_{RE}\beta_{RE}^{inf} + (1 - \hat{w}_{stock} - \hat{w}_{RE})\beta_{Corp}^{inf}$$
$$= 0.93 \times 0.5 + -0.50 \times 2 + 0.57 \times 1.5 = 0.32$$
$$\beta_{opt\ ptf}^{growth} = \hat{w}_{stock}\beta_{stock}^{growth} + \hat{w}_{RE}\beta_{RE}^{growth} + (1 - \hat{w}_{stock} - \hat{w}_{RE})\beta_{Corp}^{growth}$$
$$= 0.93 \times 3 - 0.50 \times 2 + 0.57 \times (-1) = 1.22.$$

In words, the optimal portfolio implies a positive but not excessive exposure to inflation risk and a larger, greater than one, exposure to inflation risk. Importantly, for a MV optimizer, there is a unique set of factor exposures that allows her—for a given target mean—to minimize the risk of her portfolio. It would make little sense for such an investor to insist on her factor exposures to be, say, 1.5 on the inflation risk factor and 0.5 on the growth factor. Intuitively, it may be conjectured that such a portfolio will yield a rather low mean, a target variance smaller than 9.6% a year, and possibly (barring sheer luck) a portfolio that will fail to minimize variance given the target mean of the portfolio. To see why, suppose that the investor insists on such a course of action anyway and set weights to solve:

$$\begin{cases} \tilde{w}_{stock}\beta_{stock}^{inf} + \tilde{w}_{RE}\beta_{RE}^{inf} + (1 - \tilde{w}_{stock} - \tilde{w}_{RE})\beta_{Corp}^{inf} = 1.5 \\ \tilde{w}_{stock}\beta_{stock}^{growth} + \tilde{w}_{RE}\beta_{RE}^{growth} + (1 - \tilde{w}_{stock} - \tilde{w}_{RE})\beta_{Corp}^{growth} = 0.5 \end{cases}$$

$$\Longrightarrow \begin{cases} 0.5\tilde{w}_{stock} + 2\tilde{w}_{RE} + 1.5(1 - \tilde{w}_{stock} - \tilde{w}_{RE}) = 1.5 \\ 3\tilde{w}_{stock} + 2\tilde{w}_{RE} - 1(1 - \tilde{w}_{stock} - \tilde{w}_{RE}) = 0.5 \end{cases}$$

$$\Longrightarrow \begin{cases} -\tilde{w}_{stock} + 0.5\tilde{w}_{RE} = 0 \\ 4\tilde{w}_{stock} + 3\tilde{w}_{RE} = 1.5 \end{cases} \Longrightarrow \begin{cases} \tilde{w}_{stock} = 0.5\tilde{w}_{RE} \\ 5\tilde{w}_{RE} = 1.5 \end{cases}$$

$$\Longrightarrow \begin{cases} \tilde{w}_{stock} = 0.5 + 0.5\tilde{w}_{RE} = 0.15 \\ \tilde{w}_{RE} = 0.3 \end{cases}$$

$$\Longrightarrow \tilde{w}_{corp} = 1 - 0.3 - 0.15 = 0.55$$

At this point, such an exposure-based portfolio will achieve:

$$E[R_{exp,t+1}] = 0.05 + 1.7w_{stock} + 1.65w_{RE} = 0.05 + 1.7 \times 0.15 + 1.65 \times 0.3$$
$$= 0.8\%.$$

However, it is now straightforward to calculate that the variance minimizing weights corresponding to $\bar{\mu} = 0.8\%$ are $\hat{w}_{stock} = 0.93, \hat{w}_{RE} = -0.50$, and $\hat{w}_{Corp} = 0.57$. Such weights give betas on the two macro risk indices that differ from 1.5 and 0.5:

$$\beta_{exp}^{inf} = 0.93 \times 0.5 - 0.50 \times 2 + 0.57 \times 1.5 = 0.32$$
$$\beta_{exp}^{growth} = 0.93 \times 3 - 0.50 \times 2 + 0.57 \times (-1) = 1.22,$$

which reveals the truth: taking exposures of 1.5 to inflation and 0.5 to growth cannot be MV optimizing for any investor.

Notably, this example should not be interpreted as showing that directly picking factor exposures is incorrect or misleading. Instead, the example aims at emphasizing how difficult it may be to map such a selection of preferred factor exposures into rational portfolios selected by risk-averse investors. In this sense, the potential contradiction between choosing factor betas and MV selection should be taken only as an example: as we know, an infinity of risk averse preference relationships over risky lotteries exist and yet it is not obvious how a selected configuration $\beta_{exp}^1, \beta_{exp}^2, ..., \beta_{exp}^K$ may result from (say) expected utility maximization.

In some ways, the opposition between asset vs. risk factor-based allocations derives from the existence of some informational spread between the two corresponding problems. In fact, Idrozek and Kowara (2013) prove that when there are as many risk factors as assets and hence the risk factors perfectly explain the returns of asset classes, there is no inherent advantage from either approach: we can start with either risk factors or asset classes, derive an optimal portfolio, and move from one space to the other with no gain or loss in efficiency. However, when there are many more assets than risk factors and hence the latter cannot provide a perfect fit to the former, then a difference may exist. If there is a one-to-one mapping between asset and risk factor returns, then there is no reason to expect that one set contains any less information than the other.

3.6 Summary of the model

We close by summarizing the features of the multi-index model by appealing to the list of characterizations reported above:

I.   The functional form specification $f(\cdot)$ is linear affine, similarly to the CAPM in section 2.3.

II. The number of parameters M equals $(K + 2)$ per asset/security $(K + 1$ the APT is imposed); this number must be augmented by the expectation and variance of each of the factors or of their corresponding factor-mimicking portfolio returns, for total of 2K additional parameters.

III. – IV. K should be selected on the basis of statistical methods (like in PCA), the preferences of investors in terms of what are the sources of systematic risks (the notions of "bad times") they are sensitive to, or past experience and/or the existing academic literature (for instance, theoretical models may be proposed that pin down which indices ought to appear on the RHS of (5.34)).

V. $l = 0$; however, at least since Arnott, Kelso, Kiscadden, and Macedo (1989), a literature has grown that has studied whether the risk factors themselves are somewhat predictable, which would make asset returns on the LHS of (5.34) depend on past information/variables, such as seasonal effects (monthly dummies), market conditions (large stock indices earnings yield minus the T-bill yield, market variance, and the change in the T-bill yield), and the macroeconomic state (inflation, changes in cyclical leading indicators, and money growth). Berry et al. (1988) have called these strategies *active APT bets* and emphasize that their success tends to hinge more on correctly forecasting the sign of factor movements than their future realizations.

We emphasize that in an APT interpretation, a multi-index model represents a *relative* pricing model in the sense that expected asset returns and their variances can be determined for given risk premia and variances of the factors (or their factor-mimicking portfolios), regardless of whether these are determined empirically or from appropriate theories. The CAPM is instead an overall, encompassing equilibrium model because, apart from its simplicity, it is also able to pin down the features/moments of the single risk factor, the market, for instance by $E[R_{m,t+1} - R^f] = \gamma Var[R_{m,t+1}]$.

References and Further Readings

Ang, A. *Asset Management: A Systematic Approach to Factor Investing*. New York: Oxford University Press, 2014.

Arnott, R., Kelso, C., and Kiscadden, S. R. Macedo, Forecasting Factor Returns: an Intriguing Possibility. *Journal of Portfolio Management*, 16: 28-35, 1989.

Berry, M. A., Burmeister, E., and McElroy, M. B. Sorting Out Risks Using Known Apt Factors. *Financial Analysts Journal*, 44: 29-42, 1988.

Carhart, M., M. On Persistence in Mutual Fund Performance. *Journal of Finance*, 52: 57-82, 1997.

Chen, N. F., Roll, R., and Ross, S. A. Economic Forces and the Stock Market. *Journal of Business*, 59: 383-403, 1986.

Christoffersen, P. F. *Elements of Financial Risk Management*. 2nd edition, Academic Press, 2012

Connor, G., and Korajczyk, R. A. Performance Measurement with the Arbitrage Pricing Theory: A new Framework for Analysis. *Journal of Financial Economics*, 15: 373-394, 1986.

Danthine, J. P., and Donaldson, J. B. *Intermediate Financial Theory*, Second Edition, Oxford: Academic Press, 2005

Ellis, C. D. The Loser's Game. *Financial Analysts Journal*, 31: 19-26, 1975.

Elton, E. J., Gruber, M. J., Brown, S. J., and Goetzmann, W. N. *Modern Portfolio Theory and Investment Analysis*. Hoboken: John Wiley & Sons, 2009.

Fabozzi, F., J., Vardharaj, R., and Jones, F., J. Multifactor Equity Risk Models. in *The Theory and Practice of Investment Management*, 2nd Edition, Fabozzi and Markowitz (eds.), Hoboken: John Wiley & Sons, 2011.

Fama, E., F., and French, K., R. Common Risk Factors in the Returns on Stocks and Bonds. *Journal of Financial Economics*, 33: 3–56, 1993.

Fama, E. F., and French, K. R. Size, Value, and Momentum in International Stock Returns. *Journal of Financial Economics*, 105: 457-472, 2012.

Guidolin, M., Ravazzolo, F., and Tortora, A., D. Alternative Econometric Implementations of Multi-Factor Models of the US Financial Markets. *Quarterly Review of Economics and Finance*, 53: 87-111, 2013.

Guidolin, M., and Timmermann, A. Size and Value Anomalies Under Regime Shifts. *Journal of Financial Econometrics*, 6: 1-48, 2008.

Idzorek, T. M., and Kowara, M. Factor-Based Asset Allocation vs. Asset-Class-Based Asset Allocation. *Financial Analysts Journal*, 69: 19-29, 2013.

Ilmanen, A., and Kizer, J. The Death of Diversification Has Been Greatly Exaggerated. *Journal of Portfolio Management*, 38: 15-27, 2012

Ilmanen, A., Maloney, T., and Ross, A. Exploring Macroeconomic Sensitivities: How Investments Respond to Different Economic Environments. *Journal of Portfolio Management*, 40: 87-99, 2014.

Luenberger, D. G. *Investment Science*. New York: Oxford University Press, 1997.

Lustig, H., Roussanov, N., and Verdelhan, A. Common Risk Factors in Currency Markets. *Review of Financial Studies*, 24: 3731-3777, 2011.

Markowitz, H., M. The Two Beta Trap. *Journal of Portfolio Management*, 11: 12–20, 1984.

Roll, R., and Ross, S. A., A Critical Reexamination of the Empirical Evidence on the Arbitrage Pricing Theory: A Reply. *Journal of Finance*, 39: 347-350, 1984.

Ross, S., A. The Arbitrage Theory of Capital Asset Pricing. *Journal of Economic Theory*, 13: 341-360, 1976.

Zhou, G., and Fabozzi, F. Factor Models, in *The Theory and Practice of Investment Management*, 2nd Edition, Fabozzi and Markowitz (eds.), Hoboken: John Wiley & Sons, 2011.

6 Human Capital, Background Risks, and Optimal Portfolio Decisions

"Generally speaking, investing in yourself is the best thing you can do. Anything that improves your own talents; nobody can tax it or take it away from you. They can run up huge deficits and the dollar can become worth far less. You can have all kinds of things happen. But if you've got talent yourself, and you've maximized your talent, you've got a tremendous asset that can return tenfold. (Warren Buffet in an ABC news interview in July 2009)

Summary: - 1. Simple Approaches to Labor Income in Portfolio Decisions – 2. The Case of Constant Relative Risk Aversion Preferences.

1 - Simple Approaches to Labor Income in Portfolio Decisions

So far we have modeled portfolio choices made by investors who derive "happiness" (say, terminal wealth or consumption) from capital income only, i.e., from the returns of past investments in securities and (financial) assets. It seems both legitimate and realistic to ask how and whether our results are affected by the fact that most investors are in fact either individuals or households that receive a flow of labor or entrepreneurial (we are including the self-employed) income. In this chapter, we analyze the effects of the presence of either (returns on) human capital or, more generally, *background risk*—defined as any uncertain source of income or terminal wealth that is independent of portfolio decisions that cannot be (fully) insured—on optimal asset allocation. Importantly, even though all concepts and results that we shall derive may be referred to all kinds of background risk (e.g., housing incomes and services, entrepreneurial incomes, retirement payment flows, health expenditures, etc.), in this chapter we shall preferably write about human capital, defined as the present discounted value of the expectation of life-time incomes deriving from labor or other services rendered. However, in most instances a Reader should have an easy way of replacing the human capital wording with other language, specific to other forms of background risk.

Human capital is an asset, and for young investors the value of labor income—the cash flows generated by human capital—usually dominates the rest of their financial holdings. Human capital is also risky, because earnings from work can fluctuate—and in the most unfortunate cases fall to and stay at zero. The return on human capital is often computed as the growth in wages. For instance, results may be stated as "males with one to five years of experience and a college degree have annual human capital returns of 14.2% versus 10.5% for those with some college education but no degree, and the standard deviation of human capital returns for the former is 11.3% versus 4.7% for the latter; thus, the raw Sharpe ratio (defined as mean return divided by volatility) is 1.3 vs. 2.2".[1] In comparison, the S&P 500 has a raw Sharpe ratio of around 0.6: education is a very good investment, on average.

Intuitively, human capital income yields two effects for optimal portfolio decisions:

I.   It alters the total size of the initial (present, discounted) value of lifetime wealth of an individual and this may affect her degree of (absolute or relative) risk aversion and hence the elasticity of her investments to wealth (see chapter 4 for details); note that when an investor is risk averse, her relative and absolute risk aversion coefficients cannot both be constant.

II.   It may alter the composition of the optimal portfolio if and only if the labor income process displays non-zero correlations with the returns of the assets otherwise in the investor's menu.

As far as the first effect goes, this depends entirely on an investor's preferences and therefore little can be said in advance apart from the fact that when investors find or lose a job, or is promoted/demoted within their workplace (say, your coveted post in a structured product desk), it is natural to also expect their portfolio decisions to be affected. In particular, in the case of a mean-variance optimizer, when such a behavior derives from an underlying quadratic utility function, we know from chapter 2 that such

---

[1] These claims are adapted from Ang (2014).

a felicity construct will imply IARA and hence IRRA patterns: when labor income changes and this affects lifetime, present discounted wealth by increasing (decreasing) it, then less (more) will be invested in the risky assets as whole, both in absolute and in relative terms. Of course, this is rather implausible and it must be kept in mind when assessing the relevance of the results in this chapter.

Before plunging into the algebra of this model, let's now examine the intuition of the latter effect. The plausible assumption here is that, in general, investors make the choices leading to their labor income "profile" (i.e., level, dynamics, variability, etc.) independently of their capital income. This means that rarely do individuals select jobs (or related decisions) on the basis of their portfolios; the opposite tends to apply instead: given your income profile and outlook, consumption and portfolio decisions tend to be taken. When an investor takes her labor income as a given (i.e., indeed as a background risk), then she should optimally choose securities to hedge the risks of such income process. This can be accomplished by tilting her portfolio towards assets that pay out well when labor income is below average (or zero!); to maximize the possibility of achieving this goal, an investor shall also be ready to under-weight the assets in her portfolio that pay out when she cares the least, i.e., when labor income is above average.

This is of course an application of old adage that "you do not put all eggs in the same basket." For instance, if you are an analyst in the financial or banking sectors, you will tend to under-weight equity indices that invest in financials or banking stocks. Especially—unless either you are forced into such participation schemes (often consisting in assigning shares of stock and warrants at prices below the market fair value)—you will definitely not invest in stocks and bonds issued by your own employer or parent company! The reasons are obvious: should the business of your employer go bust, you would want to avoid that also your portfolio may be negatively affected. As a result, you would rather invest in assets issued by firms that do not belong to the financials and banking sectors.

The key point that this chapter intends to make is that all assets—including human capital and housing and real estate properties—should be explicitly considered as components of the investor's overall wealth portfolio. It is the correlation structure of cash flows from these various income sources that play a crucial role in determining the optimal portfolio weights. An interesting issue that will be examined throughout this chapter is whether optimal portfolio choice models may be consistent with the standard advice given in the popular press that people in employment should invest more in risky assets (and less in safe assets) than people who are retired and that—more generally—the equity share ought to decline with age.

The story will unfold as follows. A household with labor income has an implicit holding of a non-tradable asset, human capital, which represents a claim to her stream of future labor income. The household adjusts explicit asset holdings to compensate for the implicit holding of human capital and reach the desired allocation of total wealth. Hence human capital may "crowd in or out" explicit asset holdings. If labor income is literally riskless (say, you are the king of your country), then riskless asset holdings are crowded out and the investor will tilt her portfolio strongly towards risky assets. Indeed, in some historical periods, we did see kings hiring armies of venture soldiers to conquer the world, which tends to be considered a risky enough business. In the case where the investor is constrained from borrowing to leverage her risky investments, the solution may be a corner at which the portfolio is 100% risky assets. If labor income is risky but uncorrelated with risky financial assets, then riskless asset holdings are still crowded out but less strongly. If labor income is sufficiently positively correlated with risky financial assets, then the portfolio tilt is decreased and the household compensates for risky human capital by increasing holdings of safe financial assets. Under the assumption that labor income shocks are uncorrelated or only weakly correlated with stock returns, the results will suggest that investors who expect high future labor income—discounted at some appropriate rate and measured relative to financial wealth—should display the strongest desire to hold stocks. Hence, the standard advice that risky asset holdings ought to decline as you age increases, is upheld. In fact, a famous rule of thumb is "one hundred minus your age", which says that the proportion of your portfolio invested in equities should equal the difference between your age and one hundred.

1.1 Taking a "first stab": the case of deterministic, riskless labor income

To understand in the starkest possible way what forces are at play when labor income appears in the financial planning of an investor, consider first the simple case in which labor income is riskless so that human capital is simply the present discounted value of such deterministic sums to be received in the future. Note that when labor income is riskless, then by construction it will display zero correlation with the returns on any risky assets. Moreover, a long-run investor maximizes power utility of terminal wealth (consumption) with CRRA coefficient γ and she can only invest in the risky vs. the riskless asset. In short, this is a canonical portfolio problem. Stocks have a risky log return r_{t+1} per period, with constant mean log excess return $E_t[(r_{t+1} - r^f)]$ and constant variance σ^2. Note that in this chapter $r_{t+1} \equiv \ln(1 + R_{t+1})$, where R_{t+1} is the standard notion of return used so far in the book.

Suppose in a completely counterfactual way, that human capital were totally tradable with a value of H_t. The investor's total wealth is then $W_t + H_t$. As we have seen in chapter 4, in this case the expression of the optimal asset allocation—say, the power utility tangency portfolio—for this investor when all wealth is tradable is to sell claims against her human capital and invest $\hat{\omega}_t(W_t + H_t)$ dollars of his total wealth in stocks, and the remaining $(1 - \hat{\omega}_t)(W_t + H_t)$ dollars in the riskless asset, where

$$\hat{\omega}_t = \frac{E_t[(r_{t+1} - r^f)] + \frac{1}{2}\sigma^2}{\gamma\sigma^2}. \qquad (6.1)$$

The $0.5\sigma^2$ correction at the numerator is a Jensen's inequality factor that derives from the continuously compounded definition of returns, r_{t+1}. Under non-tradable labor income, once we realize that, because labor income is riskless and the investor has implicit holdings of H_t in the riskless asset, she should adjust her financial portfolio so that her total dollar holdings of each asset equal the optimal unconstrained holdings. The optimal share of risky assets in proportion to financial wealth is then

$$\hat{\omega}_t^{H-adj} = \frac{\hat{\omega}_t(W_t + H_t)}{W_t} = \frac{E_t[(r_{t+1} - r^f)] + \frac{1}{2}\sigma^2}{\gamma\sigma^2}\left(1 + \frac{H_t}{W_t}\right), \qquad (6.2)$$

which implies that $\hat{\omega}_t^{H-adj} > \hat{\omega}_t$ because by construction, $H_t > 0$. Therefore, Bodie, Merton, and Samuelson (1992) observe that an investor endowed with riskless, non-tradable human wealth should tilt her financial portfolio toward risky assets relative to an investor who owns only tradable assets. In fact, even though an investor cannot borrow against her future labor income, the optimal dollar holdings of the riskless asset, $(1 - \hat{\omega}_t^{H-adj})(W_t + H_t) - H_t$ may be negative when H_t is very large relative to W_t. In that case, the investor may want to hold a leveraged position in stocks by borrowing at the riskless rate, even though in hindsight we understand this occurs only because the investor is trying to "undo" the large endowment of riskless cash flows that derive from labor income.

Interestingly, as a result of expression (6.2), the share of risky assets over financial wealth is increasing in the ratio of human to financial wealth (H_t/W_t). This ratio changes over the investor's life cycle. At retirement, the ratio H_t/W_t tends to zero; early in adult life the ratio is typically large— many of the Readers of this book have no financial wealth of their own (they may actually be in debt, i.e., have negative net financial worth) but they are hopefully sitting on a huge human capital value. First, they expect to receive labor incomes for many years; second, they have had little time to accumulate financial wealth. Therefore, a young, employed investor should invest more in risky assets (say, stocks) than an older, retiring investor with identical risk aversion and large financial wealth.

The ratio of human to financial wealth also changes with financial asset performances. If the stock market performs well, the investor's financial wealth grows relative to his human capital. This should lead to a reduction in the share of financial wealth invested in risky securities. Thus this model predicts a "contrarian" investment strategy that not only rebalances the portfolio regularly, but goes further to reduce the risky portfolio share after this has performed well.

This simple model with riskless labor income reveals the basic mechanisms that link together human capital and the optimal allocation to financial assets. However, it ignores some important characteristics of wealth that will complicate the analysis.[2] In particular, future labor earnings are uncertain for most investors, making human capital a risky rather than a safe, non-tradable asset. The risk characteristics of human wealth should affect the allocation of financial assets. This is what section 1.2 models, although still in a simplified format.

---

[2] A second important characteristic of human capital is that investors can influence its value by varying how much they work. The ability to vary work effort allows individuals to hold riskier portfolios because they can work harder if they need extra labor income to compensate for losses in their financial portfolios. In this chapter we do not attempt to model any additional characteristics of human capital, for instance, that individuals may deliberately choose to invest in their own human wealth, increasing its value through education, as the Reader is hopefully seeking to accomplish. They may also have some control over the risk characteristics of their human wealth through their choice of career paths: for instance, jobs in investment banking will increase the investments in financial risky assets much less than (successful) careers in academic research can.

1.2 A first formal, one-period stochastic model

Let's adopt a simple but formal static mean-variance framework to investigate these issues. As in chapter 4, suppose an investor is characterized by MV preferences defined over her terminal wealth, with risk aversion coefficient κ:

$$MV(E[W_{t+1}], Var[W_{t+1}]) = E[W_{t+1}] - \frac{1}{2}\kappa Var[W_{t+1}] \quad (6.3)$$

Of course, the same objective may be re-written in terms of overall portfolio returns (say, R^p_{t+1}) and exploiting the fact that $W_{t+1} = (1 + R^p_{t+1})W_t$. For simplicity, assume unit initial wealth. Note that κ is assumed to be constant and not to depend on labor income, which will hold only locally, for a labor income process that is not very volatile.[3,4] The asset menu is composed of N risky assets with vector of returns R_{t+1} and one riskless asset with return R^f, assumed to be constant without loss of generality, given our static, one-period framework. The investor receives labor income measured by the random variable Y_{t+1}. There are no labor supply decisions, so income is exogenous. Labor income is a non-tradable asset, i.e., as already said, you cannot borrow against future labor income (as the commitment of an individual to work is not legally enforceable). This variable is potentially correlated with returns from securities in the asset menu, $Cov[Y_{t+1}, R_{t+1}] \neq 0$, where $Cov[Y_{t+1}, R_{t+1}]$ is a $N \times 1$ vector that collects the covariance of labor income with the returns paid by each of the assets in the menu. The portfolio optimization problem may be written as:

$$\max_{\omega_t} E[W_{t+1}] - \frac{1}{2}\kappa Var[W_{t+1}]$$
$$s.t. \quad W_{t+1} = Y_{t+1} + (1 + R^f)(1 - \iota'\omega_t) + (\iota + R_{t+1})'\omega_t$$
$$= Y_{t+1} + (1 + R^f) + (R_{t+1} - R^f\iota)'\omega_t \quad (6.4)$$

Plugging in the budget constraint in the objective function, the problem becomes:

---

[3] Human capital is often also understood as to broadly include the value of privately owned firms.

[4] As we have stressed already, under quadratic utility function, the investor's ARA coefficient will be increasing in wealth and—even though the mapping between one and the other is far from trivial—to expect κ to decline in the (mean of the) labor income process may be realistic. In the following, we rule these effects out by assumption.

$$\max_{\boldsymbol{\omega}_t}(1 + R^f) + E[Y_{t+1}+(\boldsymbol{R}_{t+1} - R^f\boldsymbol{\iota})'\boldsymbol{\omega}_t] - \frac{1}{2}\kappa Var[Y_{t+1}+(\boldsymbol{R}_{t+1} - R^f\boldsymbol{\iota})'\boldsymbol{\omega}_t]$$

$$\Leftrightarrow \max_{\boldsymbol{\omega}_t} E[Y_{t+1}] + E[\boldsymbol{R}_{t+1} - R^f\boldsymbol{\iota}]'\boldsymbol{\omega}_t - \frac{1}{2}\kappa Var[Y_{t+1}] - \frac{1}{2}\kappa\boldsymbol{\omega}_t'\boldsymbol{\Sigma}\boldsymbol{\omega}_t$$
$$- \kappa Cov[Y_{t+1}, \boldsymbol{R}_{t+1}]'\boldsymbol{\omega}_t, \tag{6.5}$$

where $\boldsymbol{\Sigma} \equiv Var[\boldsymbol{R}_{t+1} - R^f\boldsymbol{\iota}] = Var[\boldsymbol{R}_{t+1}]$. This maximization program is now unconstrained and it is quadratic and globally concave. Therefore, the FOCs will be necessary and also sufficient. The variance term comes from the fact that in $W_{t+1} = Y_{t+1} + (1 + R^f) + (\boldsymbol{R}_{t+1} - R^f\boldsymbol{\iota})'\boldsymbol{\omega}_t$, $(1 + R^f)$ is a constant and $R^f\boldsymbol{\iota}$ is a vector of constants. At this point, and recalling that $\partial(\boldsymbol{y}'\boldsymbol{x})/\partial\boldsymbol{x} = \boldsymbol{y}$ and $\partial(\boldsymbol{x}'\boldsymbol{A}\boldsymbol{x})/\partial\boldsymbol{x} = 2\boldsymbol{A}\boldsymbol{x}$, the FOCs are:

$$E[\boldsymbol{R}_{t+1} - R^f\boldsymbol{\iota}] - \kappa\boldsymbol{\Sigma}\widehat{\boldsymbol{\omega}}_t - \kappa Cov[Y_{t+1}, \boldsymbol{R}_{t+1}] = 0 \tag{6.6}$$

or

$$\kappa\boldsymbol{\Sigma}\widehat{\boldsymbol{\omega}}_t = E[\boldsymbol{R}_{t+1} - R^f\boldsymbol{\iota}] - \kappa Cov[Y_{t+1}, \boldsymbol{R}_{t+1}] \tag{6.7}$$

which can be solved by pre-multiplying both sides by $(1/\kappa)\boldsymbol{\Sigma}^{-1}$, to give:[5]

$$\widehat{\boldsymbol{\omega}}_t = \boldsymbol{\Sigma}^{-1}\frac{E[\boldsymbol{R}_{t+1} - R^f\boldsymbol{\iota}]}{\kappa} - \boldsymbol{\Sigma}^{-1}Cov[Y_{t+1}, \boldsymbol{R}_{t+1}]$$
$$= \textit{Inverse of "matrix of risks"} \times \frac{\textit{Risk premia}}{\textit{Risk aversion}}$$
$$- \textit{Inverse of "matrix of risks"}$$
$$\times \textit{background risk covariances} \tag{6.8}$$

The interpretation is that the presence of labor income modifies the standard MV closed-form result if and only if the vector of covariances of labor income with asset returns is non-zero:

$$\widehat{\boldsymbol{\omega}}_t = \textit{Myopic MV asset demand} + \textit{Hedging background risk} \quad (6.9)$$

---

[5] Because $\boldsymbol{\Sigma}$ is a covariance matrix and hence positive definite (by construction, in the absence of redundant assets), $\boldsymbol{\Sigma}^{-1}$ will exist.

The desirability of the risky asset in the investor's portfolio will therefore depend not only upon its excess return (above the risk free rate) relative to its variance (risk), but also the extent to which it can be used to hedge variations in the investor's labor income. An investor will depart from the standard, tangency portfolio MV weights found in chapter 3 only because she aims at tilting her portfolio positions to buy (self-) insurance against labor income risks. Interestingly, the size of such a tilt caused by correlations between labor income and security returns shall not depend on the coefficient of risk aversion, κ.

Does labor income reduce/increase portfolio weights and how? Clearly, equation (6.8) shows that it all depends on the product $\Sigma^{-1}Cov[Y_{t+1}, R_{t+1}]$.[6] Therefore, as the result of this product depends on the data of the problem, it is difficult to state a-priori how a non-zero $Cov[Y_{t+1}, R_{t+1}]$ will affect the portfolio weights for all the assets, i.e., all N portfolio weights. Yet, notice that the variance of labor income per se, being in the background, does not affect portfolio choice: in equation (6.8), $Var[Y_{t+1}]$ fails to appear because it does not interact with portfolio weights and only the correlations between labor income and asset returns matter. Finally, also $E[Y_{t+1}]$ eventually does not affect optimal asset allocation: this comes from the fact that background choices—such as employment or retirement—are not affected by portfolio decisions and as such they do not interact with portfolio selections.

The following example illustrates these features and leads to dramatic conclusions: the same equity index may go from a benign neglect in one investor's portfolio to be in very aggressive demand just because the same investor experiences a change in the "structure" and/or outlook of her human capital returns, for fixed risk-aversion and available current wealth.

Example 6.1. Consider the monthly statistics concerning the following three equity indices and their correlations with Mary's labor income (she is an equity derivatives sales associate at a major conglomerate bank):

$$E\left[R_{t+1}^{banks} \quad R_{t+1}^{industrials} \quad R_{t+1}^{services}\right]' = [1.4\% \quad 1.0\% \quad 0.6\%]'$$

$$\Sigma \equiv Var[R_{t+1}] = \begin{bmatrix} (3.50)^2 & 5.4 & 2.2 \\ 5.4 & (3.23)^2 & 2.0 \\ 2.2 & 2.0 & (2.81)^2 \end{bmatrix}$$

---

[6] Because this product involves (the inverse of) a $N \times N$ matrix times a $N \times 1$ vector and the Reader will recall that the elements of the resulting $N \times 1$ vector are sums of each of the rows in Σ^{-1} multiplied by $Cov[Y_{t+1}, R_{t+1}]$.

The corresponding Sharpe ratios are:

$$SR^{banks} = \frac{1.4 - 0.1}{3.5} = 0.371 \quad SR^{industrials} = \frac{1.0 - 0.1}{3.23} = 0.279$$

$$SR^{services} = \frac{0.6 - 0.1}{2.81} = 0.178$$

The risk-free rate is 0.1%. The labor income process grows at a rather modest rate of 0.2% per month, it has a small variance of 0.8, and implies the following covariances with equity index returns:

$$Cov[Y_{t+1}^{Mary}, R_{t+1}^{banks}] = 3, Cov[Y_{t+1}^{Mary}, R_{t+1}^{ind}] = -0.6, Cov[Y_{t+1}^{Mary}, R_{t+1}^{serv}] = 1.6.$$

Mary is characterized by a coefficient of risk aversion of $\kappa = 0.25$. Note that

$$\Sigma^{-1} = \begin{bmatrix} 0.108 & -0.053 & -0.017 \\ -0.053 & 0.126 & -0.017 \\ -0.017 & -0.017 & 0.136 \end{bmatrix}$$

Mary's optimal risky portfolio will be as follows:

$$\begin{bmatrix} \hat{\omega}_{t+1}^{banks} \\ \hat{\omega}_{t+1}^{industrials} \\ \hat{\omega}_{t+1}^{services} \end{bmatrix} = \frac{1}{0.25} \begin{bmatrix} 0.108 & -0.053 & -0.017 \\ -0.053 & 0.126 & -0.017 \\ -0.017 & -0.017 & 0.136 \end{bmatrix} \begin{bmatrix} 1.4 - 0.1 \\ 1.0 - 0.1 \\ 0.6 - 0.1 \end{bmatrix}$$

$$- \begin{bmatrix} 0.108 & -0.053 & -0.017 \\ -0.053 & 0.126 & -0.017 \\ -0.017 & -0.017 & 0.136 \end{bmatrix} \begin{bmatrix} 3.0 \\ -0.6 \\ 1.6 \end{bmatrix} = \begin{bmatrix} 0.010 \\ 0.408 \\ -0.055 \end{bmatrix}$$

and as a result the weight in the riskless asset is: 1-0.010-0.408+0.055= 0.637. Interestingly, even though bank stocks have by far the highest Sharpe ratio, Mary is demanding them in a very small percentage. This is due to the fact that bank stocks and Mary's labor income have a very high positive correlation of $(3.0/(3.50 \times \sqrt{0.8})) = 0.958$ so that in overall terms, to Mary, buying bank stocks appears to be very risky.

Suppose now that Mary changes job and sector, becoming vice-president in risk management in one industrial corporation. Because of the promotion, Mary's salary doubles, its rate of growth becomes 0.3% per month, its variance declines to 0.6% only. Moreover, Mary's new labor income process implies the following covariances with equity index returns:

$$Cov[\tilde{Y}_{t+1}^{Mary}, R_{t+1}^{banks}] = -1, Cov[\tilde{Y}_{t+1}^{Mary}, R_{t+1}^{ind}] = 2, Cov[\tilde{Y}_{t+1}^{Mary}, R_{t+1}^{serv}] = 1.8.$$

Mary's new optimal portfolio will now be:

$$\begin{bmatrix} \tilde{\omega}_{t+1}^{banks} \\ \tilde{\omega}_{t+1}^{industrials} \\ \tilde{\omega}_{t+1}^{services} \end{bmatrix} = \frac{1}{0.25} \begin{bmatrix} 0.108 & -0.053 & -0.017 \\ -0.053 & 0.126 & -0.017 \\ -0.017 & -0.017 & 0.136 \end{bmatrix} \begin{bmatrix} 1.4 - 0.1 \\ 1.0 - 0.1 \\ 0.6 - 0.1 \end{bmatrix}$$

$$- \begin{bmatrix} 0.108 & -0.053 & -0.017 \\ -0.053 & 0.126 & -0.017 \\ -0.017 & -0.017 & 0.136 \end{bmatrix} \begin{bmatrix} -1.0 \\ 2.0 \\ 1.8 \end{bmatrix} = \begin{bmatrix} 0.581 \\ -0.127 \\ -0.104 \end{bmatrix},$$

which implies a percentage investment in the riskless asset of 0.65. Interestingly, the cash investment remains the same and the share in banks greatly increases from 1 to 58 percent, which is obviously caused by the excellent Sharpe ratio of banks; the weight in services moderately declines from -5.5 to -10.4 percent; the share of industrial stocks plunges from 41 to -13%. This is caused by the high correlation between labor incomes and industrial stock returns of $(2.0/(3.23\times \sqrt{0.6})) = 0.799$. Because everything else is the same, we can quantify the effect of the labor income hedging demand by Mary to be $|0.581 - 0.010| = 0.571$ in the case of bank stocks and $|-0.127-0.408| = 0.535$ in the case of industrial stocks.

In particular, the example emphasizes that it is hardly rational for any risk-averse, MV investor to be long in risky assets that pay out on the basis of the cash flows of the company (or bond-issuing institution) she works for. Equivalently, it only takes for any investor to express very bullish views on the risk premia of her "home asset" and/or very benign assessment on its risk (low) and hedging properties (strong) for her to find it optimal to go long in such an asset.[7] What about those investors whose wages are negatively correlated with equity returns? These people actually earn more during stock market downturns. Some examples include bankruptcy attorneys, shrewd experts who can turn around poorly performing companies, and debt collectors.

In many ways however, the conclusions derived in equations (6.6)-(6.8) seem to be insufficient to do full justice to the enormous importance that human capital and labor income decisions should have on optimal portfolio decisions. For instance, (6.8) implies that key investor characteristics such as age, professional rank, full- vs. part-time status, sex, education, etc., all have to be filtered through the lense of their impact on correlations collected in the vector $Cov[Y_{t+1}, \boldsymbol{R}_{t+1}]$, which is of course rather restrictive. In the following sections will therefore work to relax such a restrictive framework, to progressively allow these individual characteristics to potentially impact on optimal portfolios.

---

[7] To some extent, such a logic may also apply to holdings of government bonds issued in your own country, to be interpreted as the one in which you live and work, although real-life experience may suggest the opposite. In fact, with reference to US pension plans, Benartzi (2001) documents the same phenomenon on a massive scale for stock holdings by households, because these tend to hold disproportionate percentages of their wealth in stocks issued by the companies they work for.

2 - The Case of Constant Relative Risk Aversion Preferences

Let's generalize the framework of section 1 to the case in which preferences are less restrictive and in particular of the more realistic DARA/CRRA type. We keep assuming that the investor has a one period horizon, investing her wealth to support her consumption—from terminal wealth— on the next period. The investor receives next period labor income Y_{t+1}, which for analytical simplicity is assumed to be log-normally distributed:

$$y_{t+1} \equiv lnY_{t+1} \sim N(\bar{y}, \sigma_y^2). \tag{6.10}$$

We assume that labor income is uninsurable: you cannot write claims against your future income. As we shall derive in the following, the investor will be allowed to use her portfolio, by changing its structure, in order to (self-) insure any labor income shocks. Self-insurance means to tilt one's financial wealth towards assets that pay out well when background risk hits with poor realizations. Differently from section 1, to keep the problem as simple as possible, consider the case in which there are just one risk-free and one risky asset (a presumed-to-be well diversified portfolio), with continuously compounded returns of $r^f \equiv \ln(1 + R^f)$ and $r_{t+1} \equiv \ln(1 + R_{t+1})$. Furthermore,

$$r_{t+1} = E_t[r_{t+1}] + u_{t+1} \quad \text{with} \quad u_{t+1} \sim IID \ N(0, \sigma_u^2). \tag{6.11}$$

Risky returns and labor income may be correlated, in the sense that $Cov(r_{t+1}, y_{t+1}) \neq 0$. Finally, as anticipated, the investor's period t+1 utility function is of the CRRA-power utility type, with coefficient of constant relative risk aversion γ. Because we do not model any labor-leisure choice, this model is implicitly one of fixed labor supply in conjunction with a random wage in which the investor solves the following problem:

$$\max_{\omega_t} \delta E_t \left[\frac{W_{t+1}^{1-\gamma}}{1-\gamma} \right] \ subject \ to \ W_{t+1} = W_t[R^f + \omega_t(R_{t+1} - R^f)] + Y_{t+1} \tag{6.12}$$

Even though in (6.12) the argument of the felicity function keeps being defined as W_t to mean wealth, it is clear that in a single-period static problem, we could also set $C_{t+1} = W_{t+1}$ and speak of (real) consumption of the investor. After one period, at the end of her life and in the absence of heirs and bequests, as sad as this is, our investor will end up throwing a giant party for herself to eat all of her wealth by ordering hundreds of pizzas, cannolis, sushi trays, and all other goodies mentioned earlier in this book! When $\gamma > 0$, the problem (6.12) is a concave programming problem with equality constraints, in which the FOCs are both necessary and sufficient:

$$
\frac{\partial}{\partial \omega_t} E_t \left[\frac{W_{t+1}^{1-\gamma}}{1-\gamma} \right] \Bigg|_{\omega_t = \widehat{\omega}_t} = E_t \left[\frac{\partial}{\partial \omega_t} \frac{(W_t[R^f + \omega_t(R_{t+1} - R^f)] + Y_{t+1})^{1-\gamma}}{1-\gamma} \right] \Bigg|_{\widehat{\omega}_t}
$$
$$
= E_t[(W_t[R^f + \widehat{\omega}_t(R_{t+1} - R^f)] + Y_{t+1})^{-\gamma}(R_{t+1} - R^f)] = 0 \ (6.13)
$$

where the inversion of the order of expectation (integration) and differentiation is justified by the continuous and everywhere-differentiable nature of the power utility function. Equivalently, (6.13) may be written as:

$$
E_t[W_{t+1}^{-\gamma} R_{t+1}] = E_t[W_{t+1}^{-\gamma} R^f] = R^f E_t[W_{t+1}^{-\gamma}], \tag{6.14}
$$

which says that the MU-weighted expected risky asset return should equal at the optimum an identical MU-weighted riskless rate. If one log-linearizes (6.14), Campbell and Viceira (2001, 2002) show that we have:

$$
lnE_t[W_{t+1}^{-\gamma}(R_{t+1} - R^f)] = E_t[-\gamma lnW_{t+1} + ln(R_{t+1} - R^f)]
$$
$$
= E_t[(r_{t+1} - r^f)] + \frac{1}{2}Var_t[(r_{t+1} - r^f)] - \gamma Cov_t[w_{t+1}, (r_{t+1} - r^f)]
$$
$$
= E_t[(r_{t+1} - r^f)] + \frac{1}{2}\sigma_u^2 - \gamma Cov_t[w_{t+1}, r_{t+1}] \tag{6.15}
$$

because $Var_t[r_{t+1} - r^f] = Var_t[r_{t+1}] = E_t[(r_{t+1} - E_t[r_{t+1}])^2] = E_t[u_{t+1}^2] = \sigma_u^2$. At this point, useful insights can be neatly obtained only if Taylor approximations are employed which exploit our lognormal setup. In particular, we first need to modify the portfolio return expression, in the sense that because total portfolio return R_{t+1}^P equals $R^f + \omega_t(R_{t+1} - R^f)$, then:[8]

---

[8] The Taylor expansion that follows derives from the following results:

$$\ln\left(\frac{R_{t+1}^P}{R^f}\right) = r_{t+1}^P - r^f = \ln\left[1 + \omega_t\left(\frac{R_{t+1}^P}{R^f} - 1\right)\right]$$
$$= \ln[1 + \omega_t(\exp(r_{t+1} - r^f) - 1)]$$
$$= \omega_t(r_{t+1} - r^f) + \frac{1}{2}\omega_t(1 - \omega_t)(r_{t+1} - r^f)^2$$
$$+ o((r_{t+1} - r^f)^2) \tag{6.16}$$

which Campbell and Viceira (2001, 2002) show to be approximated as:

$$\ln\left(\frac{R_{t+1}^P}{R^f}\right) \cong \omega_t(r_{t+1} - r^f) + \frac{1}{2}\omega_t(1 - \omega_t)Var_t[r_{t+1} - r^f]$$
$$= \omega_t(r_{t+1} - r^f) + \frac{1}{2}\omega_t(1 - \omega_t)\sigma_u^2. \tag{6.17}$$

A similar approximation can be applied to the budget constraint of problem (6.12) re-written in terms of maximizing the utility of $W_{t+1}/Y_{t+1} = W_t R_{t+1}^P/Y_{t+1} + 1$ and using a first-order Taylor expansion of the log of the right-hand side around the mean log return of financial wealth $E_t[\ln(1 + R_{t+1}^P)]$ and of the wealth-income ratio $E_t[\ln(1 + W_{t+1}/Y_{t+1})]$:

$$\ln\left(\frac{W_{t+1}}{Y_{t+1}}\right) = w_{t+1} - y_{t+1} = \ln[1 + \exp(w_t + r_{t+1}^P - y_{t+1})]$$
$$\cong k + \xi(w_t + r_{t+1}^P - y_{t+1}), \tag{6.18}$$

which comes from the general result that $\ln(1" + " a) \cong k" + " \xi\ln(a)$ for

---

$$\frac{d\ln[1 + \omega_t(\exp(x) - 1)]}{dx} = \frac{\omega_t \exp(x)}{1 + \omega_t(\exp(x) - 1)}$$
$$\frac{d^2\ln[1 + \omega_t(\exp(x) - 1)]}{dx^2} = \frac{\omega_t \exp(x)[1 + \omega_t(\exp(x) - 1)] - [\omega_t \exp(x)]^2}{[1 + \omega_t(\exp(x) - 1)]^2}$$
$$= \frac{\omega_t(1 - \omega_t)\exp(x)}{[1 + \omega_t(\exp(x) - 1)]^2}.$$

$\xi \in (0,1)$. [9] Adding log labor income to both sides of the equation yields

$$w_{t+1} \cong k + \xi(w_t + r_{t+1}^P) + (1 - \xi)y_{t+1}, \tag{6.19}$$

i.e., (log-) end of period wealth is a constant plus a weighted average of (log) end-of-period financial wealth (equal to initial wealth plus portfolio return) and (log-) labor income. In particular, the elasticity of terminal wealth with respect to portfolio returns is ξ, while the elasticity of wealth to labor income is its complement to one, $1 - \xi$.

At this point, we know that the solution to problem (6.12) may be log-linearized to be:

$$E_t[(r_{t+1} - r^f)] + \frac{1}{2}\sigma_u^2 = \gamma Cov_t[w_{t+1}, r_{t+1}] \tag{6.20}$$

Substituting the expression in (6.19) to replace terminal wealth, yields:

$$
\begin{aligned}
E_t[(r_{t+1} - r^f)] + \frac{1}{2}\sigma_u^2 &= \gamma Cov_t[k + \xi(w_t + r_{t+1}^P) + (1 - \xi)y_{t+1}, r_{t+1}] \\
&= \gamma\xi Cov_t[r_{t+1}^P, r_{t+1}] + \gamma(1 - \xi)Cov_t[y_{t+1}, r_{t+1}] \tag{6.21}
\end{aligned}
$$

After substituting (6.17) for $r_{t+1}^P \cong r^f + \omega_t(r_{t+1} - r^f) + \frac{1}{2}\omega_t(1 - \omega_t)\sigma_u^2$, we are left with

$$
\begin{aligned}
E_t[(r_{t+1} &- r^f)] + \frac{1}{2}\sigma_u^2 \\
&\cong \gamma\xi Cov_t\left[r^f + \omega_t(r_{t+1} - r^f) + \frac{1}{2}\omega_t(1 - \omega_t)\sigma_u^2, r_{t+1}\right] \\
&\quad + \gamma(1 - \xi)Cov_t[y_{t+1}, r_{t+1}] \\
&= \gamma\xi\omega_t Cov_t[(r_{t+1} - r^f), r_{t+1}] + \gamma(1 - \xi)Cov_t[y_{t+1}, r_{t+1}] \\
&= \gamma\xi\omega_t\sigma_u^2 + \gamma(1 - \xi)Cov_t[y_{t+1}, r_{t+1}] \tag{6.22}
\end{aligned}
$$

---

[9] One can show that $\xi \equiv \frac{\exp(E[w_t + r_{t+1}^P - y_{t+1}])}{1 + \exp(E[w_t + r_{t+1}^P - y_{t+1}])}$. This log-linearization parameter can be interpreted as the elasticity of consumption with respect to financial wealth.

from which we can solve directly for ω_t:[10]

$$\hat{\omega}_t \cong \frac{1}{\xi} \frac{E_t[(r_{t+1} - r^f)] + \frac{1}{2}\sigma_u^2}{\gamma\sigma_u^2} - \left(1 - \frac{1}{\xi}\right) \frac{Cov_t[y_{t+1}, r_{t+1}]}{\sigma_u^2}$$
$$= Myopic\ asset\ demand + Hedging\ background\ risk \quad (6.22)$$

The expression in (6.22) is on the one hand very different from (6.9): the latter concerns a truly multivariate portfolio optimization problem with N assets; the former, the simple decision between one risky asset (say, some notion of a market portfolio) and the riskless asset. Moreover, while (6.22) is derived from a string of Taylor approximations and log-linearizations, (6.8) is an exact formula. Of course, the latter can be derived in this form just from assuming very special—and one may say problematic, because of their IARA and IRRA nature—preferences, while (6.22) concerns the realistic case of power, CRRA preferences.

On the other hand, the intuition of (6.9) and (6.22) are very similar. The first term on the right-hand side of (6.22) represents the fraction in the risky asset if labor income is uncorrelated with the risky asset return ($Cov_t[y_{t+1}, r_{t+1}] = 0$). It is positively related to the adjusted conditional equity premium ($E_t[(r_{t+1} - r^f)] + 0.5\sigma_u^2$) and inversely related to the investor's risk aversion coefficient, γ. As usual, the $0.5\sigma_u^2$ adjustment is a just a convexity correction due to log-normality. The second term represents the hedging component: if $Cov_t[y_{t+1}, r_{t+1}] < 0$, then since $\xi < 1$, the demand for the risky asset is increased because it can be exploited to diversify away some of the investor's labor income risk. Hedging demand arises from the desire to reduce lifetime consumption risk, and here this risk arises from the correlation between returns and labor income. Or, to express the same idea from a slightly different perspective, if the investor's labor income has a "suitable" statistical pattern vis-a-vis the stock market and hedges its fluctuations, she can reasonably take on greater financial risk.

---

[10] Samuelson (1969) and Merton (1969, 1971) demonstrate that for the horizon of the investor (i.e., T − t) to have no effect on the optimal risky-asset shares in an intertemporal portfolio choice model, requires rather special circumstances. These include power utility, IID returns, and the absence of labor income. This equivalence between the single-period and multi-period solutions is often referred to as the myopic portfolio choice solution. Hence, under these assumptions, for instance, asset shares do not differ between working and retirement years, because longer horizons have no consequence.

When $Cov_t[y_{t+1}, r_{t+1}] > 0$, a situation in which the investor's income is closely tied to the behavior of the stock market, then the investor should correspondingly reduce his position in risky equities. In fact, if the investor's coefficient of relative risk aversion is sufficiently high and ξ is large and positive (say, if the investor's portfolio contained a large position in his own firm's stock) then the investor may even optimally hold a short position in the overall risky portfolio. These remarks formalize, though in a very simple context, the idea that an investor's wage income stream represents an asset and that its statistical covariance with the equity portion of his portfolio should matter for his overall asset allocation.

It is perhaps even more striking to explore further the case where $Cov_t[y_{t+1}, r_{t+1}] = 0$: because since $\xi < 1$, even in this case the optimal fraction invested in the risky portfolio,

$$\frac{1}{\xi} \frac{E_t[(r_{t+1} - r^f)] + \frac{1}{2}\sigma_u^2}{\gamma \sigma_u^2} > \frac{E_t[(r_{t+1} - r^f)] + \frac{1}{2}\sigma_u^2}{\gamma \sigma_u^2}, \qquad (6.23)$$

exceeds the fraction the investor places in the risky portfolio were there to be no labor income at all. The intuition is that the absence of correlation between human and financial wealth income allows for a good deal of risk reduction, thereby implying a higher optimal risky asset portfolio weight. Riskless labor income creates a tilt in investor portfolios toward risky equities. This is not surprising as the labor income stream in this case contributes a risk free asset to the investor's portfolio. Behind the result in (6.23), there are two effects. One is a *wealth effect*: ceteris paribus, an investor with a labor income stream is wealthier than an investor without one, and with CRRA utility some of that additional wealth will be allocated to equities. This is complemented by a pure *portfolio substitution* effect: the risk free asset alters the overall portfolio proportions in a way that manifests itself as an increased share of financial wealth in risky assets.[11]

In the extreme case where labor income is perfectly positively correlated with the return on the risky asset, human capital becomes then an implicit investment in that asset. Hence, the investor should compensate by tilting

---

[11] The ability of an investor to adjust her labor supply—and thus her labor income—only enhances these effects. Under a flexible labor supply, the investor/worker can elect not only to save more but also to work more if she experiences an unfavorably risky return realization. Her ability to hedge averse risky return realizations is thus enriched, and stocks appear effectively less risky, see Campbell and Viceira (2002).

her financial portfolio away from such an asset. Yet, one can show that the increase in wealth is sufficient to ensure that the weight in the risky port-folio increases:

$$\hat{\omega}_t \cong \frac{1}{\xi}\frac{E_t[(r_{t+1}-r^f)]+\frac{1}{2}\sigma_u^2}{\gamma\sigma_u^2} + \left(\frac{1}{\xi}-1\right)\frac{\sigma_y}{\sigma_u} > \frac{E_t[(r_{t+1}-r^f)]+\frac{1}{2}\sigma_u^2}{\gamma\sigma_u^2}. \quad (6.24)$$

Visibly, in (6.24) the optimal weight of risky assets can be computed from the standard weight, by multiplying it by $1/\xi > 1$ and subtracting from it $(1 - 1/\xi) > 0$. The following example makes these notions more concrete.

Example 6.2. Suppose that you observe that Mary invests exactly 80% of her wealth in the market portfolio, and 20% in cash, i.e., the risk-free asset. The market portfolio is characterized by a monthly risk premium of 0.5% and a monthly volatility of 4.62%. You know that Mary is characterized by CRRA preferences with $\gamma = 5$ and her labor income is characterized by low variance, $\sigma_y^2 = (1\%)^2$. However, you ignore both her ξ, the elasticity of terminal wealth with respect to portfolio returns, and especially the corre-lation between Mary's labor income and risky market portfolio. Mary is a single-period expected utility of terminal wealth maximizer.
Because we know that

$$\hat{\omega}_t = \frac{1}{\xi}\frac{E_t[(r_{t+1}-r^f)]+\frac{1}{2}\sigma_u^2}{\gamma\sigma_u^2} - \left(1-\frac{1}{\xi}\right)\frac{Cov_t[y_{t+1},r_{t+1}]}{\sigma_u^2}$$

$$= \frac{1}{\xi}\frac{E_t[(r_{t+1}-r^f)]+\frac{1}{2}\sigma_u^2}{\gamma\sigma_u^2} + \left(\frac{1}{\xi}-1\right)\frac{\sigma_y}{\sigma_u}Corr_t[y_{t+1},r_{t+1}]$$

we can try and solve the equation

$$0.5 = \frac{1}{\xi}\frac{0.005+\frac{1}{2}(0.0462)^2}{5\cdot(0.0462)^2} + \left(\frac{1}{\xi}-1\right)\frac{0.01}{0.0462}\rho_{y,r}$$

$$= \frac{0.569}{\xi}+0.217\frac{\rho_{y,r}}{\xi} - 0.217\rho_{y,r}$$

or

$$0.5\xi - 0.217\rho_{y,r} + 0.217\rho_{y,r}\xi - 0.569 = 0.$$

This is a linear equation in two unknowns, ξ and $\rho_{y,r}$. Even though a closed-form solution is impossible, we can search for possible combinations of ξ and $\rho_{y,r}$ that satisfy the equation, at least approximately. If you try and do that (this requires using numerical methods, such as grid search in Excel), the results may be easily summarized in the plot below.

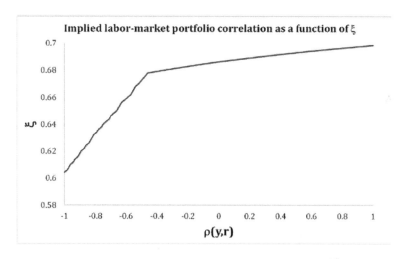

Several remarks are in order. First, note that the vertical axis concerning the values of ξ for which a solution can be found, indicates that $\hat{\omega} = 0.8$ is only compatible with values of the elasticity of terminal wealth with respect to portfolio returns approximately between 0.6 and 0.7. This means that any other value of ξ cannot characterize Mary, in the sense that if one sets ξ either below 0.6 or to exceed 0.7, then no correlation between labor income and market returns can be found to yield $\hat{\omega} = 0.8$. For ξ between 0.6 and 0.7, the plot shows that values of correlation between -1 and +1 are compatible with the observed portfolio share. For instance, when $\xi = 0.65$, then $\rho_{y,r}$ of approximately -0.66 yields an allocation to stocks equal to 80%. Implicitly, the less labor income is important to Mary, i.e., the larger ξ, the higher is the correlation between financial returns and labor income that is compatible with the relatively high share allocated to stocks that we know characterizes Mary.

What are plausible correlation values concerning labor income shocks and aggregate risky returns, as identified by the whole equity market? At an overall level—if we think of a representative agent summing up the income of all workers in the United States—the correlation of human capital with stocks is low. Cocco, Gomes, and Maenhout (2005), for example, report that the correlation of U.S. labor income with stock returns is -0.02 for those with a college degree, 0.01 for those with only a high school education, and -0.01 for those not completing their high school studies. Thus for the average investor, human capital tends to be bond-like. Perhaps the already mentioned "one hundred minus your age rule"—by which you should invest in stocks 100 minus your age—may be correct after all, at least for the average person in the US.

Under these essentially zero correlation estimates, one paradoxical implication of many related models of the life-cycle type (see Cocco, Gomes, and Maenhout, 2005) - i.e., models of the investment behavior of workers over their lifetimes - is that they normally predict that poorer households would hold more equity than rich households. To understand this point, consider that, assuming they have the same risk preferences as rich households, the total wealth of poor families is dominated by human capital. Thus they would offset this bond-like capital by preferring equities in their financial portfolios. It turns out that this prediction is highly counterfactual.

However, one ought to be careful before inferring the correlations from the data as if these were constant over time. Benzoni, Collin-Dufresne, and Goldstein (2007) and Lynch and Tan (2011) specify labor income processes that match the low correlation of labor income and stock returns for the average investor, but allow more realistic dynamics where labor income and stock returns can co-move over business cycle and longer frequencies. This is intuitive: we expect labor income and stock returns to be correlated over long frequencies as both human capital and stock capital should benefit from growing economies. Benzoni, Collin-Dufresne, and Goldstein's model co-integrated labor and stock returns, which make young human capital stock-like and old(er) human capital bond-like. Thus, the young optimally hold no equities (they actually want to short equities if they can), and equity portfolio shares increase with age. Lynch and Tan make the point that although the correlation of labor income and equities is close to zero unconditionally, it can mask pronounced conditional correlation over the business cycle. In particular, while there is not much correlation between labor income and equities overall, there is significant correlation during recession and market crashes. Guidolin and Hyde (2012) using regime switching models to capture the same idea, find that the hedging power of industrial sector returns for labor income in the US and the UK is time-varying.

Finally, let us mention that residential real estate is a source of background risk as important as human capital because in most developed countries it represents roughly half of aggregate, tangible wealth. Residential real estate also has features that make it distinct from pure financial assets. In particular, it provides a stream of housing services which are inseparable from the house itself. Houses are also indivisible assets: one may acquire a small house but not 1/2 of a medium-sized house. Cocco et al. (2005) studies the stock-bond portfolio allocation problem in the context of a model similar to the one in section 2. The only peculiarity is that the investor directly derives utility at time t from housing services so that non-durable consumption and housing services are complementary. In order to capture the idea that houses are indivisible assets, Cocco et al. (2005) imposes a minimum size constraint; to capture the fact that there are transactions costs to changing one's housing stock, the agent is assumed to receive only a fraction of the house price if she sells her housing stock; finally, the need for down-payments is also modeled.

Cocco et al. (2005) numerically solve the model to obtain a number of realistic implications. The model implies that the share in equity investments is increasing over the life cycle: early in life, housing investments keep investors' liquid assets low and they choose not to participate in the stock market; when this constrain is removed, the equity share grows with age.

References and Further Readings

Ang, A. *Asset Management: A Systematic Approach to Factor Investing*. Oxford: Oxford University Press, 2014.

Benartzi, S. Excessive extrapolation and the allocation of 401 (k) accounts to company stock. *Journal of Finance*, 56: 1747-1764, 2001.

Benzoni, L., Collin-Dufresne, P., & Goldstein, R. S. Portfolio Choice over the Life-Cycle when the Stock and Labor Markets Are Cointegrated. *Journal of Finance*, 62, 2123-2167, 2007.

Bodie, Z., Merton, R. C., and Samuelson, W. F. Labor Supply Flexibility and Portfolio Choice in a Life Cycle Model. *Journal of Economic Dynamics and Control*, 16: 427-449, 1992.

Campbell, J. Y., and Viceira, L. M. Who Should Buy Long-Term Bonds? *American Economic Review,* 91: 99-127, 2001.

Campbell, J. Y., and Viceira, L. M. *Strategic Asset Allocation: Portfolio Choice for Long-Term Investors*. New York, Oxford University Press, USA, 2002.

Cocco, J. F., Gomes, F. J., & Maenhout, P. J. Consumption and Portfolio Choice Over the Life Cycle. *Review of Financial Studies*, 18: 491-533, 2005.

Guidolin, M., and Hyde, S. Optimal Portfolios for Occupational Funds under Time-Varying Correlations in Bull and Bear Markets. *IGIER working paper* No. 455, 2012.

Lustig, H., & Van Nieuwerburgh, S. The Returns on Human Capital: Good News on Wall Street is Bad News on Main Street. *Review of Financial Studies*, 21: 2097-2137, 2008.

Lynch, A. W., and Tan, S. Labor Income Dynamics at Business-Cycle Frequencies: Implications for Portfolio Choice. *Journal of Financial Economics*, 101: 333-359, 2011.

Merton, R. C. Lifetime Portfolio Selection Under Uncertainty: The Continuous-Time Case. *Review of Economics and Statistics*, 51: 247-257, 1969.

Merton, R. C. Optimum Consumption and Portfolio Rules in A Continuous-Time Model. *Journal of Economic Theory*, 3: 373-413, 1971.

Samuelson, P. A. Lifetime Portfolio Selection by Dynamic Stochastic Programming. *Review of Economics and Statistics*, 51: 239-246, 1969.

7 Performance Measurement and Attribution

"His promises were, as he then was, mighty; but his performance, as he is now, nothing." (William Shakespeare, "Henry VIII", Act IV, scene 2, line 41, c. 1613)

Summary: - 1. Generalities – 2. Simple Performance Measures – 3 Decomposing Performance – 4. Active vs. Passive Portfolio Management.

1 - Generalities

So far in this book we have considered the asset management process mostly in an *ex-ante perspective*: for given preferences, asset menu, constraints, and the parameters/scenarios characterizing the future evolution of asset prices, we have proposed a range of methods and approaches to select optimal portfolio shares. In this final chapter, we adopt instead an *ex-post perspective*: given the same framework of choice, we ask whether ex-post, past portfolio selections of assets and the weights attributed to them, performed (usually, in risk-adjusted terms, i.e., after taking preferences into account) as well as one would expect or even require. We therefore write about performance evaluation methods.

The goal of performance analysis is to distinguish skilled from unskilled investment managers. But, how do you tell them apart? In a population of 100 investment managers, say 5 percent, or 5, should have exceptional performance by chance alone. None of the successful managers will admit to being lucky; all of the unsuccessful managers will cite bad luck. One can divide all existing managers along the dimensions of skill and luck. Those with both skill and luck are blessed. They deserve to thrive, and they will. Those with neither skill nor luck are doomed and will be wiped out by natural selection. But what about the two other categories? Those managers with skill but no luck will be unjustly expelled from the industry because their historical performance will not reflect their true skill. Finally, there is the fourth category, managers who have luck without skill. Fortunately or unfortunately, we observe only the combination of skill and luck. Both the talented and the intolerably lucky, unskilled managers will show up in the records with positive return histories. The challenge is to separate the two groups. Importantly, the mere existence of positive returns does not prove skill because important issues remain. How much risk was taken on in generating that return? Performance analysis will also involve comparing ex post returns to ex ante risk in a statistically rigorous way.

In general, there are two key requirements of a valid portfolio manager:

I.   The ability to derive above-average returns for a given risk class; superior risk-adjusted returns can be derived through either superior timing or superior security selection.

II. The ability to diversify the portfolio completely to eliminate all unsystematic risk, relative to the portfolio's benchmark.

Such an additional, final step is all the more important because a large percentage of actual asset management choices are made by professional money managers. Professional managers include mutual funds, pension funds, hedge funds, college and foundation endowments, and discretionary accounts under delegated proxies. It is then crucial to an investor utilizing one of these managers to correctly understand how the management skills have contributed to performance relative to competing funds or benchmark investments. Moreover, when restrictions have been imposed on the operations pursued by fund management (e.g., social responsibility limits to the asset menu, or specialization constraints in terms of asset classes, sectors, countries, etc.), performance measurement represents a crucial step to understand the realized, ex-post costs deriving from such restrictions.

The theory and practice of performance measurement have made tremendous steps forward in the last three decades: we have gone from simple sorts of investment vehicles on the basis of their total return in the 1970s and early 1980s, to a careful application of the key principles of modern finance theory, such as the application of risk adjustment and the implementation of multi-factor models to decompose the systematic vs. idiosyncratic sources of realized performance.

The evaluation of portfolio performance is essentially concerned with comparing the return earned by some portfolio with the return earned on one or more benchmarks. It is therefore important that the portfolios chosen for comparison are truly comparable. This means that they not only must carry similar risk, but they must also be bound by similar constraints.

For example, an institution that restricts its managers to investing in bonds rated AA or better should be evaluated by comparing their performance to bond portfolios that are unconstrained and include junk paper. We shall hope that over a sufficiently long period of time, the latter manager will achieve a higher mean realized return to compensate risk-bearing.

In earlier chapters, when we computed returns, we calculated the capital gains plus dividends from an initial investment. This looked almost obvious. Therefore, if I buy a stock (say, Lonestar) at 100 euros, hold it for 3 months, receive a dividend of 4 euros after 2 months and then re-sell at 102, the rate of return is 6% = 100x(102 + 4 - 100)/100. One may expect the same to apply to a large managed portfolio: if the total net asset value (henceforth, NAV) of Aldebaran Fund is initially 759,044,040 euros, it pays out dividends (sometimes income funds do so) for a total of 278,494 euros and at the of a 3-month period its NAV has grown to 804,308,190 euros, then one may simplistically conclude that Aldebaran's rate of return is also 6% = (804,308,190 + 278,494 - 759,044,040)/759,044,040.[1] Hence, the performance and skills displayed by the chief investment officer at Aldebaran may seem no different from the economic value generated by a simple investment in Lonestar shares.

However, you now receive additional information: over the 3 months, Aldebaran fund has faced net outflows of 5,495,500, i.e., in net terms the existing shareholders have reduced their investment in the fund by 5.5 million euros, not a negligible amount. Then we need to re-assess our initial view: the money manager at Aldebaran must have generated an increase in the fund's wealth that is not just (804,308,190 + 278,494 - 759,044,040) but instead of (804,308,190 + 5,495,500 + 278,494 - 759,044,040) = 51,038,144 and hence a net rate of return of 100x(51,038,144)/ 759,044,040 = 6.72%, which is a bit more impressive than the original 6%. What is going on? Simple, in the case of one individual security, we compute rates of return for one buy-and-hold pick that we are in control of; in the case of a mutual fund, the performance generated must be net out of new contributions and withdrawals, which may easily mask the actual outcomes from portfolio management. Importantly, this represents a necessary course of action exactly because *the inflows and outflows happen not to be under the control of the money manager.* Think of open-end mutual

---

[1] The net asset value of a fund/investment company equals the total market value of all the firm's assets divided by the total number of fund shares outstanding. The NAV for a fund is analogous to the share price of a corporation's common stock.

funds:[2] old and new shareholders independently select how much addi-tional wealth to invest and/or to dis-invest from the fund. In other words, while in the case of individual securities or simple buy-and-hold portfolios under our control, the simple definition of rate of return is sufficient, in the case of managed investment funds and products that are open—i.e., sub-ject to inflows and outflows—one needs a slightly more complex notion of return, the *time-weighted return* (henceforth, TWR). We eliminate the ef-fect of having different amounts of funds available if we calculate the rate of return in each time period and then compound the return to determine it in the overall period:

Time-weighted return of a managed, open-end portfolio: It is the geo-metric return calculated from the simple returns on every single measura-ble period within which inflows and outflows from the portfolio are not possible.[3]

The logic is that, unless the inflows and outflows are under the control of the manager (and in most cases they are not), a portfolio manager should not be rewarded or penalized for the good or bad fortune of having extra funds available at a particular time. As shown by the following example, the complexity of the calculation required by the TWR is not negligible. However, if the inflows and outflows are not related to market perfor-mance, then less frequent calculations may yield a reasonable approximation.

---

[2] A closed-end fund operates like any other public firm: its stock trades on the regular secondary market, and the market price of its shares is determined by supply and de-mand; it offers no further shares and does not repurchase the shares on demand. No new investment capital is available to the fund unless it makes another public sale of securities. Similarly, no funds can be withdrawn unless the investment company de-cides to repurchase its stock, which is quite unusual. Open-end (mutual) funds contin-uously sell and repurchase shares after their initial public offerings. They stand ready to sell additional shares of the fund at the NAV, with or without sales charge, or to buy back (redeem) shares of the fund at the NAV, with or without redemption fees.

[3] Often managed (mutual, pension, hedge, etc.) funds are sold in units. Inflows and outflows affect the number of units but any one unit reflects the same initial invest-ment. In this case tracing the performance of one unit is equivalent to determining the time-weighted rate of return.

Example 7.1. Consider the dynamics of returns on investment, inflows and outflows (as made available by the fund's depositary bank on the night before the trading day, all in thousands of euros) for the last half of December 2015 of the equity mutual fund Aldebaran:

Date	Initial Value	Inflow	Outflow	P&L (%)	Final Value
Dec. 16	684,595	2,404	4,954	3,005 (0.44)	685,050
Dec. 17	685,050	1,595	4,338	-5,549 (-0.81)	676,758
Dec. 18	676,758	674	5,650	585 (0.09)	672,367
Dec. 21	672,367	2,594	15,505	6,505 (0.99)	665,961
Dec. 22	665,961	1,586	13,695	7,505 (1.15)	661,357
Dec. 23	661,357	74	3,050	-969 (-0.15)	657,412
Dec. 28	657,412	684	1,553	1,695 (0.26)	658,238
Dec. 29	658,238	3,505	4,100	-3,505 (-0.53)	654,138
Dec. 30	654,138	5,605	2,685	7,993 (1.22)	665,051

There is a clear and probably typical pattern: even though their percentage incidence is modest (indeed, one ought to use money market funds for these purposes, not equity funds), before the Christmas holidays, investors tend to cash out of funds, possibly to finance their presents, vacations, etc.; after the holidays, some money slowly starts to trickle back into the funds. One wonders whether such patterns may cloud our ability to judge whether Aldebaran's fund manager is any good.

The question on the skills of Aldebaran's fund manager relates to the fifth column, where the daily total profits and losses of the fund have been computed as a result of trades that have been performed and of the re-evaluation of the net asset value of the fund. As one can see, the manager has been quite good: in 6 days out of 9, profits not losses have been generated and the total P&L sum is in excess of 17 million euros, almost 2 million a day. Yet, in overall terms, the wealth under management has shrunk from 684,595,000 to 665,051,000 euros, a decline of a remarkable 19,544,000 euros. However, this is not due to the manager's lack of skill, but instead to a net outflow of (55,530,000 – 18,721,000) = 36,809,000 euros possibly entirely due to the Christmas shopping spree and not to a negative judgment on the ability of the fund management to create value. Indeed, notice that:

$$\underbrace{684,595}_{Initial\ value} + \underbrace{17,265}_{Net\ P\&L\ from\ ptf.} - \underbrace{36,809}_{Net\ inflow} = \underbrace{665,051}_{Final\ value}.$$

In spite of this, one may be easily fooled into total return calculations for the fund that ignore the net inflow element, say as in the table below.

These simple returns are computed as (Final Value – Initial Value)/Initial Value, for instance 0.066% = 100x(685,050 – 684,595)/684,595. If you compute the average of the last column in the table, you get -0.318%, the corresponding geometric mean is -0.321%, which are pretty dismal *daily* performances (if you really want to annualize, you get a whopping -80%). However, the data in the original table should make us suspicious that this portfolio manager only looks bad because Aldebaran is losing funds just before Christmas, which may be normal with all the panettonis, stuffed turkeys, and struffolis bought.

Date	Initial Value	Inflow	Outflow	Final Value	Simple Return
Dec. 16	684,595	2,404	4,954	685,050	0.066%
Dec. 17	685,050	1,595	4,338	676,758	-1.210%
Dec. 18	676,758	674	5,650	672,367	-0.649%
Dec. 21	672,367	2,594	15,505	665,961	-0.953%
Dec. 22	665,961	1,586	13,695	661,357	-0.691%
Dec. 23	661,357	74	3,050	657,412	-0.597%
Dec. 28	657,412	684	1,553	658,238	0.126%
Dec. 29	658,238	3,505	4,100	654,138	-0.623%
Dec. 30	654,138	5,605	2,685	665,051	1.668%

How would the right, TWR calculations look like? They appear in the following table:

Date	Initial Value	Inflow	Outflow	P&L (%)	TW Return
Dec. 16	684,595	2,404	4,954	3,005	0.441%
Dec. 17	685,050	1,595	4,338	-5,549	-0.813%
Dec. 18	676,758	674	5,650	585	0.087%
Dec. 21	672,367	2,594	15,505	6,505	0.986%
Dec. 22	665,961	1,586	13,695	7,505	1.148%
Dec. 23	661,357	74	3,050	-969	-0.147%
Dec. 28	657,412	684	1,553	1,695	0.258%
Dec. 29	658,238	3,505	4,100	-3,505	-0.533%
Dec. 30	654,138	5,605	2,685	7,993	1.216%

These TW returns are simply computed as P&L/(Initial Value + Inflow − Outflow), for instance 0.441% = 100x3,005/(684,595 + 2,404 − 4,954). If you compute the average of the last column in the table, you get +0.294%, the corresponding geometric mean is +0.291%, which is positive and far from negligible, corresponding to approximately 73% in annualized terms. In fact, one would have a hard time to claim that Aldebaran's manager is doing a poor job, even though not enough data has been provided to claim that she is doing a good one, of course.

---

2 - Simple Performance Measures

A first important choice in performance measurement consists of whether total or systematic risk should be used to perform the risk-adjustment of the raw, time-weighted performance measures. As we have seen in chapters 2-4, investors are plausibly modeled as risk averse and in delegated portfolio management—even if the money manager herself may be risk-neutral—it seems appropriate that risk discounting be applied.

Total risk is a sensible measure for large, already well-diversified portfolios. For instance, sovereign and endowment funds may easily be ranked in this way. Such investment vehicles will normally find very little comfort in the fact that part of the risk could be diversified away if they held other assets when the portfolio under consideration contains their total assets. Total risk means that indicators based on (say) portfolio variance or standard deviation, for instance, the Sharpe ratio, should be used. Systematic risk is instead sensible when the portfolio is smaller either in size or in breadth, because constraints have been imposed on its overall diversification. For instance, a specialized domestic small cap equity fund faces severe limits to diversification. In this case, risk-adjusting on the basis of its market beta or the set of its betas estimated vs. a range of well-recognized factors, becomes sensible.

A first, simple technique works in the following way: given a fund/manager/vehicle (henceforth, FMV) to be assessed, a synthetic portfolio of assets having approximately the same amount of risk is randomly built by drawing securities for a given, wide universe of assets.[4] Such a

---

[4] We disregard comparisons of FMV performance with portfolios or competing FMVs when risk-matching is not performed and instead the comparisons just occur within

portfolio may be equally weighted (each security receives the same weight) with probabilities of inclusion that are proportional to the market cap, or value-weighted with equal probabilities of inclusion. The idea is to randomly build a large number of such benchmark portfolios, say M. The benchmark must incorporate the same restrictions that applied ex-ante to the FMV. For instance, the benchmark for a corporate bond, non-investment grade mutual fund cannot include Treasury notes or long credit default swaps. The performance of the FMV under consideration is then compared to the performance—over the same period and horizon—of the average across the M random benchmarks that have been constructed. The *difference* in realized TWR vs. the simulated benchmark average is then measured (and statistical tests of hypotheses become possible) in terms of a Montecarlo distribution. If such a distribution has a positive mean, median, or is anyway shifted towards the right, this leads to a positive assessment of the FMV's performance. If the benchmark portfolios have been accurately built, no such differences can be imputed to exposure to risk, hence the differences measure the skill of the portfolio manager.

For instance, suppose that Aldebaran has achieved a 5-year annualized return of 9%, has a total annualized standard deviation of 22%, and a beta of 1.3. One can form 10,000 random portfolios of international domestic stocks—the same asset menu from which Aldeberan has been selecting following its own mandate—that have approximately a standard deviation of 22% and a beta of 1.3 (some tolerances need to be fixed, say between 21.5 and 22.5% standard deviation and with a beta between 1.28 and 1.32). Suppose that the average TWR across such 10,000 portfolios is 7.5%. Then 0.5% represents a money management plus originated by Aldebaran. Especially if the 9% had been measured after all fees, expenses, and commissions charged by Aldebaran, these 50 bps of spread in performance represent good news. Note that in this example, the benchmark has been built applying a double sort by standard deviation and beta, which is complex but avoids a choice between total and systemic risk. This technique is sometimes referred to a *peer group comparison*.

Apart from direct comparisons, there are four different one-parameter performance measures that have been proposed in the literature. These measures differ in their definition of risk and their treatment of the ability of the investor to adjust the risk level of any fund in which she might invest. The first, already well-known measure is the *Sharpe ratio*, also called

---

broadly defined categories (e.g., "international equity", "liquidity", "income" funds etc.). A few of these methods are described by Elton et al. (2009) with skepticism.

(mean) *excess return to variability measure:*[5]

$$SR_{FMV} \equiv \frac{(T^{-1} \sum_{t=1}^{T} R_{FMV,t}) - R^f}{\sqrt{T^{-1} \sum_{t=1}^{T}[R_{FMV,t} - (T^{-1} \sum_{t=1}^{T} R_{FMV,t})]^2}}. \qquad (7.1)$$

As we known from chapter 3, the Sharpe ratio represents the slope of the capital market line and it measures the most favorable, achievable trade-off between risk premia and risk—as measured by total portfolio standard deviation. When a riskless asset exists, then the CML represents the efficient frontier. The logic of ranking FMVs based on their Sharpe ratio is that they should be as close as possible to the CML, and ideally positioned on it. The Sharpe measure looks at the decision from the point of view of an investor choosing a FMV to represent the majority her investment, in the sense that if the investor desired a risk different from that offered by a given FMV, she would modify the risk by lending and/or borrowing given the FMV selected.

Another widely employed performance measure is *CML alpha*, to be interpreted as the percentage return difference between the actual mean realized return of a given FMV and the expected return that would be anticipated if the FMV were efficient and fell on the CML. The comparison with the CML reflects the fact that a money manager can always obtain a portfolio of the desired risk on the CML through the naive strategy of placing part of the money in the market portfolio and part in the riskless asset (and, indeed, should have done so if the manager had no special selection skills). Thus, a measure of the manager's performance is how much better she performed vs. this naive strategy. Because we know from chapter 3 that—in the absence of frictions and when there is a riskless asset—the equation of the CML is

$$E[R_{PF,t}] - R^f = \frac{E[R_t^m] - R^f}{\sqrt{Var[R_t^m]}} \sqrt{Var[R_{PF,t}]}, \qquad (7.2)$$

the CML alpha is simply the intercept that reconciles the sample mean re-

---

[5] In this chapter, we assume unlimited borrowing and lending at the same riskless interest rate. The simple ranking criteria introduced fail to apply when limits to borrowing and lending exist, or borrowing and lending rates may differ. Elton et al. (2009) discuss how the criteria might be modified in this case.

turn of a given FMV with its risk as measured by its standard deviation:

$$\alpha_{FMV}^{CML} \equiv (T^{-1} \sum_{t=1}^{T} R_{FMV,t} - R^f) - \frac{(T^{-1} \sum_{t=1}^{T} R_t^m) - R^f}{\sqrt{T^{-1} \sum_{t=1}^{T} [R_t^m - (T^{-1} \sum_{t=1}^{T} R_t^m)]^2}} \times$$

$$\times \sqrt{T^{-1} \sum_{t=1}^{T} [R_{FMV,t} - (T^{-1} \sum_{t=1}^{T} R_{FMV,t})]^2} . \tag{7.3}$$

$\alpha_{FMV}^{CML} > 0$ implies that in mean-standard deviation space, a given portfolio lies above the CML and α_{FMV}^{CML} does measure this difference; $\alpha_{FMV}^{CML} < 0$ indicates that a given FMV lies below the CML. Clearly, according to this metric, portfolios ought to be ranked on the basis of their α_{FMV}^{CML}s and F with positive α_{FMV}^{CML} should be sought after. Note that the ranking of FMVs based on (7.1) and (7.3) will be different, even though both measures involve the ratio between sample, realized risk premia and realized standard deviation; however, in the case of (7.1) we care directly for the Sharpe ratio of the FMV, in the case of (7.3), the ratio between risk premium and realized volatility concerns the market portfolio. Figure 7.1 illustrates this important aspect: the distance A-A' is greater than the distance B-B', even though portfolios A' and B' lie on the same ray going through the riskless rate. Equivalently and rather visibly, $\alpha_A^{CML} > \alpha_B^{CML}$ even though $SR_A < SR_B$. Therefore we can say that a manager buying A is able to outperform a mixture of the market portfolio, and lending with the same risk as A' by more than a manager who buys B at the same risk level as B'.

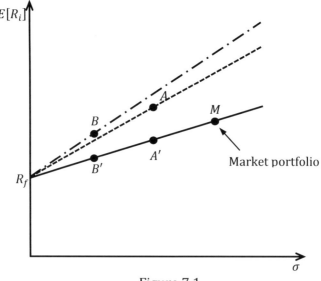

Figure 7.1

Third, another famous performance index is the *Treynor ratio*, also called (mean) *excess return to beta ratio*:[6]

$$TR_{FMV} \equiv \frac{(T^{-1} \sum_{t=1}^{T} R_{FMV,t}) - R^f}{\hat{\beta}_{FMV}}, \qquad (7.4)$$

where $\hat{\beta}_{FMV}$ is a sample estimate of the beta characterizing the FMV, computed according to the methods reviewed in chapter 5. The Treynor ratio represents the slope of the CAPM security market line, and it measures the achievable trade-off between risk premia and systematic risk. The logic of ranking FMVs based on their Treynor ratio is that they should be as close as possible to the SML, ideally positioned on it or even above it. The expression for TR_{FMV} measures the portfolio's risk premium per unit of systematic risk. All risk-averse investors would prefer to maximize this value. Note that the risk variable beta measures systematic risk and tells us nothing about the diversification of the portfolio. It implicitly assumes a completely diversified portfolio, which means that systematic risk is the relevant risk measure. Comparing a portfolio's TR_{FMV} value to a similar measure for the market portfolio—which equals the market risk premium as the market's beta equals 1—indicates whether the portfolio would plot above the SML.

The Treynor measure looks at the decision from the point of view of an in-

---

[6] When performance measurement is centered on the notion of beta, this is subject to "Roll's critique", acknowledging that beta is not unambiguously defined, also as an empirical risk measure. For instance, the beta estimated again the S&P 500 index is likely to differ from beta estimated from a regression on the MSCI International Word index. Changing the definition of the market portfolio can change both the beta and the ranking of portfolios. Roll (1980) has shown that if the proxy for the market portfolio is not a truly efficient portfolio, then the SML using this proxy may not be the true SML—the true SML could have a higher slope. In such a case, a portfolio plotted above the SML and derived using a poor benchmark could actually plot below the SML that uses the true market portfolio. For instance, Carlson (1970) and Brown and Brown (1987) have examined the overall performance of US mutual funds finding results that depended heavily on which market series were used; most fund groups outperformed the Dow Jones index but only a few had gross returns better than the S&P 500 or the NYSE composite. In fact, in performance evaluation is usually unwise to get fixated with one specific ranking. It may instead pay out to evaluate performance under several alternative definitions of the market portfolio and of beta. If the performance is robust (e.g., it appears good under a reasonable set of alternative market definitions), the user can feel confident in the result.

vestor choosing a FMV that just represents a portion of her financial wealth, and for which the overall contribution to systematic risk needs to be as efficient as possible, i.e., rewarded in a way consistent with the CAPM.[7] Interestingly, a poorly diversified portfolio could have a high ranking on the basis of the Treynor performance measure but a much lower ranking on the basis of the Sharpe performance measure. Any difference in rank would come directly from a difference in diversification.

Fourth and final, the extension of the CML alpha measure to the CAPM is *Jensen's alpha*, to be interpreted as the percentage return difference between the actual mean realized return of a given FMV and the return that would be expected if the FMV were efficient and lied on the SML. Because we know from chapters 3 and 5 that—in the absence of frictions and when there is a riskless asset—the equation of the SML is

$$E[R_{PF,t}] - R^f = \beta_{PF}(E[R_t^m] - R^f), \qquad (7.5)$$

Jensen's alpha is simply defined as the intercept that reconciles the sample return of a given FMV with its risk as measured by its beta:

$$\hat{\alpha}_{FMV}^{JENSEN} \equiv T^{-1} \sum_{t=1}^{T} (R_{FMV,t} - R^f) - \hat{\beta}_{FMV}\left[T^{-1} \sum_{t=1}^{T} (R_t^m - R^f)\right]. \quad (7.6)$$

$\hat{\alpha}_{FMV}^{JENSEN} > 0$ implies that in risk premium-beta deviation space, a given portfolio lies above the SML; $\hat{\alpha}_{FMV}^{JENSEN} < 0$ indicates that a given FMV lies below the CML. Clearly, according to this metric, portfolios ought to be ranked on the basis of their α_{FMV}^{JENSEN}s and portfolios with positive α_{FMV}^{JENSEN} are attractive. Sometimes, α_{FMV}^{JENSEN} is also referred to as the average abnormal return not explained by a FMV exposure to the market portfolio risk.[8] In fact, Roll (1980) has stressed that all it takes for it to work is for

---

[7] Interestingly, a portfolio with a negative beta and an average rate of return above the risk-free rate of return would report a negative TR_{FMV} value. In this case, the index would indicate exemplary performance. Empirically, this has been occasionally observed for money managers invested heavily in gold mining stocks during periods of great political and economic uncertainty.

[8] Some authors advise computing a variant of Jensen's alpha defined as:

$$\alpha_{FMV} \equiv T^{-1} \sum_{t=1}^{T} R_{FMV,t} - \hat{\beta}'_{FMV}\left[T^{-1} \sum_{t=1}^{T} R_t^m\right]$$

the benchmark market index to be MV efficient.

Of course $\hat{\alpha}_{FMV}^{JENSEN}$ can also be directly estimated and its statistical significance tested, when it is written as the intercept in a market line regression:

$$\left(R_{FMV,t} - R^f\right) = \alpha_{FMV}^{JENSEN} + \beta_{FMV}(R_t^m - R^f) + \epsilon_{FMV,t}. \qquad (7.7)$$

In this case, testing whether there is any average abnormal performance of the FMV portfolio is simply equivalent to perform a (t-)test of the null hypothesis of $\alpha_{FMV}^{JENSEN} = 0$.

The Jensen composite measure of performance has several advantages over the Treynor and Sharpe indices:

I.   It is easier to interpret in that an alpha value of (say) 2% indicates that the manager generated a return of 2% per period more than what was expected given the portfolio's systemic (beta) risk.

II.   Because it is directly estimated from a regression equation, it is possible to make statements about the statistical significance of the manager's skill level, or the difference in skill levels between two different managers.

III.   It is flexible enough to allow for alternative models of risk and expected return than the CAPM.

Closely related to the statistics just presented is another widely used performance measure: Goodwin's (1998) *information ratio* (also known as an signal-to-noise ratio). This statistic measures a portfolio's average return in excess of that of a benchmark portfolio divided by the standard deviation of this excess return, for instance:

$$IR_{FMV} \equiv \frac{\hat{\alpha}_{FMV}^{JENSEN}}{\sqrt{T^{-1}\sum_{t=1}^{T}[(R_{FMV,t} - R^f) - \hat{\beta}_{FMV}(R_t^m - R^f)]^2}}, \qquad (7.8)$$

Sometimes the numerator is simply stated as the difference between the sample mean excess return on a portfolio and the same quantity for some appropriate benchmark. For instance, the numerator in equation (7.8) may

which is the so-called market, or single-index model. Such α_{FMV} can still be used to sort and rank FMVs but its interpretation differs from the standard CAPM view.

be replaced with $T^{-1}\sum_{t=1}^{T}(R_{FMV,t} - R^f) - T^{-1}\sum_{t=1}^{T}(R_t^m - R^f)$, when the market portfolio represents a sensible benchmark (for instance, for an equity index fund that typically shows a correlation with large, aggregate stock indices in excess of 0.98). In this case, the standard error estimate that appears at the denominator, $\left[T^{-1}\sum_{t=1}^{T}(R_{FMV,t} - R_t^m)^2\right]^{1/2}$ is called the *tracking error* of the FMV. More generally, the information ratio is the ratio between the mean return of a portfolio in excess of a given benchmark divided by the standard deviation of such excess return.

The mean excess return at the numerator represents the investor's ability to use her talent and information to generate a portfolio return that differs from that of the benchmark against which her performance is being measured. Conversely, the denominator measures the amount of residual (unsystematic) risk that the investor incurred in pursuit of those excess returns. The tracking error of the investor's portfolio represents a "cost" of active management in the sense that fluctuations in the periodic returns represent random noise beyond an investor's control that could hurt performance. Thus, the IR can be viewed as a benefit-to-cost ratio that assesses the quality of the investor's information deflated by unsystematic risk generated by the investment process.[9]

3 - Decomposing Performance

The most commonly employed performance decomposition is due to Fama (1972). The basic premise of his technique is that the overall performance of a portfolio, which is its return in excess of the risk-free rate, can be decomposed into measures of risk-taking and security selection skill. That is,

Overall Performance = Mean Excess Return = (Portfolio Risk) + (Selectivity)

Further, if there is a difference between the risk level specified by the investor and the actual risk level adopted by the portfolio manager (in cases where these are separate individuals), this calculation can be further refined to

Overall Performance = [(Investor's Risk) + (Manager's Risk)] + (Selectivity)

The selectivity component represents the portion of the portfolio's actual

---

[9] Goodwin (1998) has noted that the Sharpe ratio is a special case of the IR where the risk-free asset is the benchmark portfolio; despite that this interpretation violates the spirit of a statistic that should have a value of zero for passively managed portfolios.

return beyond that available to an unmanaged portfolio with identical systematic risk.

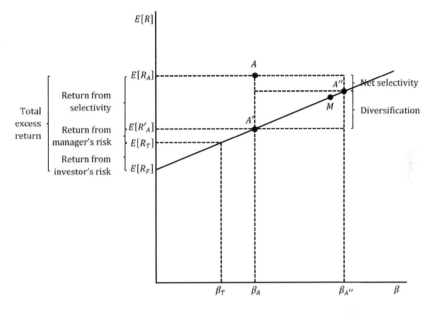

Figure 7.2

The solid line plotted in Figure 7.2 is the standard CAPM SML, representing all combinations of the riskless asset and of the market portfolio, M. One possible strategy for a money manager with a desired risk level is to achieve this level by holding a portfolio composed of the riskless asset and the market. The Jensen's measure of performance for some portfolio A is, of course, the height above the SML, or (say) A – A'. We call this distance (total) *return from selectivity*: portfolios A and A' have the same beta and thus the same systematic risk. However, A and A' do not have the same total risk. The risk of portfolio A' is completely non-diversifiable. Portfolio A, however, is not strictly a market portfolio, or its expected return would be on the SML. In the process of earning extra return, diversifiable risk must have been incurred. If this portfolio is a small part of the holdings of investors, this does not matter; if the portfolio represents the entire portfolio, it does matter. The relevant question becomes whether the extra return measured by the difference A – A' is worth the extra risk. Instead of comparing A with a naive portfolio with the same systematic risk, we can instead compare it with a naive portfolio with the same total risk. In Figure 7.2, such a portfolio is A''. Only specific calculations can isolate the coordinates of A", i.e., you are not supposed to spot the figure where this portfolios lies. The position of such a portfolio can be found thinking that because the risk on the naive portfolio with the same total risk as A is totally systematic, its total risk is $\beta_{A''}^2 Var[R_t^m]$. If A" has the same risk as A, that has greater total risk than portfolio A' has, then $Var[R_{A,t}] = \beta_{A''}^2 Var[R_t^m]$, which delivers

$$\beta_{A''} = \sqrt{\frac{Var[R_{A,t}]}{Var[R_t^m]}} > \sqrt{\frac{Var[R_{A',t}]}{Var[R_t^m]}} = \beta_A. \qquad (7.9)$$

Hence portfolio A" is located to the right of the initial, actual portfolio A. Given $\beta_{A''}$, the quantity $E[R_{A,t}] - E[R_{A'',t}]$ is a measure of the extra mean return earned on portfolio A compared to a naive portfolio with the same total risk, the *net selectivity contribution*. If we set the distance $E[R_{A'',t}] - E[R_{A',t}]$ to be the *diversification contribution*, note that

$$\underbrace{E[R_{A,t}] - E[R_{A',t}]}_{Total\ selectivity} = \underbrace{\left(E[R_{A,t}] - E[R_{A'',t}]\right)}_{Net\ selectivity} + \underbrace{\left(E[R_{A'',t}] - E[R_{A',t}]\right)}_{Diversification} \qquad (7.10)$$

The net selectivity component reveals what part, if any, of the managed portfolio return comes from selecting securities in proportions different from the market portfolio, when the total level of risk is taken into account, i.e., the fact that selecting assets with weights different from the market portfolio also changes the total risk. The diversification contribution comes from the fact that in order to reduce risk, a manager uses as a benchmark allocation the market portfolio and as such she tends to generate a mean return that comes from general movements in the market. A portfolio manager that over time tries and gets a large contribution to her performance from net selectivity is said to be *an active manager in the cross section*, i.e., one who is actively picking assets from her available menu.

The second part of a Fama-style decomposition occurs to the left, on the vertical axis of Figure 7.2 and concerns $E[R_{A,t}] - R^f$, the average portfolio excess return.[10] Assume the manager had been assigned a systematic tar-

---

[10] This further decomposition is possible only if the customers/shareholders have specified a desired level of market risk, which is typical of pension funds and profit-sharing plans. Generally, it is not possible to compute this measure for ex-post evaluations because the desired risk level is typically not available or undisclosed.

get risk level, say, β_T, where T stands for target. Then the difference in return between the benchmark portfolio with risk β_T located on the SML and the risk-free rate, $E[R_{T,t}] - R^f$, could be considered the extra return that the investor expected to earn, given the risk the investor was willing to bear, what we call *investor's reward for risk* exposure. The remaining return is $E[R_{A,t}] - E[R_{T,t}]$ is the return earned because the manager chose a different risk level than the target, the compensation for a manager's selection of risk exposure, the *manager's risk* compensation. A portfolio manager that over time receives a large contribution to her performance from risk reward is said to be *an active manager in the time series dimension*, i.e., one who is actively changing over time the amount of risk exposure around a define mandate/target level β_T. [11] Section 3.1 further explores this dimension of active portfolio management.

The following example tries to make these ideas more concrete.

Example 7.2. Consider the following data concerning the 5-year performance (annualized) of Caliman equity fund:

Average rate of return:	15.67%
Standard deviation:	13.41%
Beta (vs. MSCI Italy):	0.815
Market model R-square:	0.826
MSCI Italy return:	17.96%
St. Dev. of MSCI Italy return:	14.95%
3-month T-bills (BoT):	1.28%

Caliman is characterized by the following measures:

Sharpe ratio:	$1.073 = (15.67 - 1.28)/13.41$
Treynor ratio:	$17.66 = (15.67 - 1.28)/0.815$
CML alpha:	$-1.47 = (15.67 - 1.28) - (13.41/14.95)\times17.68$
Jensen's alpha:	$-0.02 = (15.67 - 1.28) - 0.815\times17.68$
Information ratio:	$-0.004 = -0.02/5.594$

Interestingly, the different performance measures give contrasting indications: the Sharpe and Treynor ratios are excellent in historical perspective,

---

[11] Time series activism must necessarily be time-varying because if a money manager were to systematically ignore β_T and take on a different amount of systematic risk exposure, then she would simply violate her mandate.

the CML (ex-post realized SML) alpha is rather negative, but the Jensen's alpha and the associated IR are poor, essentially nil.

Let's now work to decompose such a performance following Fama (1972). Because the market risk premium for Italy is 17.96% - 1.28% = 17.68%, the required return for risk to Caliman was 0.815(17.68) = 14.41% (its total required return is 1.28 + 14.41 = 15.69). The return for selectivity is the difference between overall performance (15.67 – 1.28 = 14.39) and the required return for risk (14.41). The results indicate that Caliman actually had an average annual return of –0.02 percent from selectivity (14.39 – 14.41). Either Caliman's managers did not try to pick stocks, or they were not very good at it.

Caliman's diversification component indicates its required return for not being completely diversified. If a fund's total risk is equal to its systematic risk, then the ratio of its total risk to the market's total risk will equal its beta. If this is not the case, then the ratio of the fund's total risk for the fund relative to the market will be greater than its beta, which implies an added return required because of incomplete diversification. For Caliman, the ratio of total risks was 13.41%/14.95% = 0.897, which is slightly in excess of the fund's beta of 0.815, indicating that the fund is not completely diversified, which is consistent with its R-square of 0.826 on the market. The fund's required return, given its standard deviation, is therefore 1.28% + 0.897x17.68 = 17.14%. Recall that the fund's required return for systematic risk exposure was 15.69%. The difference of 1.45% (= 17.14 – 15.69) is the added return required because of less than perfect diversification.

Finally, this required return for diversification is subtracted from the selectivity return to arrive at net selectivity. Caliman had a return for selectivity of –0.02 percent and net selectivity of –1.47 percent. This indicates that, after accounting for the added cost of incomplete diversification, the fund's performance was below the market line.

3.1 Market timing and tactical asset allocation

Another aspect of mutual fund performance that is often examined is the ability to time market movements. Tactical asset allocation (TAA) is a portfolio management strategy in which a manager attempts to produce active surplus returns solely through allocation decisions. Specifically, instead of trying to pick superior individual securities, TAA managers adjust their asset class exposures based on perceived changes in the relative valuations of those classes. A typical TAA fund shifts money between three asset classes—stocks, bonds, and cash equivalents—although many definitions of these categories (e.g., large cap versus small cap, long term versus short term) are also used in practice. Of course, this means that the relevant performance measurement criterion for a TAA manager is how well he is able to time broad market movements.[12]

Professional portfolio managers use one of two techniques in an attempt to improve performance through timing:

I.   By changing the percentage committed to bonds and stocks in anticipation of market changes; if the equity market is expected to increase (decrease), then the manager increases (decreases) the amount invested in common equities.

II. By adjusting the average beta on the portfolio in anticipation of changes in the market; when the stock market is expected to surge (decline), the manager increases (decreases) her portfolio beta to obtain a portfolio with a greater responsiveness to market changes.

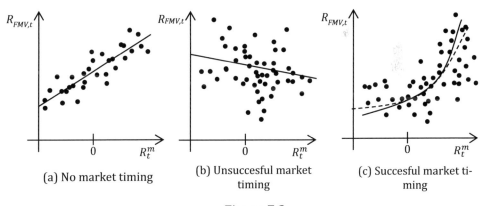

(a) No market timing

(b) Unsuccesful market timing

(c) Succesful market timing

Figure 7.3

Both the changes in the bond-stock mix and the changes in overall beta of the equity portion of the portfolio are attempts to change the average beta, the first more obvious and direct (also because safe bonds often have betas close to zero, as we have seen in chapter 5) than the latter, which instead requires trading across different stock and equity styles (also called portfolio *rotations*). Attempts to measure successful timing are best done utiliz-

---

[12] The process of selecting a target asset allocation is called *strategic asset allocation*. The variation in asset allocation around that target is called tactical asset allocation.

ing recursive beta estimates, since they will capture both changes simultaneously. A measure of a manager's timing ability is to look at a plot of portfolio beta (or also simply her bond-stock mix) compared to the market return. If there is significant timing ability, then there should be a relationship between these variables that should be apparent from the plot. Figure 7.3 documents exactly how these three cases look visually.

An alternative way to test market timing is to look directly at the FMV return compared to the market portfolio return. If the FMV did not engage in market timing, then the overall portfolio return should be highly correlated with the market and the portfolio beta should be constant implying a high regression R-square (of FMV performance on market returns). Equivalently, FMV returns should fall very close to a 45-degree line when plotted vs. market returns. If market timing was attempted but it was unsuccessful, then FMV returns should randomly fall around but also away from recorded market returns, and a regression on market returns should yield a low R-square. Finally, if market timing occurred and it was successful, then—because betas are moved up before large positive market returns and down before large negative market returns—in a FMV vs. market return space, the former should mostly fall above a 45-degree line and possibly describe a non-linear, curved and convex relationship that is flatter than the 45-degree line for negative market returns and steeper than the 45-degree line for positive market returns.[13]

3.2 Multi-index measures

The development of APT models and the related multi-index models has spurred the development of new performance measures that extend the measures commented above.[14] A first, obvious alternative to using a single benchmark is to adopt a set of *style benchmarks*, one for each FMV under

---

[13] An alternative way to analyze market timing is to fit two separate regressions of FMV vs. market returns. One regression is for the observations when the market outperforms the riskless asset (up markets) and the other is fit when the market underperforms the riskless asset (down markets): a manager with market timing should have a high up market beta and a low down market beta.

[14] Technically a problem with using an incorrect single-index benchmark is that many of the characteristics of FMVs that are studied are likely to be correlated with the omitted factors and incorrect inferences concerning the characteristics and performances will then be made. For instance, it is well known that the CAPM beta increases with the size of the companies. So the CAPM errors will correlate with the omitted factor, say either size or SMB returns.

assessment. For example, when rating mutual funds, Morningstar places every domestic stock fund—on the basis of the attributes of the securities the fund holds—into one of nine categories defined by the intersection of two dimensions, size (small, medium, or large) and growth characteristics (growth, blend, or value). This approach has gained wide acceptance and it now represents the standard of the industry. Yet, its limitations are self-evident: to force each FMV into one of M categories, where M is generally relatively small, may be quite arbitrary. For instance, mutual funds often hold securities that span multiple sets of characteristics rather than possessing only one set of characteristics.

The way to adjust for these limitations is to use a multi-index model. Sharpe (1992) proposed this type of multi-index analysis, that he called *style analysis* to customize a benchmark for each manager's returns, in order to measure the manager's contribution more exactly. The most common approach consists of simply computing a multi-factor Jensen's alpha:

$$\alpha_{FMV}^{JENSEN} \equiv T^{-1} \sum_{t=1}^{T} \left(R_{FMV,t} - R^f \right)$$

$$- \sum_{k=1}^{K} \hat{\beta}_{FMV}^k \left[T^{-1} \sum_{t=1}^{T} (FMR_{k,t} - R^f) \right], \tag{7.11}$$

where $FMR_{k,t}$ is the factor-mimicking portfolio return on the kth factor. Sharpe has also proposed a *generalized Sharpe measure*, which is simply the alpha from equation (7.6) divided by the standard deviation of the residuals from the multi-index regression model.

If one is willing to assume a multi-index (equilibrium APT) model, a more detailed decomposition of performance is possible. Sometimes, constraints are imposed in estimation thus yielding a constrained least-square estimate. First, the factor exposures are occasionally set to be non negative and sum to 1. Second, sometimes the procedure minimizes the variance of the selection returns (i.e., the regression residuals) not the sum of their squares: the objective does not penalize large mean selection returns—as regression would do—but only variance about that mean. This is a *tracking error variance minimization* problem.

4 - Active vs. Passive Portfolio Management

Traditionally, we speak of *passive portfolio management* when a money manager limits herself to buy and hold a well-diversified market index, such as the European STOXX 50, as suggested by the CAPM, among all other models of efficient markets. The prototypical passive FMV is an index equity mutual fund that buys each stock in the index in exactly the proportion it represents in the index. If BMW constitutes 4% of the index, the fund places 4% of its money in BMW stock, say.[15] Residually, an active manager would depart from such a simple buy-and-hold policy taking (net) selection risks.

At a first thought, one would expect most passive managers to underperform the index they track, on average. For instance, index funds have management fees, and transaction costs are incurred in their management. However, one factor helps performance. Index funds stand always ready to lend stock when a firm offers to buy it above market price (in a merger or stock repurchase); thus, index funds may obtain a higher price for some of its stock than is assumed when the return on the index is calculated. This results in betas slightly below one with respect to the index they track. It also means that passive managers generally do slightly better in down markets (where lending stocks is prominent and share are more frequently re-purchased) and slightly worse in up markets.

Usually, a passive manager also tends to trade on a mechanical rule by using past data; if the manager forecasts anything and acts on the forecast, we call it active management. Indeed, active management involves taking a position different from that which would be held in a passive portfolio, based on a forecast about the future. For instance, if the STOXX 50 represents a benchmark, the neutral position is to hold each stock in the proportion it represents of the index. Any difference from these proportions represents a bet based on a forecast. Although there is no wide consensus on how this can be done, one possible classification for active management

---

[15] Although exact replication is the simplest technique for constructing an index fund, many index funds are not constructed this way. Managers of index funds must face a series of decisions in designing a fund. These decisions involve a trade-off between accuracy in duplicating the index (called tracking error) and transaction costs. Does the manager buy all 50 stocks in the Euro STOXX 50 in market proportions, or are some of the stocks with the smallest market weight excluded to save on transaction costs? Often, index funds simply form a portfolio of not more than a specified number of stocks (e.g., 30), which best tracks the index historically. Standard mathematical programming algorithms can be used to do this.

styles divides active (stock) managers into three groups:

I.   Market timers change the beta(s) on their portfolio according to forecasts of how the market will do; they change the beta on the overall portfolio, either by changing the beta on the equity portfolio (by using options or futures or by swapping securities) or by changing the amount invested in short-term bonds.

II. Security selectors bet that the market weights on securities are not the optimum proportion to hold in each security; therefore, they increase the weight (make a positive bet) for undervalued securities and decrease it for overvalued securities.

III. Sector rotators shift the industrial or sectorial portfolio composition over time, based on their forecasts of what sector/industry is undervalued or overvalued.

The *efficient markets hypothesis* suggests that active managers have no skill. In its strong form, the hypothesis states that all currently known information is already reflected in security prices. Since all information is already in the prices, no additional information is available to active managers to use in generating exceptional returns. Active returns are completely random. The semi-strong version states that all publicly available information is already reflected in security prices. Active management skill is then really insider trading! The weak form of the hypothesis claims only that all previous price-based information is contained in current prices. This rules out technical analysis as skilled active management, but would allow for skillful active management based on fundamental and economic analysis.

These notions concerning active portfolio management apply equally to single- and multi-factor models. In the latter case, we define as *benchmark timing* an active management decision to vary the managed portfolio's betas with respect to the benchmarks. If we believe that a benchmark will do better than usual, then the beta is increased. If we believe a factor will do worse than usual, then the associated beta should be decreased. Benchmark timing is not tactical asset allocation, as TAA focuses on aggregate asset classes rather than specific individual stocks, bonds, etc.

These notions apply also to bond active management subject to some modifications. A prime factor needed to evaluate performance properly is a measure of risk, such as the beta coefficient for equities. This is difficult to achieve because a bond's maturity and coupon have a significant effect on the volatility of its prices. The bond's duration statistic captures the net effect of this volatility. Using this as a measure of risk, it is possible to derive a bond market line much like the security market line used to evaluate equity performance. Duration simply replaces beta as the risk variable.

As in common stock portfolio management, one passive strategy for bonds is to match an index. Some features of bond index funds differ from stock index funds and make bond index funds more difficult to manage. The first factor is the changing nature of the index. Stock indices, such as Standard & Poor's 500, change occasionally as S&P decides that different firms are more appropriate or as firms in the index merge. The composition of all widely used bond indices changes much more frequently as bonds mature and new bonds are issued. A second difference from stock indices is that many bond indices contain bonds that are illiquid and, in fact, might not be available to an investor. This means that the manager of a bond index fund will never attempt to duplicate an index exactly, but will employ one of the mathematical techniques available to maximize the correlation with the underlying bond index.

The most commonly employed active bond strategy is market timing. An estimate is made of what will happen to interest rates. If interest rates are expected to rise, prices are expected to fall and capital losses will be incurred on bonds. A fixed-income portfolio manager with superior timing ability changes the portfolio's duration in anticipation of interest rate changes by increasing the duration of the portfolio in anticipation of failing interest rates and reducing the duration of the portfolio when rates are expected to rise.

In the literature, there are considerable doubts on the potential (risk-adjusted) payoff from market timing and TAA. Grinold's (1989) *fundamental law of active management* suggests that (under restrictive assumptions, such as identical Sharpe ratios across uncorrelated securities) the portfolio Sharpe ratio increases with the square root of its *breadth*, measured by the number of independent bets in a year, multiplied by the information coefficient.[16] The *information coefficient* is the square root of the R-square in a regression of realized asset returns on the money manager's forecasts. The issues with TAA and timing factor exposures is that with a modest cross-sectional breadth—because the asset classes employed tend to be relatively few—one needs to either increase time series breadth, i.e., the number

---

[16] Grinold claims that the maximum value that can be added by an active manager is proportional to the squared maximum information ratio: $IR^2/(4k)$, where k is the coefficient of risk (variance) aversion of the investor. Goodwin (1998) gives a skeptical view on the linkage between information and Sharpe ratios.

of times in which the portfolio is revised to time beta or durations, or to operate under high information coefficients that are generally hard to find in empirical finance.[17] Of course, a very fast-paced TAA portfolio rotation may also be problematic because it will increase transaction costs and erode gross realized performance.

References and Further Readings

Brown, K., C., and Brown, G., D. Does the Composition of the Market Portfolio Rally Matter? *Journal of Portfolio Management*, 13: 26-32, 1987.

Carlson, R., S. Aggregate Performance of Mutual Funds, 1948–1967. *Journal of Financial and Quantitative Analysis*, 5: 1-32, 1970.

Elton, E. J., Gruber, M. J., Brown, S. J., and Goetzmann, W. N. *Modern Portfolio Theory and Investment Analysis*. 8th Edition. Hoboken: John Wiley & Sons, 2009.

Fama, E., F. Components of Investment Performance. *Journal of Finance* 27: 551-567, 1972.

Grinold, R., C. The Fundamental Law of Active Management. *Journal of Portfolio Management*, 15: 30-37, 1989.

Goodwin, T., H. The Information Ratio. *Financial Analysts Journal*, 54: 34-43, 1998.

Jacobs, B., I., and Levy, K. Residual Risk: How Much Is Too Much? *Journal of Portfolio Management*, 21: 10-16, 1996.

Roll, R. Performance Evaluation and Benchmark Error I. *Journal of Portfolio Management*, 6: 5–12, 1980.

Sharpe, W., F. Asset Allocation: Management Style and Performance Measurement. *Journal of Portfolio Management*, 18: 7-19, 1992.

---

[17] Goodwin (1998) studied the information ratio of 212 active institutional money managers in the US for six different equity styles. He found ratios ranging between -0.2 and 0.6. However, only 20-30% of the managers analyzed were able to exceed a ratio of 0.5, which is commonly identified with skill. Jacobs and Levy (1996) have suggested that a "good manager might have an IR of 0.5 and an exceptional manager might have an IR of 1.0" (p. 11) but they failed to explain where these numbers came from.

A Worked-Out Excel Example

We use monthly data of returns on a selection of 11 Italian equity mutual funds. The funds are selected to be "top", i.e., high performing ones, in the sense of having received scores of 3, 4, and 5 stars from Morningstar and for having a continuous record of monthly (gross, before fees and commissions) returns between March 2003 and December 2016. Moreover, these 11 funds are selected for having outperformed the average of their category on a horizon of 10 years (in 8 cases) or at least 5 years. The funds are all classified as having a pure Italian equity or at least a "balanced/aggressive" investment target. The logic of this example is that if, in risk-adjusted terms, even these funds fail to perform well, then this is an indication that it is hard to provide a solid contribution to wealth management for Italian equity mutual funds. For the same reason, we consider fund performances in gross terms, before commissions and fees. In other words, if the upper bound of the industry presents issues with one or more performance measures, then this is a serious indication of potential limitations with mutual funds as an investment vehicle. Needless to say, many of these 11 mutual funds are well-known and successful funds but it is not important for us to disclose their identities.

Over the sample period March 2003 – December 2016, we also collect data on 3-month T-bills (in Italy, BoT) returns and value-weighted MIB portfolio returns. All data are publicly available from yahoo finance Italy (https://it.finance.yahoo.com/borse-mercati). The mean return on the market portfolio is 0.46% with a standard deviation of 3.89% and the risk-free rate (assumed to be constant) return is 0.14%, which makes for a market risk premium of 0.32% and a monthly Sharpe ratio of 0.32%/3.89% = 0.08.

As a first step, we compute the Sharpe ratios for the 11 funds and proceed to rank them on this basis. The following table displays the results obtained using simple Excel functions such as AVERAGE(·) and STDEVP(·):

	Mean Return	Standard Deviation	Risk-free rate	Sharpe Ratio
Fund 1	0.43%	5.14%	0.14%	0.06
Fund 2	0.50%	5.06%	0.14%	0.07
Fund 3	0.66%	5.60%	0.14%	0.09
Fund 4	0.42%	5.16%	0.14%	0.06
Fund 5	0.48%	5.08%	0.14%	0.07
Fund 6	0.55%	3.10%	0.14%	0.13
Fund 7	0.55%	2.41%	0.14%	0.17
Fund 8	0.43%	2.04%	0.14%	0.15
Fund 9	0.33%	5.06%	0.14%	0.04
Fund 10	0.28%	1.53%	0.14%	0.09
Fund 11	0.39%	4.92%	0.14%	0.05
Market	0.46%	3.89%	0.14%	0.08

Seven funds out of 11 report a Sharpe ratio that exceeds the market's. In particular, three funds display monthly Sharpe rations in excess of 0.10, which is a strong monthly Sharpe ratio. Interestingly, the funds with the highest Sharpe ratios are also characterized by the lowest volatilities and tend to belong to the "balanced/aggressive" category. The following plot represents the 11 funds in the volatility/mean space. The two straight lines represent the Sharpe ratios of the best and the worst funds. In the latter case, the straight line is characterized by a modest slope, because fund 9 is characterized by a barely positive average excess return and Sharpe ratio.

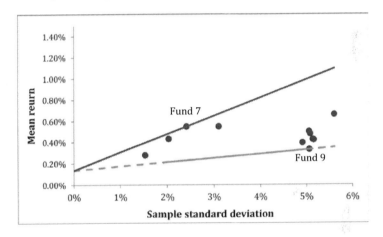

We present alphas based on the empirical CML defined by the MIB portfolio. As one would expect, because the measures are all based on total variance, the same funds that offered Sharpe ratios above the market now yield CML alphas that are positive and relatively large. In fact, 5 funds out of 11 display positive alphas. However, the rankings implied by Sharpe ratios and CML alphas are not completely identical. For instance, fund 8 appears to perform well under both criteria, but it is ranked now only third.

	Mean Return	Standard Deviation	Risk-free rate	Sharpe Ratio	Mkt Return	Mkt Volatility	Return of ptf with same σ	Differential return
Fund 1	0.43%	5.14%	0.14%	0.056	0.46%	3.89%	0.56%	-0.13%
Fund 2	0.50%	5.06%	0.14%	0.072	0.46%	3.89%	0.55%	-0.05%
Fund 3	0.66%	5.60%	0.14%	0.094	0.46%	3.89%	0.60%	0.06%
Fund 4	0.42%	5.16%	0.14%	0.056	0.46%	3.89%	0.56%	-0.14%
Fund 5	0.48%	5.08%	0.14%	0.067	0.46%	3.89%	0.55%	-0.08%
Fund 6	0.55%	3.10%	0.14%	0.133	0.46%	3.89%	0.39%	0.16%
Fund 7	0.55%	2.41%	0.14%	0.171	0.46%	3.89%	0.33%	0.21%
Fund 8	0.43%	2.04%	0.14%	0.146	0.46%	3.89%	0.30%	0.13%
Fund 9	0.33%	5.06%	0.14%	0.039	0.46%	3.89%	0.55%	-0.22%
Fund 10	0.28%	1.53%	0.14%	0.094	0.46%	3.89%	0.26%	0.02%
Fund 11	0.39%	4.92%	0.14%	0.053	0.46%	3.89%	0.54%	-0.15%

Oddly enough, five of the top 11 Italian equity mutual funds would be located below the CML built with the Italian equity market portfolio. This means that by investing in them, investors accepts a sub-optimal compensation for total risk. This is clearly discouraging, also because some of the negative CML alphas are associated to mean equity returns characterized by volatilities similar to the MIB market portfolio.

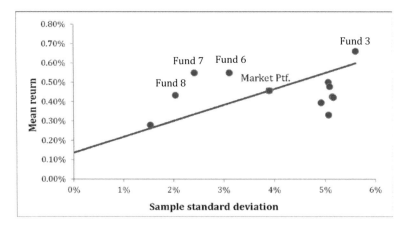

In this case, the calculations were once more straightforward, apart from the usage of the Excel function LINEST($\cdot$) that allows us to quickly compute the intercept and the slope coefficient in a regression on market excess returns. In any event, while the market has a Treynor ratio (equal to its risk premium) of 0.32%, only five funds managed to exceed such a measure. However, Fund 7 is characterized by a Treynor ratio of 0.81%, which is almost three times the market's.

	Overall Return	Standard Deviation	Risk Free rate	Mean Excess Returns	Sharpe Ratio	Beta	Intercept	Treynor Measure
Fund 1	0.43%	5.14%	0.14%	0.29%	0.056	1.299	-0.127%	0.223%
Fund 2	0.50%	5.06%	0.14%	0.36%	0.072	1.212	-0.024%	0.301%
Fund 3	0.66%	5.60%	0.14%	0.52%	0.094	1.384	0.080%	0.379%
Fund 4	0.42%	5.16%	0.14%	0.29%	0.056	1.304	-0.132%	0.220%
Fund 5	0.48%	5.08%	0.14%	0.34%	0.067	1.277	-0.068%	0.268%
Fund 6	0.55%	3.10%	0.14%	0.41%	0.133	0.726	0.180%	0.569%
Fund 7	0.55%	2.41%	0.14%	0.41%	0.171	0.513	0.249%	0.806%
Fund 8	0.43%	2.04%	0.14%	0.30%	0.146	0.435	0.158%	0.685%
Fund 9	0.33%	5.06%	0.14%	0.20%	0.039	1.279	-0.215%	0.153%
Fund 10	0.28%	1.53%	0.14%	0.14%	0.094	0.328	0.038%	0.438%
Fund 11	0.39%	4.92%	0.14%	0.26%	0.053	1.243	-0.141%	0.208%

The corresponding picture has the same structure analyzed above.

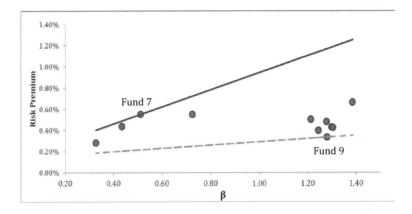

Yet, some of these 11 funds truly are top-performing funds when we adopt the typical perspective of Jensen's alpha. Using the same Excel command cited above, the following table shows that 5 funds yield alphas which are sizable—between 0.5% and 3% per annum—and statistically significant. In short, these funds are not simply generating returns that compensate their shareholder for market risks; instead, it seems that a surplus performance possibly due to skill is generated by money management. Yet, the remaining 6 funds with zero or even negative alphas do worry us: many top funds in Italy would be unable to generate a non negative average abnormal return. The picture reveals however, that the best Jensen's alphas are generated by low beta funds.

	Mean Return	Standard Deviation	Risk Free rate	Excess Returns	Beta	Intercept	Mkt Return	Mkt standard dev.	Return on a ptf of same Beta	Jensen's alpha
Fund 1	0.4%	5.1%	0.14%	0.3%	1.299	-0.001	0.5%	3.9%	0.55%	-0.13%
Fund 2	0.5%	5.1%	0.14%	0.4%	1.212	0.000	0.5%	3.9%	0.53%	-0.02%
Fund 3	0.7%	5.6%	0.14%	0.5%	1.384	0.001	0.5%	3.9%	0.58%	0.08%
Fund 4	0.4%	5.2%	0.14%	0.3%	1.304	-0.001	0.5%	3.9%	0.55%	-0.13%
Fund 5	0.5%	5.1%	0.14%	0.3%	1.277	-0.001	0.5%	3.9%	0.55%	-0.07%
Fund 6	0.5%	3.1%	0.14%	0.4%	0.726	0.002	0.5%	3.9%	0.37%	0.18%
Fund 7	0.5%	2.4%	0.14%	0.4%	0.513	0.002	0.5%	3.9%	0.30%	0.25%
Fund 8	0.4%	2.0%	0.14%	0.3%	0.435	0.002	0.5%	3.9%	0.28%	0.16%
Fund 9	0.3%	5.1%	0.14%	0.2%	1.279	-0.002	0.5%	3.9%	0.55%	-0.21%
Fund 10	0.3%	1.5%	0.14%	0.1%	0.328	0.000	0.5%	3.9%	0.24%	0.04%
Fund 11	0.4%	4.9%	0.14%	0.3%	1.243	-0.001	0.5%	3.9%	0.54%	-0.14%

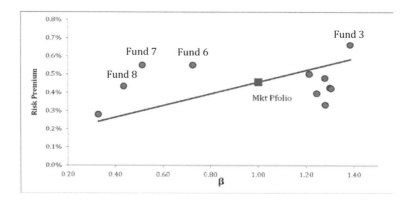

It is also interesting to investigate the information ratio for each of the 11 funds, computed as the ratio between Jensen's alpha and the standard error of each single-index regressions. The information ratios are generally disappointing and generally lower than the level that has been commonly associated with skill in the literature (0.4-0.5 or even higher). Only three funds have IRs in excess of a timid 0.1. This is an indication of modest skill at best. Moreover, six funds report negative information ratios, which is unsettling if we think these are among the 11 most successful Italian funds.

	Overall Return	Standard Deviation	Risk Free rate	Risk Premium	Market excess return	Beta	Intercept	Jensen's Alpha	St. Dev. of Abnormal return	Information Ratio
Fund 1	0.43%	5.14%	0.14%	0.29%	0.32%	1.299	-0.001	-0.13%	0.91%	-0.139
Fund 2	0.50%	5.06%	0.14%	0.36%	0.32%	1.212	0.000	-0.02%	1.82%	-0.013
Fund 3	0.66%	5.60%	0.14%	0.52%	0.32%	1.384	0.001	0.08%	1.54%	0.052
Fund 4	0.42%	5.16%	0.14%	0.29%	0.32%	1.304	-0.001	-0.13%	0.92%	-0.144
Fund 5	0.48%	5.08%	0.14%	0.34%	0.32%	1.277	-0.001	-0.07%	1.05%	-0.064
Fund 6	0.55%	3.10%	0.14%	0.41%	0.32%	0.726	0.002	0.18%	1.29%	0.140
Fund 7	0.55%	2.41%	0.14%	0.41%	0.32%	0.513	0.002	0.25%	1.36%	0.183
Fund 8	0.43%	2.04%	0.14%	0.30%	0.32%	0.435	0.002	0.16%	1.13%	0.140
Fund 9	0.33%	5.06%	0.14%	0.20%	0.32%	1.279	-0.002	-0.21%	0.91%	-0.235
Fund 10	0.28%	1.53%	0.14%	0.14%	0.32%	0.328	0.000	0.04%	0.85%	0.045
Fund 11	0.39%	4.92%	0.14%	0.26%	0.32%	1.243	-0.001	-0.14%	0.84%	-0.167

We conclude our analysis applying a Fama-style decomposition to each of the 11 funds under consideration. Rather arbitrarily, because this information is not available throughout history, we impose target betas on the funds on the basis of the average 10-year beta of the category the funds belong to according to the Italian yahoo finance site.

The very last table contains two rows of interest: the net selectivity contribution and the manager's risk taking. The net selectivity shows whether the manager displays any skills vs. the composition of the market portfolio. In only 4 funds out of 11 is net selectivity positive and large and in any event the monthly contribution is at most 21 bps, i.e., rather modest. The contribution of the manager's risk is instead systematically positive for most funds, an indication that (excluding a fund may have carried a target beta much different from its category) Italian fund managers would be capable to vary their beta risk exposure over time in rather effective ways. In the case of the rather risky fund 3, this contribution is 15 bps per month.

	Fund 1	Fund 2	Fund 3	Fund 4	Fund 5	Fund 6	Fund 7	Fund 8	Fund 9	Fund 10	Fund 11
Overall Return	0.43%	0.50%	0.66%	0.42%	0.48%	0.55%	0.55%	0.43%	0.33%	0.28%	0.39%
Standard Deviation	5.14%	5.06%	5.60%	5.16%	5.08%	3.10%	2.41%	2.04%	5.06%	1.53%	4.92%
Risk Free rate	0.14%	0.14%	0.14%	0.14%	0.14%	0.14%	0.14%	0.14%	0.14%	0.14%	0.14%
Total Excess Return	0.29%	0.36%	0.52%	0.29%	0.34%	0.41%	0.41%	0.30%	0.20%	0.14%	0.26%
Sharpe Ratio	0.056	0.072	0.094	0.056	0.067	0.133	0.171	0.146	0.039	0.094	0.053
Beta	1.30	1.21	1.38	1.30	1.28	0.73	0.51	0.44	1.28	0.33	1.24
Treynor Measure	0.22%	0.30%	0.38%	0.22%	0.27%	0.57%	0.81%	0.68%	0.15%	0.44%	0.21%
Mkt Return	0.46%	0.46%	0.46%	0.46%	0.46%	0.46%	0.46%	0.46%	0.46%	0.46%	0.46%
Mkt sd	3.89%	3.89%	3.89%	3.89%	3.89%	3.89%	3.89%	3.89%	3.89%	3.89%	3.89%
Return on Ptf with == nondiversif. risk	0.55%	0.53%	0.58%	0.55%	0.55%	0.37%	0.30%	0.28%	0.55%	0.24%	0.54%
Total risk Beta	131.9%	129.8%	143.9%	132.5%	130.5%	79.7%	62.0%	52.3%	130.0%	39.4%	126.2%
Return on Ptf with same total risk	0.56%	0.55%	0.60%	0.56%	0.55%	0.39%	0.33%	0.30%	0.55%	0.26%	0.54%
Net Selectivity	-0.13%	-0.05%	0.06%	-0.14%	-0.08%	0.16%	0.21%	0.13%	-0.22%	0.02%	-0.15%
Diversification	0.01%	0.03%	0.02%	0.01%	0.01%	0.02%	0.03%	0.03%	0.01%	0.02%	0.01%
Target Beta	0.91	0.91	0.91	0.91	0.91	0.96	0.93	0.93	0.91	0.92	0.91
Target Return	0.43%	0.43%	0.43%	0.43%	0.43%	0.44%	0.43%	0.43%	0.43%	0.43%	0.43%
Return from managers' risk	0.12%	0.10%	0.15%	0.13%	0.12%	-0.08%	-0.13%	-0.16%	0.12%	0.19%	0.11%
Return from investor's risk	0.29%	0.29%	0.29%	0.29%	0.29%	0.31%	0.30%	0.30%	0.29%	0.30%	0.29%